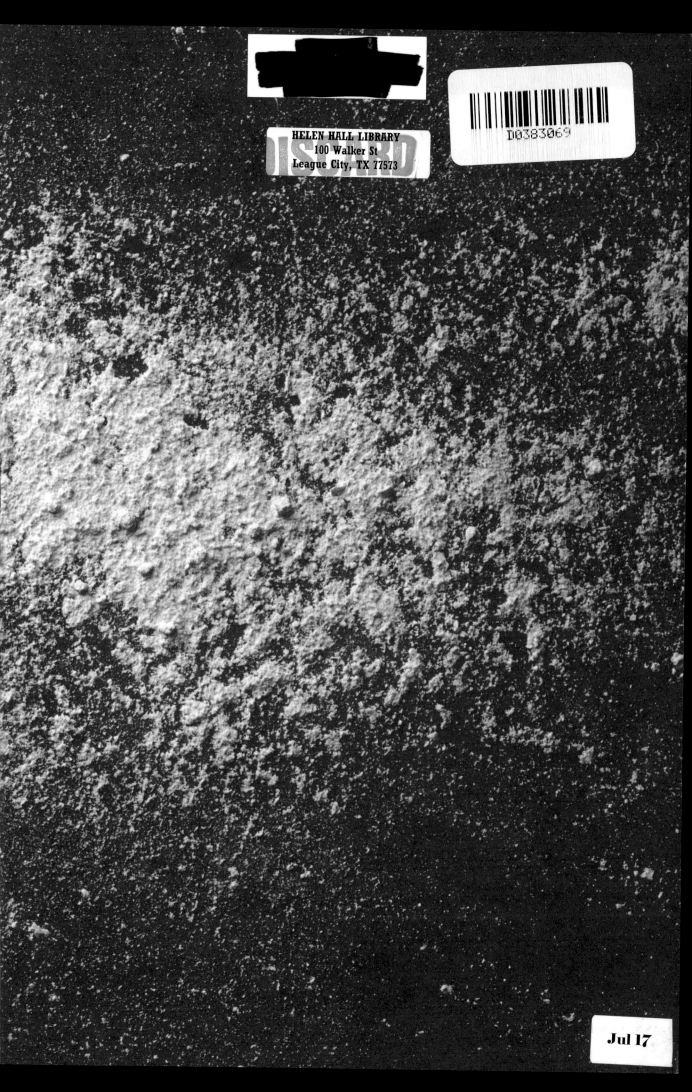

ISBN: 978-0-8487-5224-8
Library of Congress Number: 2017930523

Printed in the United States of America
10 9 8 7 6 5 4 3 2 1
First Edition 2017

EXECUTIVE EDITOR **Kate Heddings**
EDITOR **Susan Choung**
DESIGNER **Alisha Petro**
COPY EDITOR **Lisa Leventer**
PRODUCTION DIRECTOR **Joseph Colucci**
PRODUCTION MANAGERS **Stephanie
Thompson, John Markic**
EDITORIAL ASSISTANT **Taylor Rondestvedt**

FRONT COVER
PHOTOGRAPHER **Con Poulos**
FOOD STYLIST **Simon Andrews**
STYLE EDITOR **Suzie Myers**
For additional photo contributors,
see page 271.

FOOD & WINE
EDITOR IN CHIEF **Nilou Motamed**
EXECUTIVE EDITOR **Dana Bowen**
ART DIRECTOR **James Maikowski**
PHOTO EDITOR **Sara Parks**

Master Recipes

A Step-by-Step
Guide to Cooking
Like a Pro

By the Editors of

OXmoor
HOUSE®

Level One

Get ready to master these simple DIY projects. With just basic cooking chops you can learn how to pickle and can vegetables, make your own ricotta, brine and roast a turkey, bake a pandowdy (below) and more.

10

Level Two

Now that you've got the basics down, it's time to take your skills to the next level. Learn how to pull mozzarella cheese (above), cook fish sous vide, make caramel and bake perfect soufflés every time.

46

Level Three

Intermediate cooks looking to up their game will find tons to love about these kitchen projects. Learn how to master the perfect challah and Parker House rolls, whip up meringue, stuff your own sausages, make mapo tofu dumplings (below)–and even steep your own vermouth.

142

Level Four

You're a whiz in the kitchen, so get ready to challenge yourself (and wow your guests) with the most ambitious projects yet: Learn how to make ramen noodles, twist and bake babka (above), shape croissants, churn butter and more.

212

FOREWORD

Some people totally geek out over art, others about cars, but for us at FOOD & WINE, our obsession is food. Like you, we're happy to wait patiently in line for the best pizza, drive three towns over for transcendent pho and are forever on the lookout for the lushest ice cream around. It's what we do! That's why *Master Recipes* was born: to help us enthusiasts perfect those dishes that might, at first blush, seem unapproachable, from soufflés and soup dumplings to babka and baklava. And because we've collaborated with expert chefs like Daniel Boulud and Alex Guarnaschelli, star bakers, mixologists and other pros who take eating and cooking as seriously as we do, we know that these recipes are foolproof and the best of the best.

Consider this tome your pass to cooking school. It's divided into four levels, with increasingly challenging recipes, for the beginner all the way up to the expert. In each chapter you'll learn essential culinary techniques, such as pickling and canning in Level One, making luscious caramel in Level Two, cranking out fresh pasta for tender ravioli in Level Three and turning dough for the flakiest croissants in Level Four.

Whether you're still finding your way around the kitchen or feel most at home there, you'll discover lots of recipes that speak to your skill set and encourage you to stretch. And since cooking is all about engaging your senses, we wanted to bring our expert tips to life right in your kitchen. That's why we've included step-by-step photos to guide and inspire you. It's the next best thing to cooking alongside a master chef (and you won't have to share your wine).

We've done the advance work to guarantee success, so go ahead and begin with Level One or dive right into Level Four. As you master your favorites, remember to tag @foodandwine in photos of your tasty creations.

Nilou Motamed
Editor in Chief
FOOD & WINE

Kate Heddings
Executive Editor
FOOD & WINE Cookbooks

Pork-and-Crab Soup Dumplings
page 214

Ice Cream Birthday Cake
page 248

Level One

12 French Fries

14 Mac & Cheese

16 Turkey

20 Pulled Pork

22 Griddled Burgers

26 Cult Beef Cuts

30 Biscuits

32 Pickling

34 Ricotta Cheese

36 Baked
Fruit Desserts

40 Sundaes

44 Tempering
Chocolate

French Fries

At The Breslin in New York City, chef April Bloomfield serves the holy grail of thick-cut fries: insanely crispy on the outside yet tender and fluffy within. Not content with just the usual twice-fried method, she cooks her potatoes three times—boiling them first to soften them up, then double-frying. Read on for Bloomfield's foolproof tater tutorial.

Thrice-Cooked Fries

Time	1 hr active
	3 hr total
Makes	4 servings

4   large baking potatoes (¾ lb. each), scrubbed but not peeled

Vegetable oil, for frying

Kosher salt

1 Cut the potatoes into ⅓-inch-thick steak fries and transfer to a bowl of cold water **(A)**. Bring a large pot of salted water to a boil. Drain the potatoes, add them to the pot and boil just until tender, about 5 minutes **(B)**. Carefully drain the potatoes and transfer them to a paper towel–lined rack to cool. Refrigerate until chilled, about 1 hour.

2 In a large, deep skillet, heat 2 inches of oil to 250°. Set a rack over a baking sheet. Working in batches, fry the potatoes just until they begin to brown around the edges, about 8 minutes. Transfer the potatoes to the rack and let cool.

3 When all of the potatoes have been fried once, heat the oil to 350°. Fry the potatoes again, in batches, until golden and crisp, about 7 minutes per batch **(C)**. Drain the fries on a paper towel–lined baking sheet, sprinkle with salt and serve.

Mac & Cheese

Everyone has an opinion on what makes the ideal macaroni and cheese. New York City–based cookbook author Grace Parisi prefers a classic American version that's rich and creamy thanks to a quick béchamel. Small chunks of gooey cheddar and Colby flavor the dish throughout, while a sprinkling of buttery breadcrumbs gives every bite a terrific crunch.

Macaroni and Cheese with Buttery Crumbs

Time	45 min active
	1 hr 30 min total
Makes	6 servings

- 5 Tbsp. unsalted butter, plus more for greasing
- 3 Tbsp. all-purpose flour
- 2½ cups half-and-half or whole milk
- 1 lb. sharp cheddar cheese, cut into ½-inch pieces
- ½ lb. Colby cheese, cut into ½-inch pieces
- 1 Tbsp. Dijon mustard
- Pinch of freshly grated nutmeg
- Pinch of cayenne
- Kosher salt and black pepper
- 1 lb. elbow macaroni
- ¾ cup plain dry breadcrumbs

1 Preheat the oven to 350°. Generously butter a shallow 2-quart baking dish. Melt 3 tablespoons of the butter in a large saucepan. Add the flour and cook over moderate heat for 2 minutes, stirring constantly **(A)**. Add the half-and-half and cook, whisking constantly, until thickened, about 3 minutes. Add half of the cheddar and Colby cheeses and cook over low heat, stirring, until melted. Stir in the mustard, nutmeg and cayenne; season the cheese sauce with salt and black pepper.

2 Meanwhile, cook the elbow macaroni in a large pot of salted boiling water until al dente. Drain very well. Return the macaroni to the pot. Add the cheese sauce and the remaining cheese and stir until combined **(B)**. Spread the macaroni in the prepared baking dish.

3 In a small glass bowl, melt the remaining 2 tablespoons of butter in a microwave. Add the breadcrumbs, season with salt and black pepper and stir until evenly moistened. Sprinkle the buttered crumbs over the macaroni and bake for about 45 minutes, until bubbling and golden on top **(C)**. Let stand for 15 minutes before serving.

MAKE AHEAD The assembled dish can be refrigerated overnight. Bring to room temperature before baking.

WINE Buttery, full-bodied Chardonnay.

Turkey

When it comes to turkey, chefs can't seem to agree on the best way to cook it. We sought out four poultry pros and got four different answers: One chef brines, two of them dry-brine, another deep-fries. Two cook the bird whole while the other two separate the legs from the breast. Choose your own adventure for a phenomenal bird with these equally delicious techniques and recipes from Ken Oringer, Frank Stitt, Chris Cosentino and Marcus Samuelsson.

Apple-Brined Turkey

Time	1 hr active; 3 hr 45 min total plus 25 hr brining and drying
Makes	8 servings

BRINE

- 3 cups apple juice
- 2 cups light brown sugar
- 1 cup kosher salt
- 1 green apple, quartered
- ½ navel orange
- 2 Tbsp. coriander seeds
- 2 Tbsp. fennel seeds
- 2 Tbsp. Old Bay seasoning
- 1 Tbsp. whole allspice berries
- 1 Tbsp. whole black peppercorns
- 8 sage leaves
- 4 tarragon sprigs
- 1 medium bunch of thyme
- 2 garlic cloves, crushed
- 2 whole cloves
  - One 15-lb. turkey, legs and breast separated (see Note)

HERB BUTTER

- 6 sticks unsalted butter (1½ lbs.), at room temperature
- 3 Tbsp. each chopped thyme and parsley
- 2 Tbsp. each chopped chives and sage
  - Kosher salt and pepper

1 Brine the turkey In a large pot, combine all of the ingredients except the turkey and add 4 cups of water. Bring to a boil, stirring to dissolve the sugar. Remove from the heat and add 12 cups of cold water. Let stand until cool. Add the turkey and refrigerate for 12 hours.

2 Set a rack over a rimmed baking sheet. Remove the turkey from the brine and transfer it to the prepared rack; pat the turkey dry with paper towels and refrigerate it uncovered for 12 hours.

3 Make the herb butter In a medium bowl, blend all of the ingredients except the salt and pepper.

4 Roast the turkey Set a clean rack over a clean baking sheet and set a large rack in a large roasting pan. Gently separate the turkey skin from the breast meat. Rub half of the herb butter over the breast meat under the skin. Spread the remaining herb butter all over the skin of the breast and legs; season with salt and pepper. Set the breast in the prepared roasting pan and tuck the wings under it. Transfer the legs to the prepared baking sheet. Let stand at room temperature for 1 hour.

5 Preheat the oven to 400°. Roast the turkey for about 2 hours, basting every 15 minutes with the melted herb butter and tenting the breast with foil after 30 minutes, until an instant-read thermometer registers 165° in the thickest part of the breast and 180° in the inner thighs. Let rest for 30 minutes. Carve and serve. *–Ken Oringer; Toro, Boston and New York City*

NOTE Ask your butcher to separate the legs from the turkey.

WINE Spiced Pinot Noir.

Slow-Roasted Turkey with Herb Salt

Time	30 min active; 5 hr 45 min total plus 2 days dry-brining
Makes	8 servings

- 2 Tbsp. kosher salt
- 1 Tbsp. pepper
- ½ Tbsp. dried thyme
- ½ Tbsp. dried savory
- 1 tsp. dried sage
- ½ tsp. dried rosemary
- ½ tsp. dried marjoram
- 2 tsp. finely grated lemon zest
- One 14-lb. organic turkey, rinsed and patted dry
- 1 onion, quartered
- 1 celery rib, cut into 2-inch pieces
- 4 garlic cloves, crushed
- 1 stick unsalted butter, melted and cooled

1 Set a rack over a rimmed baking sheet. In a small bowl, mix the salt and pepper with all of the dried herbs and the lemon zest. Rub the herb salt all over the turkey cavity. Transfer the turkey to the baking sheet and refrigerate uncovered for 2 days.

2 Transfer the turkey to a clean rack set over a clean baking sheet; let stand at room temperature for 1 hour.

3 Preheat the oven to 400°. Stuff the turkey with the onion, celery and garlic. Tuck the wings under the breast and tie the legs together with kitchen twine. Brush the turkey all over with the butter. Put it in the oven and immediately reduce the temperature to 275°. Roast the turkey for about 3 hours and 15 minutes, basting occasionally, until an instant-read thermometer inserted in the inner thighs registers 165°. Cover the turkey with foil and let rest for 1 hour. Carve and serve. *–Frank Stitt; Highlands Bar and Grill, Birmingham, Alabama*

WINE Rhône-style red blend.

MAXIMUM FLAVOR

Dry-brining a turkey requires neither a massive, leak-proof cooler nor the fridge space for an enormous bucket. Much like a dry rub for barbecue, a handful of spices and a healthy dose of salt concentrate the flavor for a well-seasoned and juicy bird.

Four-Herb Turkey with Crispy Skin

Time	30 min active; 4 hr 15 min total plus overnight dry-brining
Makes	10 servings

TURKEY

2 carrots, chopped

2 onions, chopped

3 celery ribs, chopped

4 Granny Smith apples, quartered

1 bunch each of thyme and rosemary

One 18-lb. organic turkey, legs and breast separated (see Note)

¼ cup apple cider vinegar

Kosher salt and pepper

HERBED FAT

2 cups cold rendered duck fat or softened butter

2 Tbsp. each finely chopped thyme and sage

2 tsp. finely chopped rosemary

1 fresh bay leaf, minced

2 tsp. finely grated lemon zest

1 tsp. coarse sea salt

1 tsp. pepper

1 Prepare the turkey In a large bowl, toss the carrots, onions, celery, apples, thyme and rosemary. Rub the turkey inside and out with the vinegar; season with salt and pepper. Add one-third of the vegetable mixture to a large pot. Top with the turkey legs and half of the remaining vegetable mixture. Set the turkey breast on top and scatter the remaining vegetables over the breast. Cover and refrigerate overnight.

2 Make the herbed fat In a medium bowl, combine all of the ingredients and mix well. Keep chilled but still spreadable.

3 Roast the turkey Remove the turkey from the pot. Spread half of the vegetable mixture in a roasting pan and the other half on a rimmed baking sheet. Set the turkey breast on the vegetables in the roasting pan and the legs on the baking sheet. Let stand at room temperature for 1 hour.

4 Preheat the oven to 350°. Separate the turkey skin from the breast meat. Spread the herbed fat under the skin of the breast, pressing to distribute it evenly. Tuck the wings under the breast. Roast the legs for 2 hours and the breast for 2 hours and 15 minutes, basting occasionally. The turkey is done when an instant-read thermometer inserted in the inner thighs registers 165° and the thickest part of the breast registers 160°. Let rest for 30 minutes. Carve and serve. –*Chris Cosentino; Cockscomb, San Francisco*

NOTE Ask your butcher to separate the legs from the turkey.

WINE Fruit-dense, full-bodied Chardonnay.

Deep-Fried Turkey with Berbere Spices

Time	30 min active
	2 hr 15 min total
Makes	6 servings

Canola oil, for deep-frying

1 head of garlic, halved crosswise

2 rosemary sprigs

One 10- to 12-lb. turkey, rinsed

1 Tbsp. garlic powder

1 Tbsp. smoked paprika

2 tsp. kosher salt

2 tsp. celery salt

2 tsp. ground cumin

2 tsp. black pepper

1 tsp. ground ginger

½ tsp. cayenne

1 In a turkey deep fryer, heat the oil with the garlic halves and rosemary to 350° following the manufacturer's instructions; discard the garlic and rosemary. Put the turkey on a rack set over a rimmed baking sheet and thoroughly dry it inside and out with paper towels.

2 In a small bowl, mix all of the remaining seasonings. Gently separate the turkey skin from the breast meat and rub some of the spice mix under the skin. Rub the remaining spice mix all over the outside of the turkey.

3 Following the manufacturer's instructions, carefully lower the turkey into the hot oil. Fry the turkey for about 3½ minutes per pound, until an instant-read thermometer inserted in the thickest part of the breast registers 160°. Carefully transfer the fried turkey to a clean rack set over a rimmed baking sheet and let the bird rest for 1 hour. Carve and serve. –*Marcus Samuelsson; Red Rooster, New York City*

WINE Fragrant, berry-rich Oregon Pinot Noir.

Pulled Pork

Sean Brock of Husk in Charleston, South Carolina, is a Carolina-barbecue scholar. The traditional process usually involves pit-roasting a whole hog for days until the meat is tender enough to pull apart, but Brock cooks just the shoulder, which has the best flavor and fat-to-meat ratio. Bonus: It only takes about half a day. Here, his simpler method for pulled pork, plus three key sauces.

Carolina Pulled Pork with Eastern Carolina Sauce

Time	1 hr active
	14 hr 30 min total
Makes	12 to 14 servings

1   cup Dijon mustard
2   Tbsp. dark brown sugar
2   Tbsp. kosher salt
2   Tbsp. pepper
1   Tbsp. sweet paprika
1   Tbsp. onion powder
    One 12- to 14-lb. bone-in pork shoulder, with skin
    About 50 hardwood charcoal briquettes
8   cups small hardwood smoking chips, soaked in water for 30 minutes and drained
    Eastern Carolina Sauce or variation (recipes below), for serving

1 Preheat the oven to 275°. In a medium bowl, whisk the mustard with the brown sugar, salt, pepper, paprika and onion powder. Set the pork shoulder, fat side up, in doubled 14-by-18-inch disposable aluminum roasting pans. Brush the pork with the mustard mixture **(A)**. Roast, uncovered, for 12 hours, until the meat is very tender and is pulling away from the shoulder bone.

2 Tilt the pan and pour the roasting juices into a medium bowl; you should have about 1¼ cups **(B)**. Refrigerate the juices for 30 minutes. Skim off the fat before using.

3 Meanwhile, light 10 of the charcoal briquettes. When the coals are hot, cover them with the remaining 40 briquettes. When all the coals are hot, arrange 6 cups of the soaked wood chips around the coals **(C)**. Set the roasting pan on the grill grate over the coals and wood chips. Cover the grill, partially open the air vents and smoke the pork shoulder for 30 minutes **(D)**.

4 Carefully remove the pork and the grill grate and stir the coals a few times. Scatter the remaining 2 cups of soaked wood chips over the coals. Replace the grill grate and return the pork to the grill. Cover and smoke for 30 minutes longer.

5 Transfer the pork to a work surface and let rest for 30 minutes. Pull the meat off the bones; discard the bones, gristle, skin and fat. Using tongs and a fork, or your fingers, finely shred the meat and transfer it to a large bowl **(E)**. Toss the shredded meat with ¼ cup of the reserved roasting juices and serve with one of the three barbecue sauces below **(F)**.

EASTERN CAROLINA SAUCE

In a medium bowl, combine 1 cup of the reserved roasting juices (from Step 2 of the recipe above) with 1 cup white wine vinegar and 1 cup cider vinegar. Add 1 Tbsp. dark brown sugar and 1 Tbsp. sweet smoked paprika, stirring to dissolve the sugar. Season with salt, pepper and hot sauce and serve.

WESTERN CAROLINA VARIATION Make the Eastern Carolina Sauce. Stir in 1 cup ketchup. Simmer over moderate heat for 30 minutes, until thickened. Season with salt and pepper.

SOUTH CAROLINA VARIATION Make the Eastern Carolina Sauce. Stir in 1 cup yellow mustard. Simmer over moderate heat for 30 minutes, until thickened slightly. Season with salt and pepper.

A

B

C

D

E

F

STORIED SEASONING

Brock says the tangy Eastern Carolina sauce dates to the 1500s, when Spanish settlers in coastal North Carolina spiked their pork with a hit of vinegar.

Griddled Burgers

For superjuicy burgers with a delicious crust, pros like Adam Fleischman, founder of Umami Burger, know a griddle beats a grill. "You get a more even sear, and the fat bastes the patty instead of dripping through the grate," he says. To demonstrate the griddle's superiority, Fleischman shares two of his signature creations.

Cheddar-and-Onion Smashed Burgers

Time	30 min
Makes	4 burgers

16   thin bread-and-butter pickle slices, patted dry

Four 4-inch potato buns, buttered and toasted

1¼   lbs. ground beef chuck (30 percent fat)

Kosher salt and pepper

2   small onions, sliced paper-thin

4   oz. sharp cheddar cheese, sliced

Umami dust (recipe follows), for sprinkling (optional)

1 Heat a cast-iron griddle until very hot. Layer the pickle slices on the bottom buns.

2 Without overworking the meat, loosely form it into 4 balls and place them on the griddle. Cook the meatballs over moderately high heat for 30 seconds. Using a sturdy large spatula, flatten each ball into a 5-inch round patty **(A)**. Season the patties with salt and pepper and cook for 2 minutes, until well seared. Press a handful of sliced onions onto each patty. Using the spatula, carefully flip each burger so the onions are on the bottom **(B)**. Top with the cheese and cook for 2 minutes **(C)**. Cover with a roasting pan and cook just until the cheese is melted, 1 minute more. Transfer the burgers with the onions to the buns and sprinkle with umami dust, if using. Top with the buns and serve.

BEER Hoppy pale ale: Dale's Pale Ale.

WINE Juicy, peppery California Zinfandel.

(continued on page 25)

PATTY TLC

Burger purists handle ground meat as little as possible; over-working the beef can create a tight, meatloaf-like texture.

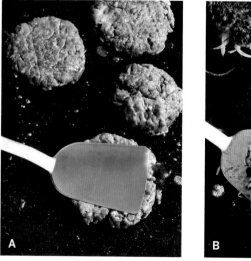

Umami Burgers with Port and Stilton

Time	40 min
Makes	4 burgers

1 cup ruby port
2 lbs. mixed ground beef brisket, skirt steak and sirloin steak (20 percent fat)
Kosher salt and pepper
½ cup Stilton cheese (3 oz.), softened
Umami dust (recipe below), for sprinkling (optional)
4 brioche hamburger buns, buttered and toasted

1 In a small saucepan, cook the port over moderate heat until reduced to 2 tablespoons, about 15 minutes.

2 Heat a cast-iron griddle until very hot. Form the meat into four 4-by-1-inch patties without packing too tightly. Season generously with salt and pepper. Add the patties to the griddle, cover with a roasting pan and cook over moderately high heat for 4 minutes, until very crusty. Flip the patties and cook, covered, for 2 minutes longer; top with the Stilton and cook uncovered for 1 minute. Transfer the patties to a plate and sprinkle with the umami dust, if using; let rest for 2 minutes and set on the bottom buns. Drizzle with the reduced port, top with the buns and serve.

BEER Malty brown ale: Brooklyn Brewery Brown Ale.

WINE Cherry-rich Washington Merlot.

UMAMI DUST

To make a simplified version of umami dust (the secret behind Umami Burger's super-savory patties), use a spice grinder to pulse 3 Tbsp. bonito flakes, ½ oz. crumbled dried kombu and ½ oz. dried shiitake mushrooms into a powder. All of these ingredients are available at Asian markets or from amazon.com.

BUILD A BETTER BURGER

Bun Tender is ideal: Crusty buns make biting through a burger too difficult.

Beef grind Fat content of 20 to 30 percent is critical for a juicy patty. Look on the label or ask your butcher.

Patty-to-bun ratio For the perfect balance, every bite should be half patty, half bun.

Toppings Go classic (pickles and onions) or creative (aioli or a Thousand Island–style dressing).

Cult Beef Cuts

It may be time to take a break from glitzy bone-in rib eyes and other premium steaks. Butcher Jeremy Stanton of The Meat Market in Great Barrington, Massachusetts, champions cuts from the chuck (shoulder). "Chuck has the stigma of being tough," he says, "but it has some very flavorful steaks and delivers great value." Read on for Stanton's recipes for his three favorite cuts from the chuck—eye roast, flat iron and teres major—all worth seeking out from artisanal butchers.

Beef Chuck Eye Roast with Paprika-Herb Rub

Time	25 min active
	1 hr 45 min total
Makes	8 servings

1 Tbsp. ground bay leaves
1 Tbsp. pepper
1 Tbsp. chopped thyme
2 tsp. sweet paprika
½ tsp. ground cumin
   One 3-lb. chuck eye roast
   Extra-virgin olive oil, for drizzling
   Kosher salt
4 garlic cloves, minced
3 Tbsp. vegetable oil

1 Preheat the oven to 375°. In a small bowl, mix the bay leaves, pepper, thyme, paprika and cumin. Drizzle the roast generously with olive oil and season with salt. Rub the garlic and spice mixture over the roast and let stand for 10 minutes.

2 Using butcher's twine, tie the roast to give it a uniform shape. In an ovenproof skillet, heat the vegetable oil. Add the roast and cook over moderate heat until lightly browned all over, about 12 minutes.

3 Transfer the skillet to the upper third of the oven and roast the meat for 1 hour, until an instant-read thermometer inserted in the center registers 130°. Transfer the roast to a carving board and let rest for 10 minutes. Discard the twine. Using a thin, sharp knife, thinly slice the beef across the grain and serve.

SUMAC-ROSEMARY RUB VARIATION Combine ¼ cup dried ground sumac (available online from penzeys.com), 2 Tbsp. chopped rosemary leaves, 1 Tbsp. pepper and 4 minced garlic cloves; rub all over the roast with a small amount of olive oil.

WINE Herb-and-cassis-scented Cabernet Sauvignon.

(continued on page 29)

CHOICEST CHUCK CUTS

Chuck eye roast This 2- to 4-pound roast comes from the chuck portion of the rib eye muscle. Ask the butcher to trim connective tissue and tie the meat for uniform cooking.

Flat iron steak Great for marinating and grilling, the flat iron sits on the shoulder blade next to the teres major—in fact, it's known as a **blade steak** when sliced against the grain.

Teres major This ultra-lean steak, sometimes referred to as the **mock tender,** sits on the shoulder blade. Its similarity to the tenderloin makes it a great substitute for filet mignon.

Lemon-and-Garlic-Marinated Flat Iron Steak

Time	30 min plus 24 hr marinating
Makes	2 servings

One 1-lb. beef flat iron steak
Kosher salt and pepper
2   Tbsp. extra-virgin olive oil
6   garlic cloves, minced
4   scallions, chopped
4   bay leaves, broken into pieces
2   lemons, very thinly sliced
Vegetable oil, for brushing

1 In a glass baking dish, season the steak with salt and pepper and rub with the olive oil. Spread the garlic, scallions and bay leaves all over the steak. Cover both sides of the steak with lemon slices. Cover and refrigerate for 24 hours.

2 Light a grill and brush with vegetable oil. Scrape off the seasonings and bring the steak to room temperature. Season with salt and pepper and grill over moderately high heat until medium-rare within, $3\frac{1}{2}$ minutes per side. Transfer to a carving board and let rest for 5 minutes. Thinly slice across the grain and serve.

RED WINE VINEGAR VARIATION In a resealable plastic bag, combine $\frac{1}{4}$ cup extra-virgin olive oil, 3 Tbsp. red wine vinegar, $\frac{1}{2}$ tsp. crushed red pepper and $\frac{1}{4}$ cup chopped parsley; add the seasoned steak to the bag and refrigerate for at least 6 hours and up to 12 hours.

WINE Juicy, berried Syrah.

Beef Medallions with Bacon and Morels

Time	35 min
Makes	4 servings

8   slices of bacon
2   beef teres majors (about 1 lb. each), cut into 8 medallions
Kosher salt and pepper
2   Tbsp. vegetable oil
16   fresh morels, rinsed, or dried morels soaked in boiling water for 30 minutes, drained and rinsed
4   large scallions, cut into ½-inch lengths
½   cup Madeira
¾   cup mushroom stock or low-sodium broth
2   Tbsp. cold unsalted butter

📷 opposite page

Wrap a slice of bacon around each beef medallion and secure with toothpicks. Season with salt and pepper. In a skillet, heat the oil until shimmering. Add the medallions and cook over moderately high heat until browned on the bottom, 2 minutes; turn and cook for 1 minute. Add the morels and scallions and cook over moderate heat until the scallions are tender. Transfer the meat to a plate. Cook the vegetables for 2 minutes more, add the Madeira and simmer for 2 minutes. Add the meat and stock and simmer over moderately low heat, turning, until an instant-read thermometer inserted in the center of the meat registers 140°, about 3 minutes. Transfer the meat to plates; discard the toothpicks. Remove the skillet from the heat and swirl in the butter. Season with salt and pepper, spoon over the meat and serve.

CARROT-AND-ONION VARIATION Substitute 2 medium carrots that have been cut into 1-inch matchsticks, and 1 halved and sliced medium onion, for the morels and scallions; ½ cup dry white wine for the Madeira; and ¾ cup beef stock for the mushroom stock. Garnish with parsley.

WINE Tart cherry–inflected, earthy Barolo.

LEARNING TO LOVE CHUCK

"The chuck has a lot of connective tissue, and many different muscle groups that are all intertwined," says Stanton. For the most tenderness, he suggests asking the butcher for chuck that's been dry-aged for at least 21 days.

Biscuits

"Saturday mornings at the deli are all about biscuits," says Matt Neal of Neal's Deli in Carrboro, North Carolina. "Our neighbors, friends, the farmers—everyone is always clamoring for them. Some people get two filled biscuits at a time, but that's a lot." Learn how to make Neal's wildly popular jumbo biscuits and choose one (or a couple) of the signature fillings—classic strawberry jam; cheddar and a breakfast-sausage patty; or warm, sliced pastrami—for an over-the-top sandwich.

Oversize Breakfast Biscuits

Time	30 min active
	1 hr total
Makes	6 biscuits

2   cups all-purpose flour, plus more for dusting

1   tsp. kosher salt

1   Tbsp. plus ¼ tsp. baking powder

½   tsp. baking soda

2   Tbsp. chilled solid vegetable shortening

5   Tbsp. unsalted butter—3 Tbsp. thinly sliced, 2 Tbsp. melted

1   cup buttermilk

1 Preheat the oven to 475°. Position a rack in the upper third of the oven. In a large bowl, whisk the 2 cups of flour with the salt, baking powder and baking soda **(A)**. Using a pastry blender, cut in the shortening until the mixture resembles coarse meal **(B)**. Using your fingers, rub in the sliced butter, leaving large flakes of coated butter **(C)**. Freeze the mixture until very cold, about 15 minutes.

2 Stir in the buttermilk until a raggy dough forms. Transfer the dough to a lightly floured work surface and press or roll into a 9-by-7-inch rectangle, about ¾ inch thick **(D)**. Fold the rectangle in thirds like a letter **(E)**, then fold the rectangle in half to make a little package **(F)**. Press or roll out the dough to a 9-by-7-inch rectangle again. Repeat the folding process once more, then roll the dough out one more time to a 9-by-7-inch rectangle. Using a 3½-inch round cutter, stamp out 4 biscuits **(G)**. Pat the scraps together and stamp out 2 more biscuits.

3 Arrange the biscuits on a large baking sheet and brush the tops with the melted butter **(H)**. Bake for about 14 minutes, shifting the baking sheet halfway through, until the tops and bottoms are golden and the biscuits are cooked through **(I)**.

STRAWBERRY JAM BREAKFAST BISCUIT Spread 1 rounded Tbsp. strawberry jam on a split breakfast biscuit.

PASTRAMI BREAKFAST BISCUIT Pile about 2 oz. warm sliced pastrami on a split breakfast biscuit.

SAUSAGE-CHEDDAR BREAKFAST BISCUIT Pan-fry a 3-oz. breakfast-sausage patty and set it on the bottom half of a breakfast biscuit. Top with 1½ oz. sliced sharp or mild white cheddar. Cover with the biscuit top. Bake the sandwich at 350° for about 5 minutes, until heated through.

MAKE AHEAD The biscuits can be made up to 3 days ahead and reheated.

PRO MOVE

When he's rolling out the dough, Neal gives it two turns (see Step 2) to evenly distribute the butter and make the biscuits extra-flaky.

A

B

C

D

E

F

G

H

I

Pickling

Linton Hopkins of Holeman and Finch in Atlanta cans all year, putting up more than 300 jars each season. Here, he shares his technique for two of his favorites: cucumber pickles and sunchoke pickle relish. The key to vegetables that stay crunchy long after jarring? Brining.

Bread-and-Butter Pickles

Time	1 hr 15 min
	plus overnight salting
Makes	6 pts

- 1 cup kosher salt
- 5½ lbs. Kirby cucumbers, sliced crosswise on a mandoline ⅛ inch thick
- 5 cups cider vinegar
- 5 cups sugar
- 1¼ lbs. onions, thinly sliced
- 2 Tbsp. yellow mustard seeds
- 1 Tbsp. celery seeds
- 1 Tbsp. turmeric
- 1 Tbsp. coarsely cracked black pepper

1 In a very large bowl or pot, dissolve the salt in 1½ gallons of water. Add the cucumbers, cover and soak overnight in the refrigerator **(A)**.

2 In a large, heavy, nonreactive pot, combine the vinegar and sugar and cook until the sugar dissolves. Stir in the remaining ingredients. Drain the cucumbers and add them to the pot. Stir gently and bring to a boil, then turn off the heat. Ladle the hot cucumbers and their liquid into 6 sterilized 1-pint canning jars, leaving ½ inch of space at the top **(B)**. Close with the lids and rings.

3 Set a metal rack in a large pot, fill with water and bring to a boil. Using canning tongs, carefully set the filled jars on the rack; make sure the jars are covered by at least 1 inch of water. Boil the jars for 10 minutes **(C)**. Using the tongs, carefully remove the jars from the water and let stand until the lids seal (they will look concave). Store in a cool, dark place for up to 1 year. Refrigerate after opening.

BEYOND THE JAR

Hopkins has endless uses for these sweet and tangy pickles—he even deep-fries them to make pickle chips.

Sunchoke Pickle Relish

Time	30 min active
	2 hr total
Makes	2 qts

- ½ cup kosher salt
- 1¼ lbs. sunchokes, scrubbed and cut into ½-inch dice
- 1 large Vidalia or other sweet onion (about 1¼ lbs.), finely diced
- 1 large red bell pepper, cut into ¼-inch dice
- ½ cup mustard powder
- ¼ cup all-purpose flour
- 1 qt. apple cider vinegar
- 2 cups sugar
- 1 Tbsp. turmeric
- 1 tsp. yellow mustard seeds
- 1 tsp. black pepper
- 1 tsp. celery seeds

1 In a large bowl, dissolve the salt in 4 cups of water. Add the sunchokes and let stand for 1 hour **(A)**.

2 Drain the sunchokes and return them to the bowl. Add the onion and bell pepper and toss **(B)**. Transfer the vegetables to 2 sterilized quart-size canning jars.

3 In a small bowl, stir the mustard powder and flour with ½ cup of water to make a paste. In a large saucepan, combine all of the remaining ingredients and bring to a boil. Whisk in the mustard-flour paste until smooth. Simmer until thickened, about 10 minutes. Pour the hot liquid over the sunchokes and tap the jars to release any air bubbles **(C)**.

4 Cover the jars (not too tightly) and use canning tongs to transfer them to a deep pot of boiling water. Boil the jars for 25 minutes **(D)**. Using the tongs, carefully remove the jars from the water; let stand until the lids seal.

LOCAL SPECIALTY

Sunchoke relish is on every table in Georgia and South Carolina, says Hopkins. "When I was a boy, I thought they were the funniest artichokes," he recalls; in fact, they are the knotty roots of sunflowers, with a sweet, crunchy taste.

Ricotta Cheese

So much creamier and tastier than any store-bought version, homemade ricotta is also surprisingly easy to prepare. Chef Daniel Patterson, co-founder of the Locol restaurants in L.A. and Oakland, makes his the base for a lemony pudding that can be served sweet or savory.

Lemon-Ricotta Pudding

Time	20 min active
	1 hr 30 min total
Makes	4 servings

RICOTTA

½ gal. whole milk

1 cup heavy cream

3 Tbsp. plus 1 tsp. white vinegar, plus more if needed

PUDDING

Unsalted butter, for greasing

¾ cup heavy cream

Finely grated zest of 1 lemon

Kosher salt and pepper

2 large eggs, lightly beaten

1 Make the ricotta Line a strainer with a double layer of cheesecloth and set it over a large bowl. In a large saucepan, heat the milk and cream over moderately high heat to 180°. Remove from the heat and slowly add the vinegar until you see the milk separate; add more vinegar as needed **(A)**. Cover the saucepan and let stand for 2 minutes.

2 Pour the contents of the saucepan into the prepared strainer **(B)**. Shake the strainer vigorously to remove the water (a.k.a. whey). You should have about 2 cups of ricotta; let cool.

3 Make the pudding Preheat the oven to 325°. Butter four 1-cup ramekins. In a large bowl, whisk 1¾ cups of the ricotta with the heavy cream and lemon zest, breaking up any large ricotta curds; season with salt and pepper. Whisk in the eggs.

4 Pour the pudding into the prepared ramekins and set them in a baking dish. Add enough hot water to the dish to reach halfway up the sides of the ramekins. Bake just until set, about 55 minutes. Let the puddings cool to room temperature or refrigerate until chilled. Serve the puddings in the ramekins.

MAKE AHEAD The puddings can be refrigerated overnight.

WAYS TO SERVE

This versatile, lemony pudding can be served as a starter with a cherry tomato–and–basil salad or at the end of a meal with honey or strawberries. Any leftover ricotta is excellent spread on toast.

A

B

Baked Fruit Desserts

Pie-obsessed Kansas City residents flock to Megan Garrelts's Bluestem and Rye all week long for her Dutch apple and banana cream pies. At home, however, Garrelts favors simpler cobblers or pandowdies. These all-American fruit desserts topped with pieces of dough are easier to make than pie and even better showcases for your juiciest farm-stand finds.

Blueberry-Nectarine Pandowdy

Time	45 min active
	3 hr total
Makes	8 servings

SUGAR COOKIE DOUGH

- ¾ cup all-purpose flour
- ¼ tsp. baking powder
- ¼ tsp. kosher salt
- 4½ Tbsp. unsalted butter, softened
- ½ cup sugar
- ¼ tsp. pure vanilla extract
- 1½ tsp. finely grated lemon zest plus 1½ tsp. fresh lemon juice
- 1½ tsp. finely grated lime zest plus 1½ tsp. fresh lime juice
- 2 Tbsp. beaten egg (½ large egg)

PANDOWDY

- Unsalted butter, for greasing
- ½ cup sugar
- ½ tsp. ground cinnamon
- 4 cups sliced nectarines (4 to 5)
- 4 heaping cups blueberries
- ¼ cup cornstarch
- 1 Tbsp. finely grated orange zest plus ½ cup fresh orange juice
- 2 tsp. finely grated peeled fresh ginger
- 2 tsp. brandy
- 1 tsp. ground ginger
- ½ tsp. ground cardamom
- ½ tsp. grated nutmeg
- Heavy cream, for brushing
- Ice cream, for serving

1 Make the sugar cookie dough In a medium bowl, sift the flour with the baking powder and salt. In a large bowl, beat the butter and sugar with a hand mixer at medium-high speed until light and fluffy, about 3 minutes. Beat in the vanilla, lemon zest, lemon juice, lime zest and lime juice, scraping down the side of the bowl as necessary. Beat in the egg. With the mixer at low speed, beat in the dry ingredients, scraping down the side of the bowl as necessary; the dough will be very soft.

2 Scrape the dough out onto a sheet of plastic wrap and roll into a 9-inch log. Flatten the log into a 2-inch-wide rectangle, about 1 inch tall. Refrigerate until very firm, at least 2 hours.

3 Make the pandowdy Preheat the oven to 350°. Butter a 9-by-13-inch glass, ceramic or metal baking dish and sprinkle with 2 tablespoons of the sugar; turn to coat the pan with sugar.

4 In a small bowl, mix 2 tablespoons of the sugar with the cinnamon. In a large bowl, toss the nectarines and blueberries with the remaining ¼ cup of sugar and the cornstarch, orange zest, orange juice, grated ginger, brandy, ground ginger, cardamom and nutmeg **(A)**. Spread the fruit in the prepared baking dish **(B)**.

5 Using a sharp knife, cut the rectangle of cookie dough into ¼-inch-thick slices **(C)**. Arrange the slices over the fruit in a graphic or random pattern; they will spread during baking. Brush the dough with heavy cream and sprinkle with the cinnamon sugar **(D, E)**. Bake until the cookie dough is golden brown and the fruit is bubbling, about 45 minutes. Serve the pandowdy warm, with ice cream **(F)**.

NOTE Cutting rectangles from a slice-and-bake log makes the soft dough easy to work with.

(continued on page 39)

A

B

C

D

E

F

TAKE A BITE OUT OF AMERICAN HISTORY

Pandowdies (you've got to love the name) belong to the family of Colonial American dough-topped fruit desserts that includes cobblers, betties, crisps, grunts, slumps and buckles.

Mixed-Fruit Cornmeal Cobbler

Time	45 min active
	2 hr 30 min total
Makes	8 servings

CORNMEAL BISCUITS

- 1¾ cups all-purpose flour
- ¼ cup corn flour
- ¼ cup fine cornmeal
- ¼ cup granulated sugar
- 2 tsp. finely grated lemon zest
- 1½ tsp. baking powder
- ⅛ tsp. baking soda
- 1 tsp. kosher salt
- 1 stick cold unsalted butter, cubed, plus more for greasing
- ½ cup plus 2 Tbsp. buttermilk

COBBLER

- ½ cup honey
- ½ cup light brown sugar
- ¼ cup fresh lemon juice
- 1 Tbsp. ground cinnamon
- ½ tsp. kosher salt
- ⅓ cup cornstarch mixed with ¼ cup water
- 8 cups raspberries, pitted cherries and sliced plums
- Heavy cream, for brushing
- 2 Tbsp. turbinado sugar
- Lemon thyme sprigs, for garnish
- Whipped cream, for serving

1 Make the biscuits In a food processor, combine the all-purpose flour, corn flour, cornmeal, granulated sugar, lemon zest, baking powder, baking soda and salt; pulse to blend. Add the cubed butter and pulse until the mixture resembles coarse meal. With the machine on, drizzle in the buttermilk. Turn the dough out onto a work surface and knead just until it comes together. Pat the dough into a 1-inch-thick disk, wrap in plastic and refrigerate until firm, at least 1 hour.

2 Preheat the oven to 350°. Butter a 3-quart baking dish. On a lightly floured work surface, roll out the dough ½ inch thick. Using a 2-inch biscuit cutter, stamp out rounds, rerolling the scraps.

3 Make the cobbler In a large bowl, mix the honey with the brown sugar, lemon juice, cinnamon and salt. Stir and add the cornstarch mixture, then add the fruit and toss gently. Spread the fruit in the prepared baking dish and top with the biscuits. Brush the biscuits with cream and sprinkle with the turbinado sugar. Bake until the fruit is bubbling and the biscuits are golden, about 45 minutes. Garnish with lemon thyme and serve warm, with whipped cream.

TOP THAT!

This cornmeal-biscuit dough is light and not too sweet. Cut the biscuits in any size rounds, or in fanciful shapes if you prefer.

Sundaes

At San Francisco's Mr. and Mrs. Miscellaneous, everyone can indulge their nostalgic love of the ice cream sundae. Owners Annabelle Topacio and Ian Flores create classic toppings, each with one smart twist that makes it taste exactly as you remember but also mysteriously better. For instance, the berries in the strawberry sauce are lightly cooked with a vanilla bean. "We want to satisfy your memory," says Topacio, "and at the same time blow your mind."

Butterscotch Sauce

Time	15 min plus cooling
Makes	3 cups

¾ cup packed dark brown sugar

¾ cup granulated sugar

6 Tbsp. Lyle's Golden Syrup

1¼ tsp. kosher salt

1 stick unsalted butter, diced

1 cup plus 2 Tbsp. heavy cream, at room temperature

1 Tbsp. pure vanilla extract

¾ tsp. fresh lemon juice

In a medium saucepan, combine both sugars with the syrup and salt. Cook over moderate heat, stirring occasionally, until the mixture is molten and beginning to bubble at the edge, about 6 minutes. Simmer, stirring, for 1 minute more, then stir in the butter. Attach a candy thermometer to the side of the pan and cook until the sauce reaches 240°, about 2 minutes. Carefully stir in the cream until incorporated and bring to a rolling boil. Remove from the heat and stir in the vanilla, lemon juice and 1½ tablespoons of water. Let the sauce cool completely, then transfer it to a container and refrigerate. Serve warm or at room temperature.

Hot Fudge Sauce

Time	30 min
Makes	3 cups

5 oz. semisweet chocolate, coarsely chopped

3 oz. unsweetened chocolate, coarsely chopped

6 Tbsp. unsalted butter

1 cup plus 2 Tbsp. light corn syrup

¾ cup sugar

¾ tsp. kosher salt

2 tsp. pure vanilla extract

1 In a medium heatproof bowl, combine both chocolates with the butter. Set the bowl over a medium saucepan of simmering water and stir until the chocolate and butter are melted and blended. Remove the bowl and set aside. Pour off the water.

2 In the same saucepan, combine the corn syrup, sugar, salt and 2 cups of water and bring to a boil over high heat. Reduce the heat to moderate and whisk in the melted chocolate. Cook, stirring occasionally, until the sauce is thick and shiny, 18 to 20 minutes. Remove from the heat and stir in the vanilla. Use immediately or let cool completely and refrigerate. Rewarm in a microwave before serving.

Strawberry Sauce

Time	20 min plus chilling
Makes	3 cups

2 lbs. strawberries, hulled and quartered

2 cups sugar

½ tsp. finely grated lemon zest

1 vanilla bean, seeds scraped

Combine all of the ingredients in a medium saucepan. Stir to coat the strawberries with sugar and bring to a boil over high heat. Reduce the heat to moderate and simmer, stirring occasionally, until the strawberries begin to break down and the sauce is thickened, 10 to 12 minutes. Remove from the heat and let cool completely, then refrigerate. Serve cold or at room temperature.

(continued on page 43)

Fresh Pineapple Sauce

Time	20 min plus chilling
Makes	3 cups

- 2 cups finely chopped fresh pineapple
- 2 cups pineapple juice
- 1 cup sugar
- 1 cup light corn syrup
- Finely grated zest of 1 lemon plus 2 tsp. fresh lemon juice
- ½ tsp. kosher salt
- 2 tsp. Campari

In a medium saucepan, combine all of the ingredients except the Campari and bring to a boil over high heat. Reduce the heat to moderate and simmer for 5 minutes. Stir in the Campari and cook, stirring occasionally, until the sauce is thick and shiny, about 10 minutes. Remove from the heat and let cool completely, then refrigerate. Serve cold.

MAKE AHEAD The pineapple sauce can be refrigerated for up to 2 weeks.

Wet Mixed Nuts

Time	30 min plus cooling
Makes	3 cups

- 1 cup walnuts
- ½ cup pecans
- ½ cup blanched hazelnuts
- ½ cup pure maple syrup
- ½ cup Lyle's Golden Syrup
- ½ cup light corn syrup
- ¼ cup sugar
- ½ vanilla bean, seeds scraped

1 Preheat the oven to 350°. Spread the walnuts, pecans and hazelnuts on a rimmed baking sheet and bake for 10 minutes, until toasted. Let cool, then coarsely chop.

2 In a medium saucepan, combine the three syrups with the sugar, vanilla seeds and ½ cup of water. Bring to a boil over high heat, then reduce the heat to moderate and simmer until thickened, about 8 minutes. Remove from the heat and stir in the chopped nuts. Let cool completely, then transfer to a container and refrigerate for up to 2 weeks. Serve at room temperature.

NEXT-LEVEL TOPPINGS

Topacio and Flores add Campari to their pineapple sauce for a hint of bitterness and vibrant color. Their take on the classic wet nuts topping was inspired by a tart filling; golden syrup (treacle) and maple syrup give the nuts a complex sweetness.

Tempering Chocolate

"I'm more addicted to chocolate than I am to sugar," says Jacques Torres, the celebrated pastry chef who's been nicknamed Mr. Chocolate. At his eponymous shops in New York City, Torres creates all kinds of confections, such as the addictive chocolate-coated corn flakes here. For the best flavor and glossiest sheen, start by tempering high-quality chocolate like Valrhona or Callebaut.

Chocolate Corn-Flake Clusters

Time	40 min
Makes	about 4 dozen clusters

1 lb. semisweet or bittersweet chocolate

4 cups corn flakes

1 Chop the chocolate into ¹/₂-inch pieces with a serrated or other large knife **(A)**. Microwave two-thirds of the chocolate for 30 seconds at high power, then stir with a rubber spatula **(B)**. Continue to microwave the chocolate in 30-second intervals, stirring each time **(C)**. Stop microwaving the chocolate when it is fully melted **(D)**.

2 Stir in the remaining one-third of chocolate until melted. The melted chocolate should now register between 104° and 113° on an instant-read thermometer **(E)**. If you don't have an instant-read thermometer, a simple method of checking tempering is to apply a small quantity of chocolate to a piece of paper or to the point of a knife **(F)**. If the chocolate has been correctly tempered it will harden evenly and show a good gloss within 5 minutes.

3 Pour the corn flakes into a large bowl, then pour about half of the tempered chocolate over them. Using a rubber spatula, quickly fold the corn flakes into the chocolate until they're evenly coated **(G)**. The tempered chocolate will immediately begin to set. Once the chocolate has set, repeat with the remaining chocolate to give the corn flakes a second coat. Using a spoon, quickly scoop small mounds of the chocolate-covered corn flakes onto a parchment paper–lined baking sheet **(H)**. Allow the chocolate to harden, then serve **(I)**.

NOTE If your kitchen is very hot, you can place the baking sheet in the refrigerator for about 5 minutes to allow the chocolate to harden. Do not leave them in the refrigerator for more than 10 minutes; if they get too cold, condensation will form on them when they are removed from the refrigerator due to the difference in temperature between the cold chocolate and the warm air. This will cause the chocolate to turn white. While this doesn't affect the taste, it does ruin the appearance.

MAKE AHEAD Store the corn-flake clusters in an airtight container in a cool, dry place. They will keep for 2 weeks, if you can resist eating them.

TEMPERING TIPS

Use the best-quality bittersweet chocolate that you can find. Any leftover tempered chocolate can be tempered again later.

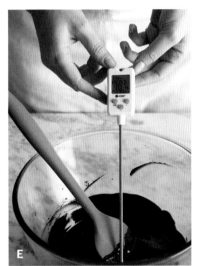

Level Two

48 Mozzarella

50 Tempura

52 Beef Jerky

54 Stock

56 Hot & Sour Soup

58 Vietnamese Pancakes

60 Hand-Cut Noodles

64 Thin-Crust Pizza

68 Risotto

70 Fish Stew

74 Gumbo

76 Sushi

78 Soft-Shell Crabs

80 Sous Vide Cooking

82 Fried Chicken

84 Tikka Masala

86 Pho

90 Thai Curry

92 Duck à l'Orange

94 Osso Buco

96 Next Great Lamb Cuts

100 Sauerkraut

104 Rye Bread

106 Popovers

108 Soufflé

112 Yogurt

116 Layer Cake

120 Pie Crust

124 Baklava

126 Pastry Puffs

128 Caramel Sauce

130 Ice Cream

132 Candy

138 Barrel-Aged Cocktails

Mozzarella

Homemade mozzarella is warm, tender, milky and easier to make than you might think. Sal Lamboglia, a chef at Bar Primi in New York City, starts with store-bought curds. He softens them with very hot water, then starts pulling (stretching the pieces like taffy and folding them over and around to form balls of delicate cheese). "Eat it within the hour," he says. As if anyone could wait.

Fresh Mozzarella

Time	30 min
Makes	2 lbs

2   lbs. mozzarella cheese curds (see Note), cut into ½-inch pieces

2   Tbsp. kosher salt

Tomato slices, basil leaves, extra-virgin olive oil, sea salt and pepper, for serving

1 In a large heatproof bowl, soak the cheese curds in lukewarm water for 10 minutes to bring them to room temperature. Pour off the water. Toss the cheese curds with the kosher salt **(A)**.

2 Heat 2 quarts of water to 170° (measured on a candy thermometer). Slowly pour the water around the edge of the bowl until the cheese curds are completely submerged; be sure not to pour the water directly on the curds **(B)**. Let the curds stand in the hot water, without stirring, until they begin to melt together into a mass, about 1 minute **(C)**.

3 Using 2 wooden spoons or spatulas, pull the curd up from the bottom and fold it over onto itself until it's smooth and silky and forms tender strands, about 3 minutes **(D)**.

4 Fill a large bowl with cold water. Pull a fist-size piece of the warm curd and form it into a ball by stretching and tucking it under and into itself **(E)**. Pinch off the ball and drop it into the cold water. Repeat with the remaining curd.

5 Slice the mozzarella and serve with tomatoes, fresh basil, a drizzle of olive oil and a sprinkling of sea salt and pepper **(F)**. Or wrap the mozzarella balls in plastic and refrigerate for up to 3 days.

NOTE Mozzarella curd is available in many large stores that make their own mozzarella, or online from caputobrotherscreamery.com and saxelbycheese.com.

A

B

C

D

E

F

CHOOSE WISELY

Be sure to use only mozzarella curds, as other kinds will not yield the same results.

Tempura

Pulling batter-coated tempura hot out of the oil makes vegetables—even kale—absolutely irresistible. New York City–based recipe developer Kay Chun creates a batter that fries up ultralight and shatteringly crisp. Her secret weapon: fizzy club soda. (The bubbles produce an incredible airy texture.) A tangy ponzu-based sauce is perfect for dipping.

Vegetable Tempura with Ginger-Ponzu Dipping Sauce

Time	45 min
Makes	10 to 12 servings

- 1 small eggplant (8 oz.), cut into 1-inch pieces
  Kosher salt
- ½ cup ponzu sauce
- 1 Tbsp. fresh lime juice
- 2 Tbsp. julienned ginger (½-inch lengths)
- 2 Tbsp. thinly sliced scallion
  Vegetable oil, for frying
- 2 cups all-purpose flour
- ¼ cup cornstarch
- 1 tsp. baking powder
- 2 cups cold club soda
- 1 small Delicata squash (1 lb.)—halved lengthwise, seeded and sliced crosswise ⅛ to ¼ inch thick
- 1 small Japanese sweet potato (8 oz.), sliced crosswise ⅛ inch thick
- 1 lemon, sliced crosswise ⅛ inch thick
- 12 small kale leaves (optional)

1 In a colander, toss the eggplant with 1 teaspoon of salt and let stand for 15 minutes. Rinse and squeeze gently to remove excess water **(A)**.

2 Meanwhile, in a small bowl, stir together the ponzu sauce, lime juice, ginger and scallion. Set aside the dipping sauce **(B)**.

3 In a Dutch oven, heat 1½ inches of oil to between 365° and 370°. In a large bowl, whisk together the flour, cornstarch, baking powder and 1 teaspoon of salt. Gently whisk in the club soda just until a batter forms. Do not overmix; some lumps are OK **(C)**. Working in batches, dip the eggplant, squash, sweet potato and lemon slices into the batter, letting the excess drip off **(D)**. Carefully lower the vegetables and fruit into the hot oil **(E)**. Fry, turning occasionally, until cooked through, light golden and crispy, about 2 minutes **(F)**. Let the oil to return to 365° to 370° between batches. Transfer the tempura to a paper towel–lined wire rack set over a baking sheet to drain. Repeat with the kale, if using (be careful; the oil will splatter), frying a few leaves at a time. Season the tempura with salt and serve with the dipping sauce **(G, H)**.

WINE Light, citrusy white, such as Muscadet.

BATTER UP

The tempura batter is also fabulous on onion rings, broccoli florets and asparagus spears—or try it on leafy herbs like Japanese shiso and Korean perilla.

Beef Jerky

Real beef jerky isn't the smoky stick of preserved mystery meat you may think it is. Case in point: Rachel Graville of Iris Café in Brooklyn has a cult following for her handcrafted artisanal versions. She starts with lean beef (fat interferes with the drying process), then slices it by hand. For the seasonings, she urges not to overdo it. "You want to be able to taste the beef," she says.

Sweet and Spicy Jerky

Time	30 min active 10 hr 30 min total plus cooling
Makes	about ¾ lb

1½	cups brewed strong coffee
1½	cups Coca-Cola
2	whole star anise pods
2	cups soy sauce
½	cup Asian fish sauce
½	cup fresh lime juice
¼	cup sambal oelek
2	lbs. trimmed beef top round or bottom round, about 1½ inches thick

1 Make the marinade In a saucepan, boil the coffee, Coca-Cola and star anise until reduced by half, about 10 minutes **(A)**. Pour the reduction into a large bowl and let cool to room temperature, stirring often. Add the soy sauce, fish sauce, lime juice and sambal oelek and stir well **(B)**.

2 Prepare the meat Cut the beef into ¼-inch-thick slices, either with or against the grain **(C)**. Add the beef to the marinade, a few slices at a time, stirring well to coat each slice **(D)**. Cover and refrigerate for 6 to 8 hours.

3 Dry the meat Preheat the oven to 200°. Set a large wire rack on each of 3 large rimmed baking sheets. Remove the beef from the marinade and pat dry with paper towels. Arrange the beef on the racks, leaving ¼ inch between slices **(E)**. Bake for about 4 hours, until the jerky is firm and almost completely dry, but still chewy. Let cool completely on the racks before serving **(F)**.

MAKE AHEAD The dried-beef jerky can be refrigerated in an airtight container for up to 6 weeks.

Black Pepper Jerky

Time	30 min active 10 hr 30 min total plus cooling
Makes	about ¾ lb

3	cups amber ale or lager
2	cups soy sauce
½	cup Worcestershire sauce
2	Tbsp. cracked black peppercorns
2	lbs. trimmed beef top round or bottom round, about 1½ inches thick
2	Tbsp. coarsely ground black pepper

1 Make the marinade In a large bowl, combine the ale or lager with the soy sauce, Worcestershire sauce and cracked black peppercorns.

2 Prepare the meat Cut the beef into ¼-inch-thick slices, either with or against the grain. Add the beef to the marinade, a few slices at a time, stirring well to coat each slice. Cover and refrigerate for 6 to 8 hours.

3 Dry the meat Preheat the oven to 200°. Set a large wire rack on each of 3 large rimmed baking sheets. Remove the beef from the marinade and pat dry with paper towels. Arrange the beef on the racks, leaving ¼ inch between slices. Sprinkle with the coarsely ground black pepper. Bake for about 4 hours, until the jerky is firm and almost completely dry, but still chewy. Let cool completely on the racks before serving.

MAKE AHEAD The dried-beef jerky can be refrigerated in an airtight container for up to 6 weeks.

JERKY BASICS

Slicing Graville slices meat by hand. She likes the imperfections of the artisanal approach.

Marinating The beef gets saltier the longer it marinates; soak it for no more than 8 hours.

Drying Graville prefers a home dehydrator like Nesco American Harvest but says that a 200° oven works just as well for first-timers.

Stock

If you want to make a truly memorable soup, starting with homemade stock is a must. Here, two stellar versions: a traditional one from André Soltner, the revered chef and dean of classic studies at the International Culinary Center in New York City; plus, a quick pressure-cooker option from Momofuku founder David Chang with an extra-concentrated flavor from freeze-dried chicken.

Classic Chicken Stock

Time	20 min active
	2 hr 20 min total
Makes	3 qts

1 gal. cold water
   One 4-lb. chicken
2 leeks, coarsely chopped
2 carrots, coarsely chopped
2 celery ribs, coarsely chopped
2 unpeeled garlic cloves
1 medium onion, coarsely chopped
4 parsley sprigs
2 thyme sprigs
1 bay leaf

📷 opposite page

Combine all of the ingredients in a large pot and bring to a boil. Reduce the heat, partially cover and simmer for 1 hour, skimming as necessary. Transfer the chicken to a rimmed baking sheet and let cool slightly. Remove all of the meat from the chicken and return the bones and skin to the pot; reserve the meat for another use. Partially cover and simmer the stock for 1 hour longer. Strain the stock and let cool. Skim off the fat before using. —*André Soltner*

MAKE AHEAD The stock can be refrigerated for up to 3 days or frozen for up to 1 month.

David Chang's Freeze-Dried Chicken Stock

Time	15 min active
	1 hr total
Makes	2½ qts

5 qts. water
1 large onion, chopped
1 fennel bulb, chopped
4 scallions, chopped
4 garlic cloves, smashed and peeled
1 Tbsp. coriander seeds
2 oz. dried kombu
2 chicken drumsticks
2 chicken thighs
4 cups (4 oz.) dried shiitake mushrooms
4 oz. freeze-dried chicken (see Note)

1 In a large pot, combine the water, onion, fennel, scallions, garlic and coriander and bring to a boil. Cover and simmer over low heat for 10 minutes.

2 Strain the broth and return it to the pot. Add the kombu. Cook over very low heat (140°) for 10 minutes. Discard the kombu.

3 Transfer the broth to a pressure cooker. Add the drumsticks, thighs, shiitake and freeze-dried chicken. Close and seal the pressure cooker and bring it to full pressure according to the manufacturer's instructions. Cook for 25 minutes. Strain and let cool. —*David Chang*

NOTE Freeze-dried chicken is available from campmor.com.

MAKE AHEAD The stock can be refrigerated for up to 3 days or frozen for up to 1 month.

Hot & Sour Soup

If you've only had this soup in a takeout container, then read on. Ed Schoenfeld, Chinese-food expert and owner of RedFarm in New York City, creates an exceptional silky version that's ready in the time it takes for delivery. Traditional ingredients like earthy tree ear fungus, tender bamboo shoots and lily buds—all available at Chinese markets and online—make it wonderfully complex.

Silky Hot and Sour Soup

Time	40 min
Makes	4 servings

- 12 dried lily buds (see below)
- ½ oz. dried tree ear fungus (¼ cup; see below)
- 1 qt. low-sodium chicken broth
- 2 Tbsp. distilled white vinegar, plus more for seasoning
- 2 Tbsp. medium-dark soy sauce, plus more for seasoning
  Kosher salt
- 2 Tbsp. cornstarch
- 2 large eggs
- ½ cup shredded bamboo shoots
- ½ cup shredded cooked chicken, pork or ham
- 3½ oz. shredded spiced thick dry tofu (1 cup; see below)
- 1½ tsp. finely ground white pepper
  Toasted sesame oil, for drizzling
  Chopped scallions and cilantro, for garnish

1 In a small heatproof bowl, cover the lily buds with hot water and let stand until softened, about 30 minutes **(A)**. Cut off and discard the tough tips. In another small heatproof bowl, cover the dried tree ear fungus with hot water and let stand until softened, about 20 to 30 minutes **(B)**. Rinse, drain and coarsely chop **(C)**.

2 Meanwhile, in a large saucepan, bring the chicken broth to a boil **(D)**. Add the 2 tablespoons each of vinegar and soy sauce and ½ teaspoon of salt. In a small bowl, whisk the cornstarch with 3 tablespoons of water, then add the mixture to the boiling broth, stirring constantly **(E)**. Let the broth return to a simmer and cook until it thickens, about 3 to 4 minutes.

3 In a bowl, beat the eggs with a pinch of salt. Bring the soup to a full rolling boil and, using a circular motion, pour in the beaten eggs **(F)**. Wait 5 seconds, then turn off the heat and stir the soup to distribute the eggs throughout.

4 Add the lily buds, tree ear fungus, bamboo shoots, chicken, tofu and white pepper **(G)**. Simmer over moderate heat until the flavors meld, about 2 minutes. Season with soy sauce, vinegar and salt **(H)**.

5 Ladle the soup into 4 bowls. Drizzle with sesame oil, garnish with scallions and cilantro and serve **(I)**.

INGREDIENT INTEL

Lily buds With an earthy, sweet taste, these unopened buds of the day lily are very popular in China.

Tree ear fungus Dried dark brown to black fungi (a.k.a. wood ear mushrooms) with a mild flavor.

Spiced thick dry tofu Pressed to remove all moisture, these tofu cakes get their distinctive flavor from Chinese five-spice powder.

A

B

C

D

E

F

G

H

I

Vietnamese Pancakes

These lacy savory bánh xèo pancakes from Marcia Kiesel, co-author of *Simple Art of Vietnamese Cooking*, represent everything we love about the Southeast Asian cuisine: Studded with pork and shrimp and folded around sprouts, they're hot and crisp, cold and juicy, and invigoratingly aromatic.

Happy Pancakes (Bánh Xèo)

Time	1 hr
Makes	about 10 pancakes

DIPPING SAUCE

- 2 Thai red chiles or 1 medium jalapeño, thickly sliced
- 2 medium garlic cloves, thickly sliced
- 2 Tbsp. sugar
- 2 Tbsp. Asian fish sauce
- 2 Tbsp. fresh lime juice

PANCAKES

- 1¾ cups rice flour
- ¼ tsp. turmeric
- 1 scallion, thinly sliced
- ¾ cup plus 3 Tbsp. vegetable oil
- 1 lb. boneless pork loin, cut crosswise into very thin slices
- ½ lb. medium shrimp, shelled and deveined
- ½ small onion, thinly sliced
- 10 medium mushrooms, sliced
  Kosher salt and pepper
- 2½ cups mung bean sprouts

1 Make the dipping sauce In a mortar, pound the chiles, garlic and sugar to a paste. Stir in the fish sauce, lime juice and 2 tablespoons of water.

2 Make the pancakes In a bowl, whisk together the rice flour and 2 cups of cold water. Mix in the turmeric and scallion **(A)**.

3 In a large nonstick skillet, heat 1½ tablespoons of the vegetable oil over high heat. Add 3 slices of pork, 3 shrimp and a few slices of onion and mushroom. Season with ⅛ teaspoon each of salt and pepper. Cook for 1 minute **(B)**. Stir the rice flour mixture again and ladle ⅓ cup into the pan; tilt the pan to evenly distribute the batter. Cover and cook until the sides of the pancake turn deep brown and curl up, 5 minutes. Scatter ¼ cup of the bean sprouts over the pancake, fold it in half and slide it onto a warm platter **(C)**. Keep warm in a low oven while you repeat with the remaining ingredients. Serve the pancakes warm, with the dipping sauce on the side.

WINE Zesty Grüner Veltliner.

Hand-Cut Noodles

Inspired by the udon he learned to make in Tokyo, David Chang of New York City's Momofuku Noodle Bar makes rustic hand-cut noodles that come together in just minutes. He slices the dough into uneven strips, which he then cooks quickly in a vegetarian broth that's deeply flavored with umami-rich shiitake mushrooms. Keep reading to get your slurp on.

Shiitake and Swiss Chard Soup with Hand-Cut Noodles

Time	30 min active
	1 hr 30 min total
Makes	8 servings

One 1-oz. sheet of dried kombu (see Note)

3 oz. dried shiitake mushrooms, finely ground in a food processor

2 cups all-purpose flour

½ cup soy sauce

¼ cup mirin

6 oz. fresh shiitake mushrooms, stemmed and caps thinly sliced

1 lb. Swiss chard—stems finely chopped, leaves coarsely chopped

Kimchi and honey, for serving

📷 page 62

1 In a large pot, combine the kombu with 14 cups of water and bring to a simmer. Cook over low heat, without boiling, for 30 minutes **(A)**. Discard the kombu and bring the cooking broth to a boil. Add the ground mushrooms and return to a boil **(B)**. Remove from the heat, cover and let steep for 30 minutes.

2 Meanwhile, in a stand mixer fitted with the dough hook, mix the flour and ¾ cup of water at medium speed just until the flour is moistened **(C)**. Increase the speed to medium-high and beat until a smooth, firm, elastic dough forms, 8 to 10 minutes. Wrap the dough in plastic; let stand for 30 minutes **(D)**.

3 Strain the broth into a heatproof bowl. Wipe out the pot and return the broth to it. Add the soy sauce and mirin and bring to a boil. Add the fresh shiitake and Swiss chard and cook just until tender, about 2 minutes; keep warm **(E)**.

4 On a lightly floured surface, roll the dough out ⅛ inch thick **(F)**. Using a pastry wheel, slice the dough into uneven strips **(G)**. Bring the broth back to a boil and add the noodles **(H)**. Cook, stirring, until the noodles are tender and the soup is slightly thickened, 5 minutes. Ladle the soup into bowls and garnish with kimchi and a little honey **(I)**.

NOTE Kombu, a type of kelp often used to flavor Japanese soups, is available at Japanese markets and at some supermarkets and health-food stores.

DOUBLE THE MUSHROOMS, DOUBLE THE FLAVOR

Chang infuses this fabulous kombu broth with dried shiitake; fresh shiitake intensify the flavor.

A

B

C

D

E

F

G

H

I

Shiitake and Swiss
Chard Soup with
Hand-Cut Noodles
page 60

Thin-Crust
Margherita Pizza
page 66

Thin-Crust Pizza

Thomas McNaughton, the chef and dough master at San Francisco's Flour + Water, is renowned for his ethereal Neapolitan-style pies. They bake up tender inside and crisp outside, even in a standard home oven. The key is using a small amount of yeast for a long, slow rise, resulting in complex, nuanced flavors. Learn how to make his dough, perfect pizza sauce and three toppings.

Slow-Rising Pizza Dough

Time	1 hr 15 min active 3 days total
Makes	five 10-inch pizzas

1¾ lbs. 00 flour (5½ cups; see Note), plus more for dusting

0.75 g. active dry yeast (½ tsp.; see Note)

2 cups warm water

27 g. kosher salt (3 Tbsp.)

Perfect Pizza Sauce and toppings (recipes follow)

1 Make the dough Lightly dust a very large bowl with flour. In a small bowl, whisk the yeast with ¼ cup of the water and let stand until foamy, about 5 minutes.

2 In a stand mixer fitted with the dough hook, combine the 1¾ pounds of flour with the yeast mixture and the remaining 1¾ cups of water and mix at low speed for 1 minute. Increase the speed to medium and mix until all of the flour is incorporated, about 4 minutes. Add the salt and mix at medium speed until a soft, smooth dough forms, about 5 minutes longer.

3 Scrape the dough out onto a lightly floured work surface and form it into a large ball. Transfer the dough to the prepared bowl and cover the bowl securely with plastic wrap so that it's airtight. Let the dough stand in a warm place until it has doubled in bulk, about 8 hours. Refrigerate the dough for at least 8 hours or overnight.

4 Let the pizza dough return to room temperature in the bowl, about 2 hours.

5 Lightly dust 2 large baking sheets with flour. Scrape the dough out onto a lightly floured work surface and punch it down. Using a sharp knife, cut the dough into 5 even pieces. Form the pieces into balls and transfer them to the prepared baking sheets **(A, B)**. Using the tip of a paring knife, gently pop any air bubbles on the surface of each ball. Securely cover the dough balls by sliding each baking sheet into a clean 13-gallon plastic kitchen bag and tying them closed. Let the dough stand in a warm place until it has a little more than doubled in bulk, about 8 hours **(C)**. Refrigerate the dough for at least 8 hours or overnight.

6 Shape and assemble the pizza Set a pizza stone on a rack in the top third of the oven. Preheat the oven to 500° for at least 45 minutes. Meanwhile, remove the baking sheets from the refrigerator and let the dough stand for 20 minutes.

7 Working on a floured surface and using your fingers, press and stretch a dough ball out to a 10-inch round, working from the center toward the edge; avoid pressing on the outermost edge **(D)**. Transfer the dough to a lightly floured pizza peel **(E)**. Add sauce and toppings to the dough as desired, making sure to leave a 1-inch border around the edge **(F)**.

(continued on page 66)

LESS IS MORE

"Flour, salt, water and yeast—that's it," says McNaughton about this supersimple dough recipe, the same one he uses to make his amazing restaurant pies.

TURN UP THE HEAT

Set your oven to the highest temperature possible. If you have a convection feature, turn it on to circulate the hot air around the pizza.

JUST A LITTLE SPRINKLE

Dust the peel sparingly with flour; if you use too much, it will stick to the bottom of the pizza and burn.

8 Bake the pizza Turn the oven to broil for 5 minutes, then return it to 500°. Slide the pizza onto the pizza stone, opening and closing the oven door as quickly as possible. Bake until the bottom is lightly charred and the toppings are bubbling, about 6 minutes for a chewier crust and 8 minutes for a crispier one; avoid opening the oven door during baking. Repeat with the remaining pizza dough and toppings.

NOTE *Doppio zero*, or "00" flour, a fine Italian flour, is available at specialty food shops and online from amazon.com. To accurately weigh small quantities, use a scale that counts in 0.01-gram increments, such as one from American Weigh ($25; amazon.com).

PIZZA TOPPINGS

PERFECT PIZZA SAUCE Pass one 28-oz. can whole San Marzano tomatoes through a food mill. Blend the puree with 1 Tbsp. extra-virgin olive oil and season with salt.

MARGHERITA Spread ½ cup Perfect Pizza Sauce onto the dough and top with ¼ lb. thinly sliced fresh mozzarella cheese, 10 fresh basil leaves, a drizzle of extra-virgin olive oil and a light grating of Parmigiano-Reggiano.

SAUSAGE AND OLIVE Spread ⅓ cup Perfect Pizza Sauce onto the dough and top with 2 oz. uncooked crumbled Italian sausage, ¼ cup pitted and halved Gaeta olives, 1 tsp. chopped capers, ½ tsp. chopped oregano and ¼ cup shaved Pecorino Sardo cheese.

SQUASH AND ARUGULA Skip the sauce. Grate Parmigiano-Reggiano over the dough and top with ¾ cup shredded Fontina cheese, 2 oz. thinly sliced summer squash (about ½ small squash), 1 tsp. chopped rosemary and 1 or 2 chopped Calabrian red chiles. Scatter ½ cup arugula leaves on the pizza after baking.

WINE Vivid, lightly earthy Chianti Classico.

CRUST HELPER

Nathan Myhrvold's *Modernist Cuisine* recommends a steel slab instead of a pizza stone because it retains heat better. $89; bakingsteel.com.

Risotto

A good risotto should have plump grains of flavor-packed rice suspended in a thick, creamy sauce. Cookbook author Grace Parisi achieves just that with her Milanese risotto, which gets a brilliant hue and subtle aroma from saffron. Parisi's hard-learned steps for success? Coat the grains in olive oil, season the stock and let the rice absorb the broth slowly.

Milanese Risotto

| Time | 30 min |
| Makes | 6 servings |

5½ cups chicken stock, preferably homemade

2 Tbsp. extra-virgin olive oil

1 small onion, finely chopped
   Kosher salt and pepper

1½ cups arborio rice (10 oz.)
   Pinch of saffron threads

½ cup dry white wine

½ cup freshly grated Parmigiano-Reggiano cheese

1 Tbsp. unsalted butter

2 Tbsp. chopped flat-leaf parsley

1 In a medium saucepan, bring the chicken stock to a simmer; keep warm. In a large saucepan, heat the olive oil. Add the onion, season with salt and pepper and cook over moderate heat, stirring, until softened, about 5 minutes **(A)**. Add the rice and cook for 1 minute, stirring to thoroughly coat.

2 Crumble the saffron into the wine and add it to the rice. Cook, stirring, until the wine is absorbed. Add 1 cup of the warm stock and cook over moderate heat, stirring constantly, until nearly absorbed **(B)**. Continue adding the stock ½ cup at a time, stirring constantly and waiting until the stock is nearly absorbed between additions.

3 The risotto is done when the rice is al dente and suspended in a thick, creamy sauce, about 20 minutes total. Season the risotto with salt and pepper, then stir in the cheese, butter and parsley **(C)**. Serve immediately.

WINE Earthy, medium-bodied Italian red.

Fish Stew

An aromatic broth is the secret to a phenomenal fish stew. "Once you make the broth, you can do a million things with it," says Mark Sullivan of Spruce in San Francisco. Each of his regional variations has its own distinct character, but they're all built the same way, starting with a rich fish stock and ending with flavorful extras like fennel pollen and mint or a luscious garlicky aioli. Following this formula, you can riff on these recipes with whatever is freshest at your market.

Master Fish Stock

Time	30 min active 2 hr 45 min total
Makes	about 3½ qts

- 1 lb. fish head and bones, gills removed
- Ice water
- ¼ cup olive oil
- 1 medium yellow onion, coarsely chopped
- 1 medium fennel bulb, coarsely chopped
- 4 celery ribs, coarsely chopped
- 4 garlic cloves, halved
- ½ lb. mussels, scrubbed and debearded
- ½ lb. littleneck clams, scrubbed
- One 750-ml bottle dry white wine
- 4 qts. chicken stock or low-sodium chicken broth
- 1 lemon, thinly sliced
- 6 thyme sprigs
- 6 parsley sprigs
- 1 bay leaf
- 1 tsp. white peppercorns

1 In a large bowl, cover the fish head and bones with ice water and let soak for 1 hour. Drain well.

2 In a large stockpot, heat the olive oil. Add the onion, fennel, celery and garlic and cook over low heat, stirring occasionally, until softened but not browned, about 15 minutes. Add the fish head and bones along with the mussels, clams, white wine and chicken stock. Simmer over low heat for 1 hour, skimming off the foam as it rises to the surface.

3 Remove the pot from the heat and stir in the lemon, thyme and parsley sprigs, bay leaf and peppercorns. Let steep for 30 minutes.

4 Strain the broth through a fine sieve and refrigerate until ready to use.

(continued on page 72)

A BETTER BROTH

"You're never going to get a great fish stew without a great broth," Sullivan says. The fish head and bones lend flavor and body; they're soaked first to remove blood and impurities, ensuring a pristine stock with pure flavor.

Sicilian Fish Stew

Time	45 min
Makes	4 servings

AROMATICS

- 2 Tbsp. extra-virgin olive oil
- ¼ cup minced shallot
- 2 Tbsp. minced seeded tomato
- 2 Tbsp. golden raisins
- 1 Tbsp. minced garlic
- 1 Tbsp. drained capers
- ½ tsp. ground coriander

LIQUIDS

- 3 cups Master Fish Stock (p. 70)
- ¼ cup dry vermouth

SEAFOOD

- Four 4-oz. skinless halibut fillets
- 3 lbs. colossal head-on shrimp
- 1 lb. littleneck clams, scrubbed
- ½ lb. mussels, scrubbed and debearded

GARNISHES

- ⅓ cup thinly sliced pitted Sicilian green olives
- Chopped mint
- Fennel pollen

1 In a large pot, heat the olive oil. Add the remaining aromatics and sauté over moderately high heat until fragrant, about 1 minute.

2 Add the liquids and bring to a simmer. Add the seafood in stages, in order of cook time: Cook the halibut and shrimp until opaque, flipping once, about 8 minutes; and the clams and mussels until they open, 3 to 4 minutes. Discard any clams or mussels that don't open.

3 Ladle the stew into bowls and top with the garnishes.

SERVE WITH Plain baguette toasts.

STEW GO-WITH: BAGUETTE TOASTS

Plain Preheat the oven to 425°. Arrange eight ½-inch-thick baguette slices, cut on the diagonal, on a baking sheet. Drizzle the bread with extra-virgin olive oil and toast until lightly golden, about 5 minutes.

Garlic Rub the toasts with a halved garlic clove.

Garlic-tomato Rub the toasts with a halved garlic clove, then with a halved tomato.

Provençal Fish Stew (Bourride)

Time	50 min
Makes	4 servings

AROMATICS

2   Tbsp. extra-virgin olive oil
¼   cup minced shallot
2   Tbsp. minced seeded tomato
    Pinch of saffron threads

LIQUIDS

4   cups Master Fish Stock (p. 70)
¼   cup Pernod

SEAFOOD

    Four 4-oz. skinless halibut fillets
3   lbs. colossal head-on shrimp
1   lb. littleneck clams, scrubbed
½   lb. mussels, scrubbed and debearded
4   large sea scallops

GARNISHES

    Aioli (recipe at right)
    Chopped tarragon

📷 page 71

1 In a large pot, heat the olive oil. Add the remaining aromatics and sauté over moderately high heat until fragrant, about 1 minute.

2 Add the liquids and bring to a simmer. Add the seafood in stages, in order of cook time: Cook the halibut and shrimp until opaque, flipping once, about 8 minutes; the clams and mussels until they open, 3 to 4 minutes; and the scallops until just cooked through, 2 to 3 minutes. Discard any clams or mussels that don't open.

3 Using a slotted spoon, transfer the seafood to 4 serving bowls. Pour half of the broth into a large bowl and vigorously whisk in ½ cup of the aioli until smooth. Pour the aioli-enriched broth back into the pot and whisk once more, then pour it over the seafood in the serving bowls. Garnish with tarragon. Pass the remaining aioli at the table.

SERVE WITH Garlic baguette toasts.

AIOLI

In a mini food processor, combine 1 garlic clove with 1 large egg yolk, 2 Tbsp. fresh lemon juice and 1 Tbsp. water. With the machine on, slowly drizzle in 1 cup extra-virgin olive oil. Season with salt. Makes about 1¼ cups.

Catalan Fish Stew

Time	45 min
Makes	4 servings

AROMATICS

2   Tbsp. extra-virgin olive oil
¼   lb. dry Spanish chorizo, finely diced
¼   cup minced shallots
2   Tbsp. minced seeded tomato
2   Tbsp. minced piquillo pepper
    Pinch of pimentón de la Vera

LIQUIDS

3   cups Master Fish Stock (p. 70)
¼   cup dry sherry

SEAFOOD

3   lbs. colossal head-on shrimp
1   lb. littleneck clams, scrubbed
1   lb. mussels, scrubbed and debearded
½   lb. cleaned squid, bodies thinly sliced

GARNISHES

¼   cup unsalted roasted almonds, chopped
    Chopped flat-leaf parsley

1 In a large pot, heat the olive oil. Add the remaining aromatics and sauté over moderately high heat until fragrant, about 1 minute.

2 Add the liquids and bring to a simmer. Add the seafood in stages, in order of cook time: Cook the shrimp until opaque, flipping once, about 8 minutes; the clams and mussels until they open, 3 to 4 minutes; and the squid until just cooked through, 2 to 3 minutes. Discard any clams or mussels that don't open.

3 Ladle the stew into bowls and top with the garnishes.

SERVE WITH Garlic-tomato baguette toasts.

Gumbo

"There are a lot of bad gumbos out there because people are afraid to take the roux where it needs to go," says Slade Rushing about the classic base of flour and fat. Where it "needs to go" is from a pale beige to deep mahogany. At Brennan's in New Orleans, Rushing prepares a gumbo that's rich and soulful. It all starts with a deep brown roux that "smells like a roomful of toasted hazelnuts."

Seafood Gumbo

Time	1 hr 20 min active
	3 hr 50 min total
Makes	8 servings

CRAB STOCK

- 2 gal. water
- 1 onion, quartered
- 1 head of garlic, halved
- 2 bay leaves
- 1 Tbsp. whole black peppercorns
- 6 live blue crabs

GUMBO

- 1 cup canola oil
- ½ cup all-purpose flour
- ¾ lb. andouille sausage, finely chopped (2 cups)
- 1 large onion, finely chopped
- 2 celery ribs, finely chopped
- 1 red bell pepper, finely chopped
- 1 green bell pepper, finely chopped
- ½ cup finely chopped garlic (12 large cloves)
- ½ lb. okra, thickly sliced
- 1 lb. tomatoes, finely chopped
- ½ tsp. filé powder (see Note)
- ⅛ tsp. Creole seasoning, such as Zatarain's
- 2 thyme sprigs
- 1 bay leaf
- 1 Tbsp. kosher salt
- 1 lb. jumbo lump crabmeat, picked over
- 1 lb. large shrimp, shelled and deveined
- 2 dozen freshly shucked oysters
  Hot sauce, such as Crystal or Tabasco
  Basmati rice and sliced scallions, for serving

1 Make the crab stock In a large pot, combine all of the ingredients except the crabs and bring to a boil. Add the crabs and simmer briskly over moderate heat for 1 hour, skimming as necessary. Strain the stock into a pot. You should have about 12 cups; add water if necessary, or reserve any extra for another use. Discard the crabs.

2 Make the gumbo In a large pot, heat the oil. Whisk in the flour and cook over moderately low heat, whisking constantly, until the roux is deep mahogany brown with a nutty aroma, about 40 minutes.

3 Stir in the andouille, onion, celery, red and green bell peppers, garlic and okra and cook, stirring occasionally, until the vegetables soften, about 10 minutes. Add the tomatoes, filé powder, Creole seasoning, thyme, bay leaf, salt and the 12 cups of crab stock. Simmer over moderate heat, stirring occasionally, until reduced and thickened, about 1½ hours.

4 Stir in the crabmeat, shrimp, oysters and 2 tablespoons of hot sauce and cook until the shrimp are white throughout, about 3 minutes. Discard the thyme sprigs and bay leaf. Ladle the gumbo into bowls and top with rice. Garnish with scallions; serve with hot sauce.

NOTE Filé powder, made from ground sassafras leaves, gives gumbo its distinctive earthy, vegetal flavor. It's available from amazon.com.

MAKE AHEAD The gumbo can be prepared 3 days ahead through Step 3. Reheat gently and cook the seafood just before serving.

WINE Fragrant, honeyed Loire Valley Chenin Blanc.

Sushi

Making maki rolls may seem daunting, but it requires just three things: high-quality ingredients, a bamboo mat and practice. Masaharu Morimoto, *Iron Chef* star and owner of Morimoto restaurants around the world, raises the sushi bar for home cooks with his foolproof technique.

Maki Rolls

Time	45 min active
	1 hr 40 min total
Makes	48 maki rolls

SUSHI RICE

2   cups short-grain Japanese rice

¼   cup sake-mash vinegar or white wine vinegar

¼   cup rice vinegar

¼   cup sugar

2   Tbsp. kosher salt

FILLINGS

1   lb. sushi-grade salmon or tuna (see Fish Prep Tips, below)

Crabmeat from Dungeness, blue or king crabs, picked over (optional)

1   cucumber, seeded and thinly julienned, including some of the skin (optional)

1   ripe Hass avocado, cut into ¼-inch-thick slices (optional)

MAKI ROLLS

8   sheets of nori (4-by-7½-inches each)

2   tsp. wasabi

Gari (thin slices of pickled young ginger) and good-quality soy sauce, for serving

---

FISH PREP TIPS

To be eaten safely, sushi-grade fish must be handled correctly: It should be frozen for at least one day to kill any parasites. For the best flavor and texture in oily, strong-smelling fresh fish, such as salmon and mackerel, rub the fillets with fine sea salt and let stand for 30 minutes; rinse the fish well, pat dry and sprinkle all over with rice vinegar.

1 Make the sushi rice Rinse the rice 5 times, then drain in a colander and let dry for 15 minutes. Cook the rice in a rice cooker. Alternatively, in a medium saucepan, combine the rice with 2 cups of cold water and bring to a boil over high heat. Cover and cook over moderate heat for 10 minutes. Reduce the heat to low and cook for 10 minutes longer. Remove from the heat and let stand, covered, for 15 minutes.

2 Meanwhile, in a small saucepan, combine both vinegars with the sugar and salt and warm over moderate heat, stirring to dissolve the sugar.

3 Transfer the rice to a very large bowl. Sprinkle ½ cup of the seasoned vinegar all over the rice: Drizzle onto a spatula while waving it back and forth **(A)**. Using a slicing motion with the spatula, gently separate the rice grains while mixing in the seasoning. Fan the rice while mixing it to help it dry. Wipe down any stray grains from the side of the bowl. Cover the rice with a damp towel to keep warm.

4 Prepare the fish If a piece of tuna is sinewy, simply scrape the meat off the sinews with a sharp knife. Slice the fish across the grain into strips about 4 inches long and ¼ inch thick **(B)**.

5 Spread the rice for the maki Carefully wave a sheet of nori over an open flame until crisp and fragrant, then transfer to a bamboo mat. Wet your hands in water that's seasoned with rice vinegar, then scoop up ½ cup of sushi rice. Gently form the rice into a loosely packed, palm-width log and place it at one edge of the nori **(C)**. Begin spreading the rice across to the other side.

6 Add the wasabi and filling Continue to spread the rice all over the nori, rewetting your hands as necessary, until an even layer covers all but a ¼-inch border at the top edge. Spread about ¼ teaspoon of wasabi lengthwise along the middle of the rice **(D)**. Lay about 2 ounces of the filling (a single ingredient or a combination) along the center of the rice **(E)**.

7 Roll the maki Roll the bamboo mat up and away from you, curling the nori and rice around the filling; use your fingers to hold the filling in place as you roll **(F)**. Secure the roll with the ¼-inch flap of nori. Once the roll is sealed, gently squeeze, pressing gently on the top and sides, to compress the roll slightly and form a rough square shape. Press on each end of the roll to make a neat surface **(G)**.

8 Cut the maki Transfer the roll to a work surface. Dip the tip of a long, sharp knife into vinegar water; let the water run down the length of the blade. Using a long slicing motion, cut the maki in half, then cut each half into thirds to form six even pieces, rewetting the blade as needed **(H, I)**. Repeat with the remaining ingredients. Serve with gari and soy sauce.

A

B

C

D

E

F

G

H

I

Soft-Shell Crabs

We count the days till this seasonal delicacy is available. At North Pond in Chicago, Bruce Sherman pairs the crispy fried crabs with salty slices of pancetta on small rounds of brioche slathered with homemade remoulade (mayonnaise mixed with mustard, capers, cornichons and herbs). Here, that dish is simplified and reimagined as a hefty sandwich.

Soft-Shell Crab Sandwiches with Pancetta and Remoulade

Time	45 min
Makes	4 sandwiches

½ cup mayonnaise
3 cornichons, finely chopped
1 Tbsp. minced red onion
2 tsp. chopped tarragon
1 tsp. capers, chopped
1 tsp. Dijon mustard
Kosher salt and pepper
4 slices of pancetta (2 oz.)
4 jumbo soft-shell crabs
2 Tbsp. unsalted butter
2 Tbsp. extra-virgin olive oil
All-purpose flour, for dusting
4 large brioche buns, split and toasted
One 5-oz. bunch of arugula, trimmed
1 large tomato, thinly sliced

1 In a small bowl, whisk the mayonnaise, cornichons, red onion, tarragon, capers and mustard. Season the remoulade with salt and pepper.

2 In a large skillet, arrange the pancetta slices in a single layer. Place a flat pot lid, slightly smaller than the skillet, directly on the pancetta to weigh it down. Cook over moderate heat, turning once, until the pancetta is crisp, about 6 minutes. Drain the pancetta on paper towels; wipe out the skillet.

3 Using scissors, snip the eyes off the crabs. Lift each side of the top shell and remove the gills underneath **(A)**.

4 In the skillet, melt the butter in the oil. Season the crabs with salt and pepper and dust them generously with flour **(B)**. Add the crabs to the skillet and cook over high heat, turning once, until crisp, about 7 minutes **(C)**.

5 Spread the remoulade on the cut sides of the buns. Arrange the pancetta on the bottoms and top with the arugula, tomato slices and crabs. Close the sandwiches, cut them in half and serve.

WINE Vivid, red cherry–inflected rosé, such as one from California's Russian River Valley.

A

B

C

Sous Vide Cooking

Cooking food sous vide—simmering it in vacuum-sealed plastic bags in precisely heated water baths—seems like a trick only fancy chefs with immersion circulators can pull off. But home cooks can re-create the incredibly moist, flavorful results with just a countertop vacuum packer and a pot fitted with a candy thermometer. Read on to learn how to sous vide radishes until they're sweet-firm and turn salmon fillets buttery-soft and rare in just 12 minutes.

Radishes Three Ways

Time	15 min active
	35 min total
Makes	4 servings

25 to 30 assorted radishes, such as French breakfast, watermelon and daikon—quartered or sliced so that all are ½ inch thick (5 cups; see Note below)

Sea salt and white pepper

Zest and juice of 2 lemons

Zest and juice of ½ navel orange

1   shallot, finely chopped

1   Tbsp. sugar

1   tsp. rice vinegar

Extra-virgin olive oil

1 In a pot fitted with a candy thermometer, preheat a water bath to 181°. In a medium bowl, season one-third of the radishes with salt and white pepper. Transfer them to a 1-gallon vacuum-pack bag, arranging them in a single layer, and vacuum-seal. Submerge the bag in the water bath and cook at 181° for 20 minutes. Fill a bowl with ice water. Transfer the bag to the ice bath; let cool.

2 Meanwhile, in another medium bowl, combine the lemon zest and juice with the orange zest and juice, shallot, sugar and vinegar. Whisk in 1 cup of olive oil; season the vinaigrette with salt and white pepper.

3 In a grill pan, heat a thin layer of olive oil. Add another one-third of the radishes and cook over moderately high heat, turning, until browned and just tender, about 7 minutes; transfer to plates with the sous vide radishes and remaining fresh radishes, drizzle with the vinaigrette, sprinkle with salt and serve. –*Viet Pham and Bowman Brown; formerly of Forage, Salt Lake City*

Salmon with Cucumbers

Time	15 min active
	45 min total
Makes	4 servings

2   seedless cucumbers, peeled—1 sliced crosswise ¼ inch thick, 1 halved, seeded and julienned

Kosher salt and black pepper

Four 6-oz. center-cut skinless salmon fillets, chilled (see Note)

White pepper

8   oz. plain nonfat Greek yogurt

½   cup coarsely chopped dill

2   Tbsp. extra-virgin olive oil

Juice of 1 lemon

1 In a pot fitted with a candy thermometer, preheat a water bath to 122° for rare salmon, 160° for medium. Light a grill or heat a grill pan. Season the sliced cucumber with salt and black pepper. Grill over high heat, turning once, until lightly charred, about 2 minutes. Transfer to a plate.

2 Season the salmon with salt and white pepper; transfer to four 1-quart vacuum-pack bags and vacuum-seal. Submerge the bags in the water bath and cook at the desired temperature for 12 minutes.

3 In a blender, blend the yogurt with the dill; season with salt and black pepper. In a small bowl, toss the julienned cucumber with the olive oil and lemon juice; season with salt. Remove the fillets from the bags and transfer to plates. Top with the grilled and julienned cucumber, dollop with the dill sauce and serve. –*Maria Hines; Tilth, Seattle*

SERVE WITH Steamed couscous.

NOTE For safe sous vide cooking, use only the freshest ingredients, chill them in the refrigerator before sealing in plastic and cook them right after sealing or keep them in the refrigerator; unseal them promptly after cooking.

WINE Greek white, such as Assyrtiko.

Fried Chicken

"People say my chicken reminds them of the fried chicken their families made when they were young," says Josh Galliano of Companion bakery in St. Louis. "And that's a hell of a compliment." A sweet-tea brine, a buttermilk soak and a deep-fry in lard—that's the "traditional flavor," according to Galliano. Here, he details the steps behind his finger-lickin' recipe.

Creole-Spiced Fried Chicken

Time	1 hr active 13 hr total
Makes	8 servings

10 bags English Breakfast or other black tea

¼ cup kosher salt

2 Tbsp. sugar

¾ cup JG Creole Spice Mix (recipe below)

 Two 3½-lb. chickens, cut into 8 pieces each

2 cups buttermilk

¼ cup Louisiana-style hot sauce, such as Crystal or Tabasco

2 large eggs

2 cups all-purpose flour

2 cups fine cornmeal

¼ cup cornstarch

 Rendered pork lard or canola oil, for frying (see Note)

1 Make the tea brine Fill a large saucepan with 8 cups of water and add the tea bags, salt, sugar and 2 tablespoons of the Creole spice mix. Bring just to a boil, stirring to dissolve the salt and sugar; let steep for 10 minutes. Discard the tea bags and let the brine cool completely. Submerge the chicken in the brine, cover and refrigerate for at least 6 hours.

2 Make the buttermilk soak In a large bowl, whisk the buttermilk with the hot sauce, eggs and 2 tablespoons of the Creole spice mix. Drain the chicken, discarding the brine. Add the chicken to the buttermilk mixture, turning to coat completely. Cover and refrigerate for at least 6 hours or overnight.

3 Fry the chicken Preheat the oven to 250°. Line a large rimmed baking sheet with wax paper. In a large bowl, whisk the flour with the cornmeal, cornstarch and remaining ½ cup of Creole spice mix. Remove the chicken from the buttermilk, letting the excess drip back into the bowl. Dredge the chicken in the flour mixture, then transfer it to the prepared baking sheet.

4 In a large, heavy saucepan, heat 1½ inches of lard to 350°. Set a rack over a rimmed baking sheet. Add half of the coated chicken to the lard and fry at 300°, turning occasionally, until golden brown and an instant-read thermometer inserted in the thickest part of each piece registers 155°, 15 to 18 minutes. Transfer the fried chicken to the rack and keep warm in the oven while you fry the second batch.

NOTE Frying chicken in lard makes the crust light, crunchy and less likely to get soggy. Look for rendered fresh lard at butcher shops and farmers' markets.

WINE Lively, citrusy sparkling wine.

JG CREOLE SPICE MIX

In a medium bowl, whisk together ½ cup paprika, ¼ cup plus 2 Tbsp. kosher salt, 2 Tbsp. each garlic powder, onion powder and black pepper, 1 Tbsp. each dried thyme, dried oregano and dried basil, 2 tsp. cayenne, 1½ tsp. sugar and ½ tsp. crushed red pepper. Makes 1½ cups.

KICKING IT UP

The spice mix recipe makes ¾ cup more than you'll need for the chicken. You can also triple or quadruple it to use in gumbo or jambalaya, or mix it one-to-one with light brown sugar to use as a dry rub for brisket, ribs or pulled pork.

Tikka Masala

Legend has it that this dish was invented at a restaurant in Punjab when a British patron complained that his chicken tikka was too dry—the chef doctored it with a can of tomato soup and spices. This version from cookbook author Grace Parisi ditches the canned soup for a fresh-tasting, slightly spicy tomato cream sauce that's straight-up addictive.

Chicken Tikka Masala

Time	45 min active 1 hr 45 min total plus overnight marinating
Makes	4 servings

MASALA MARINADE

- 1 cup plain low-fat yogurt
- 2 garlic cloves, minced
- 1 Tbsp. finely grated fresh ginger
- 1½ tsp. ground cumin
- 1½ tsp. ground coriander
- ¼ tsp. ground cardamom
- ¼ tsp. cayenne
- ¼ tsp. ground turmeric
  Kosher salt and black pepper

CHICKEN

- 2½ lbs. skinless, boneless chicken thighs, fat trimmed
  Kosher salt and black pepper
- 2 Tbsp. plus 1 tsp. vegetable oil
- ¼ cup blanched whole almonds
- 1 large onion, finely chopped
- 2 garlic cloves, minced
- 1 tsp. minced fresh ginger
- 1½ Tbsp. garam masala
- 1½ tsp. pure chile powder
- ½ tsp. cayenne
  One 35-oz. can peeled tomatoes, finely chopped, juices reserved
  Pinch of sugar
- 1 cup heavy cream

1 Make the masala marinade In a large glass or stainless steel bowl, combine the yogurt, garlic, ginger, cumin, coriander, cardamom, cayenne and turmeric. Season with salt and black pepper **(A)**.

2 Prepare the chicken Using a sharp knife, make a few shallow slashes in each piece of chicken **(B)**. Add the chicken to the marinade, turn to coat and refrigerate overnight.

3 Preheat the broiler and position a rack about 8 inches from the heat. Remove the chicken from the marinade; scrape off as much of the marinade as possible **(C)**. Season the chicken with salt and black pepper and spread the pieces on a baking sheet. Broil the chicken, turning once or twice, until just cooked through and browned in spots, about 12 minutes. Transfer to a cutting board and cut it into 2-inch pieces **(D)**.

4 Meanwhile, in a small skillet, heat 1 teaspoon of the oil. Add the almonds and cook over moderate heat, stirring constantly, until golden, about 5 minutes **(E)**. Transfer the almonds to a plate and let cool completely. In a food processor, pulse the almonds until finely ground.

5 In a large enameled cast-iron casserole, heat the remaining 2 tablespoons of oil until shimmering. Add the onion, garlic and ginger and cook over moderate heat, stirring occasionally, until tender and golden, about 8 minutes. Add the garam masala, chile powder and cayenne and cook, stirring, for 1 minute **(F)**. Add the tomatoes with their juices and the sugar and season with salt and black pepper. Cover partially and cook over moderate heat, stirring occasionally, until the sauce is slightly thickened, about 20 minutes **(G)**. Add the cream and ground almonds and cook over low heat, stirring occasionally, until thickened, about 10 minutes longer. Stir in the chicken; simmer gently for 10 minutes, stirring frequently, and serve **(H, I)**.

VARIATION The marinade and sauce here are also delicious with shrimp, lamb and vegetables.

SERVE WITH Steamed basmati rice, rice pilaf or warm naan.

WINE Bright, fruity rosé.

FUN FACT

The most popular curry in the U.K. is chicken tikka masala. It accounts for one in every seven sold.

Pho

Bunker, which started as a tiny Vietnamese restaurant in an industrial stretch of New York City, has become a cult favorite for its chicken pho. Chef Jimmy Tu gently poaches the bird until it's cooked just enough so the meat can be removed from the bones, then shreds the meat and simmers it in the finished soup so it's tasty and tender. He builds flavor in stages, adding aromatics, then spices, and finally fresh garnishes for a burst of brightness right before serving.

Chicken Pho

Time	1 hr active
	4 hr total
Makes	4 servings

PHO

	Kosher salt
	One 3½-lb. chicken
2	whole star anise pods
2	cardamom pods
1	tsp. coriander seeds
	One 2½-inch cinnamon stick
1	tsp. black peppercorns
½	tsp. white peppercorns
1	tsp. goji berries
2	shallots, halved
1	small onion, quartered
1	leek, halved lengthwise and cut into 2-inch pieces
1	Tbsp. crushed rock sugar or dark brown sugar
1	Tbsp. Asian fish sauce

GARNISHES

¼	cup canola oil
3	medium shallots, thinly sliced (1 cup)
6	oz. dried rice noodles (see Rice Noodle Basics, p. 88)
¼	cup sliced scallions
¼	cup chopped cilantro
	Bean sprouts, basil sprigs, mint sprigs, thinly sliced jalapeños and lime wedges, for serving

1 Start the pho In a large stockpot, bring 5 quarts of water to a boil. Add 1 tablespoon of salt and the chicken, breast side down **(A)**. Place a heatproof plate over the chicken to keep it submerged and bring to a boil **(B)**. Reduce the heat and simmer the chicken for 30 minutes; it will not be cooked through. Transfer the chicken to a bowl of ice water and let cool completely **(C)**. Drain well and pat dry.

2 Meanwhile, in a large cast-iron skillet, combine the star anise, cardamom, coriander, cinnamon stick, black and white peppercorns and goji berries **(D)**. Cook over moderately low heat, stirring, until very fragrant, about 3 minutes. Transfer to a small bowl.

3 In the same skillet, combine the shallots, onion and leek. Cook over moderate heat, stirring occasionally, until deep golden, about 10 minutes **(E)**.

4 Remove all of the meat from the chicken and coarsely shred it.

5 Simmer the broth Return all of the chicken skin and bones to the broth in the stockpot **(F)**. Add the pan-roasted shallot, onion and leek mixture and bring to a boil. Cover and simmer over moderately low heat for 1 hour.

6 Stir the toasted spices and goji berries into the broth. Cover and simmer for 1 hour longer. Add the rock sugar and simmer for another 30 minutes.

7 Strain the broth into a large bowl, pressing on the solids **(G)**. Pour the broth into a clean saucepan; discard the solids.

8 Make the garnishes In a large skillet, heat the oil. Add the shallots and cook over moderate heat, stirring, until golden brown, 5 to 7 minutes **(H)**. Using a mesh skimmer, transfer the shallots to a paper towel–lined plate to drain. Let cool.

(continued on next page)

ALL ABOUT THE BIRD

Because pho is largely about the flavor of the broth, using a high-quality chicken here is key.

9 Soak the noodles in a large bowl of boiling water until pliable, 8 to 10 minutes.

10 Finish the pho Bring the broth to a simmer. Stir in the shredded chicken and cook until just white throughout, 1 to 2 minutes. Stir in the fish sauce and season the broth with salt **(l)**.

11 Drain the rice noodles and transfer to large bowls. Ladle the broth and chicken over the noodles. Top with the scallions and cilantro. Garnish with the crispy shallots, bean sprouts, basil, mint and jalapeños and serve with lime wedges.

MAKE AHEAD The poached chicken and finished broth can be refrigerated separately overnight.

WINE Fragrant northern Italian white, such as Pinot Bianco.

RICE NOODLE BASICS

Linguine-width rice noodles are sometimes sold as rice sticks. The dried kind need to be handled carefully but are otherwise easy to use: Just soak until pliable, then add to the broth. Tu prefers dried to fresh because fresh noodles can be made with preservatives.

Thai Curry

Every good cook has a favorite, foolproof dish. For British food writer and BBC star Nigel Slater, it's a fragrant and spicy green curry chicken that's so flavorful, you'll stop ordering takeout once you learn how to prepare it. The recipe makes extra curry paste, with a hit of fish sauce for a sweet-salty bite; use it to jazz up everything from simple soups to weeknight stews.

Green Curry Chicken

Time	1 hr 15 min
Makes	6 servings

CURRY PASTE

- 4 stalks of fresh lemongrass, bottom 4 inches thinly sliced
- 6 jalapeños, seeded and coarsely chopped
- 3 garlic cloves, smashed
- 2 shallots, thinly sliced
-   One 2-inch piece of peeled fresh ginger, thinly sliced
- ¼ cup chopped cilantro
- 1 Tbsp. Thai fish sauce
- 1 Tbsp. fresh lime juice
- 1 tsp. minced lime zest
- 1 tsp. ground cumin
- 1 tsp. ground coriander
- ½ tsp. pepper

CURRY

- 3 Tbsp. peanut oil
- 1½ lbs. skinless, boneless chicken thighs, cut into ½-inch-wide strips
- ½ lb. shiitake mushrooms, stemmed, caps quartered
-   One 14-oz. can coconut milk
- 2 cups chicken stock or low-sodium broth
- 8 lime leaves or 1-inch-wide strips of lime zest
- 1 Tbsp. brined green peppercorns, drained
- 2 Tbsp. Thai fish sauce
- 1 cup chopped cilantro
- ½ cup shredded basil
-   Steamed rice and lime wedges, for serving

1 Make the curry paste In a food processor, combine all of the ingredients and pulse to a paste **(A)**.

2 Make the curry In a large, heavy casserole, heat the peanut oil. Add half of the chicken and cook over high heat until browned all over, about 6 minutes. Transfer the chicken to a plate. Repeat with the remaining chicken **(B)**. Add the mushrooms to the casserole and cook over moderately high heat until softened and just beginning to brown, about 4 minutes **(C)**. Add the coconut milk, stock, lime leaves, peppercorns, 1 tablespoon of the fish sauce, ½ cup of the cilantro, ¼ cup of the basil and a heaping ¼ cup of the curry paste **(D)**. Bring to a boil and simmer over low heat for 10 minutes. Return the chicken and any accumulated juices to the casserole **(E)**. Add 1 tablespoon of the curry paste and simmer for 5 minutes **(F)**. (Reserve the remaining curry paste for another use.)

3 Just before serving, add the remaining 1 tablespoon of fish sauce, ½ cup of cilantro and ¼ cup of basil **(G)**. Serve the chicken curry in deep bowls, with rice and lime wedges **(H)**.

WINE Citrusy Sauvignon Blanc.

Duck à l'Orange

Chef Ludo Lefebvre of Petit Trois in L.A. may be a rule breaker, but he has an unexpected soft spot for retro French classics. Here, he modernizes duck à l'orange by cooking the breast and tender leg confit separately, then serving them in a North African–inspired sauce of fresh orange juice simmered with honey, orange blossom water and the spice blend ras el hanout.

Spiced Duck à l'Orange

Time	1 hr 30 min plus overnight drying
Makes	4 servings

5 Tbsp. dark honey, such as buckwheat

1 cup fresh orange juice

⅓ cup chicken stock or low-sodium broth

¼ cup apple cider vinegar

2 Tbsp. orange blossom water

1 Tbsp. ras el hanout (see Note)

4 Tbsp. unsalted butter

Kosher salt and white pepper

4 confit duck legs

Four 8-oz. duck breasts, air-dried overnight (see below)

2 blood oranges or oranges

2 cups amaranth leaves or baby spinach leaves

Mint leaves, for garnish

1 Make the sauce In a small saucepan, bring the honey to a boil over high heat. Add the juice, stock, vinegar, orange blossom water and ras el hanout. Return to a boil and cook over moderately high heat until reduced by half (to about 1 cup), 16 to 18 minutes. Off the heat, whisk in 2 tablespoons of the butter. Season with salt and pepper; keep warm.

2 Cook the duck Meanwhile, preheat the oven to 425°. Place the duck legs on a foil-lined rimmed baking sheet and roast until heated through and browned, 14 to 16 minutes. Transfer to a plate and tent with foil to keep warm.

3 Using a paring knife, deeply score the skin of each duck breast every ½ inch in a crosshatch pattern; season with salt. In a large skillet, arrange the duck breasts skin side down. Place the skillet over moderately low heat and cook, without turning, until some of the fat has rendered and the skin is golden brown, 14 to 16 minutes. Turn the breasts and cook until medium-rare (130° internal temperature), 2 to 3 minutes longer. Transfer to a cutting board and let rest. Drain the fat from the skillet and save for another use; reserve the skillet.

4 Finish the dish On a cutting board, trim the ends from each blood orange and then slice away all the peel and pith. Cut each orange crosswise into ¼-inch slices, then halve the slices.

5 Return the skillet to high heat and melt the remaining 2 tablespoons of butter. Add the amaranth leaves and swirl the skillet until they are wilted and fragrant, 20 seconds. Slice the duck breasts. Arrange the breasts and the amaranth on plates and drizzle with the sauce. Top with the duck legs and orange slices and garnish with mint leaves.

NOTE Ras el hanout is a North African spice mixture that usually includes ginger and anise. It's available at some grocery stores (McCormick makes a version) and from kalustyans.com.

MAKE AHEAD The sauce can be refrigerated for up to 5 days.

WINE Spiced, red-berried southern Rhône red.

HOW TO AIR-DRY DUCK

For supercrisp, golden skin, refrigerate the breasts uncovered on a rack overnight to remove moisture.

A

B

C

D

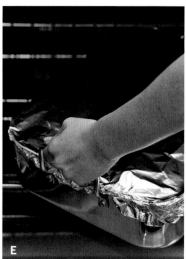

E

F

G

H

I

Osso Buco

Chef Ethan Stowell of Tavolàta in Seattle sticks to Italian tradition when making the Milanese specialty osso buco. He braises veal shanks until meltingly tender and then tops them with a citrusy gremolata (orange and lemon zest mixed with garlic and parsley). Stowell insists that scooping out every bit of marrow from the bones is a must for "a mouthful of fatty goodness."

Osso Buco with Citrus Gremolata

Time	1 hr active
	4 hr total
Makes	8 servings

8 meaty veal shanks, cut 1½ inches thick (7 lbs.)
   Kosher salt and pepper
6 Tbsp. extra-virgin olive oil
6 carrots, cut into ¼-inch dice
6 celery ribs, cut into ¼-inch dice
2 onions, cut into ¼-inch dice
6 garlic cloves—4 whole, 2 minced
3 bay leaves
4 cups chicken stock or low-sodium broth
2 cups dry white wine
   One 15-oz. can diced Italian tomatoes
6 thyme sprigs
   Two 2½-inch strips of orange zest, minced
   Two 2½-inch strips of lemon zest, minced
2 Tbsp. minced flat-leaf parsley

1 Preheat the oven to 375°. Season the veal shanks with salt and pepper **(A)**. In a very large, deep skillet, heat 3 tablespoons of the olive oil until shimmering. Working in batches, cook the veal over moderately high heat until browned on both sides, about 8 minutes total per batch. Transfer the osso buco to a large roasting pan **(B)**.

2 Add the remaining 3 tablespoons of olive oil to the skillet. Add the carrots, celery, onions, 4 whole garlic cloves and the bay leaves and cook over moderate heat until softened, about 12 minutes **(C)**. Add the chicken stock, white wine, tomatoes and thyme sprigs and bring to a boil. Pour the vegetables and liquid over the veal **(D)**. Cover the roasting pan with foil, transfer to the oven and braise the shanks for about 2½ hours, until very tender **(E)**.

3 Meanwhile, in a small bowl, mix the orange zest, lemon zest, parsley and the 2 minced garlic cloves. Lightly season the gremolata with salt and pepper **(F)**.

4 Transfer the veal shanks to a baking sheet and cover with foil. Carefully strain the cooking liquid into a large bowl **(G)**. Reserve the vegetables; discard the bay leaves and thyme sprigs. Pour the cooking liquid back into the roasting pan and boil over high heat until it is reduced by half, about 25 minutes. Season the sauce with salt and pepper. Stir in the reserved vegetables and simmer over moderately low heat for 2 minutes **(H)**. Transfer the osso buco to shallow bowls. Spoon the sauce and vegetables on top and sprinkle lightly with the gremolata **(I)**. Serve with the remaining gremolata at the table.

SERVE WITH Polenta.

MAKE AHEAD The osso buco can be refrigerated for up to 2 days.

WINE Cherry-inflected, aromatic Barbera d'Alba.

PERFECT PARTY DISH

Osso buco is ideal for entertaining because the flavor only gets better after a day in the fridge.

Next Great Lamb Cuts

Eating just the most popular cuts of lamb, such as the chops, is like visiting only the major tourist destinations in a city: You miss out on so much. Tony Maws, a master of whole-animal cooking at his restaurant Craigie on Main in Boston, shares his secrets for cooking overlooked parts. For the leg and ribs, that means roasting; for the neck, slow braising; and for leg steaks, quick searing.

Vadouvan-Spiced Lamb Ribs

Time	10 min active
	3 hr total plus 8 hr curing
Makes	4 servings

1½ Tbsp. vadouvan (see Note)
1 Tbsp. kosher salt
1 Tbsp. sugar
One 3½-lb. rack of lamb ribs

📷 opposite page

1 In a small bowl, whisk the vadouvan, salt and sugar. Set the ribs on a rimmed baking sheet and rub the spice mixture all over them; refrigerate, covered, for 8 hours or overnight.

2 Preheat the oven to 300°. Roast the ribs for 2½ hours, until browned and tender; transfer to a carving board and let rest for 10 minutes. Cut into 2-rib pieces and serve.

NOTE Vadouvan, a French curry spice blend flavored with shallots and garlic, is available at specialty food stores and laboiteny.com.

WINE Spicy southern French red.

Slow-Roasted Leg of Lamb

Time	15 min active
	7 hr 15 min total
Makes	8 to 10 servings

One 9-lb. bone-in leg of lamb
Kosher salt and pepper
Canola oil, for greasing
1 qt. chicken stock or low-sodium broth
1 750-ml bottle dry white wine
5 thyme sprigs
5 parsley sprigs

1 Preheat the oven to 275°. Season the lamb with salt and pepper. In a large, oiled roasting pan, sear the lamb over moderately high heat until browned. Add the chicken stock, white wine and herb sprigs, transfer to the oven and cook for 2 hours, basting every hour.

2 Cover the pan with foil and cook for 5 hours longer, until the meat is tender and pulling away from the bone.

WINE Powerful Australian Shiraz.

(continued on page 99)

RIB TIP

Lamb ribs can be fatty, so it's best to get them from small farms where the animals tend to be younger and leaner.

Braised Lamb Neck with Turnip

Time	45 min active
	3 hr total
Makes	6 servings

Six 1½-inch-thick, bone-in lamb necks

Kosher salt and pepper

2 Tbsp. canola oil

2 celery ribs, chopped

1 carrot, chopped

1 large onion, chopped

1 turnip, peeled and chopped

1 Tbsp. tomato paste

1 anchovy fillet

2 cups dry white wine

2 cups chicken stock

1 cup raisins

1 bay leaf and 1 sprig each of parsley, cilantro and rosemary, tied in cheesecloth

📷 opposite page

1 Preheat the oven to 300°. Season the lamb with salt and pepper. In a casserole, heat the oil until shimmering. Add the lamb and cook over moderately high heat, turning, until browned, about 10 minutes; transfer to a plate.

2 Pour off all but 2 tablespoons of the fat from the casserole. Add the celery, carrot, onion, turnip, tomato paste and anchovy and cook, stirring, until the vegetables just start to soften, about 5 minutes. Stir in the wine, scraping up any browned bits, and simmer for 3 minutes. Add the stock, raisins and herb bundle and bring to a boil.

3 Return the lamb to the casserole, cover and braise in the oven for 2 hours, until the meat is very tender. Discard the herb bundle and season the lamb with salt and pepper. Serve.

SERVE WITH Buttered noodles.

WINE Juicy Oregon Pinot Noir.

Lamb Steak Frites

Time	30 min
Makes	4 servings

Two 1¼-lb. lamb leg steaks, cut about 1¼ inches thick

½ tsp. ground cumin

½ tsp. ground fennel seeds

Kosher salt and pepper

2 Tbsp. canola oil

4 small thyme sprigs

2 garlic cloves

6 Tbsp. unsalted butter, cubed

1 shallot, minced

1 cup dry red wine

1 cup chicken stock

French fries, for serving

1 Rub the lamb with the cumin and fennel; season with salt and pepper. In a cast-iron skillet, heat the oil until smoking. Add the lamb and cook over high heat, turning once, until browned, 3 minutes. Reduce the heat to moderate. Add the thyme, garlic and 4 tablespoons of the butter and cook for 5 minutes, basting the lamb with the butter. Turn the steaks and cook, basting, until an instant-read thermometer inserted in the thickest part registers 130°, about 5 minutes; transfer to a carving board and let rest for 10 minutes. Thickly slice against the grain.

2 Pour off all but 1 tablespoon of the fat from the skillet. Add the shallot and cook over moderately high heat until softened, 1 minute. Add the wine and simmer until syrupy, 4 minutes. Add the stock and simmer until slightly reduced, 3 minutes. Off the heat, whisk in the remaining 2 tablespoons of butter; season with salt and pepper. Serve with the lamb and french fries.

WINE Earthy, peppery Sangiovese.

BRAISING BEAUTY

Lamb necks are fantastic when braised. The meat gets succulent and tender as it cooks in the braising liquid, while the bones, in turn, enrich and flavor the broth.

Sauerkraut

Made the old-fashioned way, sauerkraut is a healthy superfood. Fermentation pro Alex Hozven of Cultured Pickle Shop in Berkeley, California, shows how to make three kinds of this probiotic-rich pickled food at home. Aside from the great taste, another benefit of DIY sauerkraut is that it's guaranteed to be live, which isn't true of all store-bought versions.

Homemade Sauerkraut with Caraway and Apples

Time	1 hr active; 5 hr total plus up to 6 weeks fermenting
Makes	2 qts

4 lbs. green cabbage, very thinly sliced on a mandoline or finely shredded in a food processor

1 Granny Smith apple—peeled, cored and very thinly sliced on a mandoline

2 Tbsp. plus 1 tsp. fine sea salt

1 Tbsp. caraway seeds

½ Tbsp. juniper berries (optional)

1 Combine all of the ingredients in a very large bowl. Squeeze the cabbage to release some liquid. Press a heavy plate on the cabbage to weigh it down and let stand at room temperature, tossing and squeezing the cabbage 4 or 5 more times, until it has released enough liquid to cover, about 4 hours.

2 Pour the cabbage and its liquid into a clean ceramic crock or tall glass container. Top the cabbage with a clean plate that just fits inside the crock. Place a glass or ceramic bowl on the plate and put a heavy can in the bowl; the cabbage should be completely submerged in its brine by at least ½ inch. Cover the crock with a clean kitchen towel and set it in a cool, dark place to ferment for about 6 weeks.

3 Every 3 days, clean and replace the plate that sits on the cabbage, carefully skimming any foam or mold that forms on the surface of the liquid. Discard the cabbage and its liquid if it's foul-smelling, or if anything brown, moldy or slimy has penetrated below what can easily be scraped off the surface. If too much liquid evaporates before the sauerkraut is sufficiently fermented, dissolve ½ teaspoon of sea salt in 1 cup of spring water and add it to the crock. When the sauerkraut is ready, it should have a light crunch and a bright, pleasantly tangy taste, with an acidity similar to that of a lemon.

SERVE WITH Roast pork–and–mustard sandwich.

MAKE AHEAD The sauerkraut can be refrigerated in its brine in a glass or ceramic jar for up to 6 months. Drain before serving.

(continued on page 102)

THE PICKLE'S PROGRESS

"Try the kraut at different stages to see its evolution from one week to the next," says Hozven. "The longer it ferments, the more acidic—and shelf-stable—it gets."

Indian-Spiced Sauerkraut

Time	1 hr active; 5 hr total plus up to 6 weeks fermenting
Makes	2 qts

- 4 lbs. green cabbage, very thinly sliced on a mandoline or finely shredded in a food processor
- 1 Tbsp. each whole cumin seeds and coriander seeds
- ½ Tbsp. each whole fennel seeds and black peppercorns
- 1 tsp. each whole brown mustard seeds and fenugreek seeds
- 1 tsp. each turmeric and paprika
- 2 Tbsp. plus 1 tsp. fine sea salt

1 Combine all of the ingredients in a very large bowl. Squeeze the cabbage to release some liquid. Press a heavy plate on the cabbage to weigh it down and let stand at room temperature, tossing and squeezing the cabbage 4 or 5 more times, until it has released enough liquid to cover, about 4 hours.

2 Pour the cabbage and its liquid into a clean ceramic crock or tall glass container. Top the cabbage with a clean plate that just fits inside the crock. Place a glass or ceramic bowl on the plate and put a heavy can in the bowl; the cabbage should be completely submerged in its brine by at least ½ inch. Cover the crock with a clean kitchen towel and set it in a cool, dark place to ferment for about 6 weeks.

3 Every 3 days, clean and replace the plate that sits on the cabbage, carefully skimming any foam or mold that forms on the surface of the liquid. Discard the cabbage and its liquid if it's foul-smelling, or if anything brown, moldy or slimy has penetrated below what can easily be scraped off the surface. If too much liquid evaporates before the sauerkraut is sufficiently fermented, dissolve ½ teaspoon of sea salt in 1 cup of spring water and add it to the crock. When the sauerkraut is ready, it should have a light crunch and a bright, pleasantly tangy taste, with an acidity similar to that of a lemon.

SERVE WITH Potato-and-lentil salad with fresh herbs.

BALANCING ACT

For the sauerkraut above, Hozven worked with an herbalist to create an ayurvedic spice blend designed to improve digestion and balance within the body.

Seakraut

Time	1 hr active; 5 hr total plus up to 6 weeks fermenting
Makes	2 qts

4   lbs. green cabbage, very thinly sliced on a mandoline or finely shredded in a food processor

One 4-inch piece of fresh burdock root (see below), peeled and thinly sliced crosswise on a mandoline

1   small golden beet, finely shredded

¼   cup dry hijiki or arame seaweed (see below)

2   Tbsp. plus 1 tsp. fine sea salt

1 Combine all of the ingredients in a very large bowl. Squeeze the cabbage to release some liquid. Press a heavy plate on the cabbage to weigh it down and let stand at room temperature, tossing and squeezing the cabbage 4 or 5 more times, until it has released enough liquid to cover, about 4 hours.

2 Pour the cabbage and its liquid into a clean ceramic crock or tall glass container. Top the cabbage with a clean plate that just fits inside the crock. Place a glass or ceramic bowl on the plate and put a heavy can in the bowl; the cabbage should be completely submerged in its brine by at least ½ inch. Cover the crock with a clean kitchen towel and set it in a cool, dark place to ferment for about 6 weeks.

3 Every 3 days, clean and replace the plate that sits on the cabbage, carefully skimming any foam or mold that forms on the surface of the liquid. Discard the cabbage and its liquid if it's foul-smelling, or if anything brown, moldy or slimy has penetrated below what can easily be scraped off the surface. If too much liquid evaporates before the sauerkraut is sufficiently fermented, dissolve ½ teaspoon of sea salt in 1 cup of spring water and add it to the crock. When the sauerkraut is ready, it should have a light crunch and a bright, pleasantly tangy taste, with an acidity similar to that of a lemon.

SERVE WITH Beet, watercress and mixed-green salad.

INGREDIENT INTEL

Popular in China, Japan and Korea, burdock is a root vegetable with an earthy, nutty flavor. It's sold at many Asian markets, but if you can't find it, substitute another root vegetable, like carrot.

Hijiki is a seaweed with a neutral flavor, sold in dry black strips, while arame is a dark brown sea vegetable that has long strands and a slightly sweet, mild flavor. "Hijiki and arame retain a good texture during fermentation," explains Hozven of this kraut inspired by the Japanese macrobiotic diet. Both ingredients are available at Asian markets, health food stores and online from amazon.com.

Rye Bread

Lionel Vatinet of La Farm Bakery in Cary, North Carolina, is a master French baker, but the bread he's most proud of is a dense, aromatic rye—the kind that's practically a religion in Scandinavia. Learn how to make the ultra-crusty, extra-flavorful loaf that won over his Norwegian father-in-law.

Scandinavian Rye Bread

Time	35 min active
	5 hr 45 min total
Makes	one 9-by-5-inch loaf

½ cup rye berries, rinsed and drained

5¼ cups warm water

½ cup millet, rinsed and drained

1 envelope (¼ oz.) active dry yeast

4 cups whole-grain rye flour, preferably stone-ground heirloom (carolinaground.com)

1 cup bread flour

2 Tbsp. fine sea salt

1¼ cups rolled oats

Vegetable oil, for greasing

1 In a small saucepan, cover the rye berries with 2 cups of the water and bring to a boil. Simmer gently over moderately low heat until all of the water has been absorbed and the rye berries are al dente, about 40 minutes. Spread the rye berries on parchment paper and let cool completely.

2 Meanwhile, in another small saucepan, cover the millet with 1 cup of the water and bring to a boil. Reduce the heat to moderately low and simmer until all of the water has been absorbed and the millet is halfway to tender, 12 minutes. Spread the millet on parchment paper; let cool completely **(A)**.

3 In a stand mixer fitted with the paddle, mix the yeast with the remaining 2¼ cups of water; let stand until foamy, 10 minutes. Add both flours and the salt; mix at low speed for 5 minutes. Increase the speed to medium and mix for 2 minutes. Mix in the cooled rye berries and millet along with ¾ cup of the oats **(B)**. Scrape the dough into a greased large bowl and cover with plastic wrap. Let stand in a warm spot until doubled, 2 hours.

4 Scatter the remaining ½ cup of oats on a work surface and scrape the dough onto them. Roll the dough until coated with the oats, then pat into a large brick shape **(C)**. Transfer the dough to a greased 9-by-5-inch loaf pan and cover with a damp kitchen towel. Let stand in a warm spot until slightly risen, about 1½ hours.

5 Preheat the oven to 450°. Bake the bread until lightly browned on top and an instant-read thermometer inserted in the center registers 200°, 1 hour. Transfer to a rack; let cool for 30 minutes. Unmold and let cool completely.

A

B

C

Popovers

Light, hollow popovers are America's answer to the U.K.'s Yorkshire pudding. Crusty and nicely browned, with an impressive mushroom-shaped pouf, a really good one is guaranteed to make guests swoon. Cookbook author Grace Parisi shares tips on how to perfect the brunch specialty in this citrusy rendition baked in a simple muffin pan.

Orange Popovers

Time	10 min active 40 min total
Makes	12 popovers

3 large eggs, at room temperature
1 Tbsp. sugar
1 tsp. finely grated orange zest
1¼ cups milk
4 Tbsp. unsalted butter, melted
1¼ cups all-purpose flour
½ tsp. baking powder
½ tsp. kosher salt

1 Preheat the oven to 425°. In a large bowl, whisk the eggs with the sugar and orange zest. Whisk in the milk and 3 tablespoons of the melted butter **(A)**. In another bowl, whisk the flour with the baking powder and salt **(B)**. Whisk the wet ingredients into the dry ingredients until only small lumps remain **(C)**.

2 Brush the cups of a 12-cup muffin tin (preferably not nonstick) with the remaining 1 tablespoon of melted butter **(D)**. Heat the muffin tin in the oven for 5 minutes; the butter will turn a nutty brown. Carefully fill the muffin cups halfway with the popover batter **(E)**. Bake the popovers for about 30 minutes, until they are risen and browned. Turn the popovers out onto a platter and serve them right away **(F)**.

SERVE WITH Preserves or jam.

BUILDING A HIGH RISE

Popovers don't always rise as
they should. For foolproof ones,
add a bit of baking powder to
the batter and use a regular (not
nonstick) muffin tin.

Soufflé

An exquisitely puffy soufflé can seem like a small miracle. Master chef Jacques Pépin is a pro at making both sweet and savory versions. The most important thing, he says, is the timing. For instance, you must use the beaten egg whites right away or they'll deflate. Read on for more advice on how to re-create these stunners in your own kitchen.

Gruyère Cheese Soufflé

Time	25 min active 1 hr total
Makes	4 servings

- 3 Tbsp. unsalted butter, plus more for greasing
- 2 Tbsp. freshly grated Parmigiano-Reggiano cheese
- 3½ Tbsp. all-purpose flour
- 1 cup cold whole milk
- 5 large eggs, separated
- ½ tsp. kosher salt
- ½ tsp. pepper
- 3 oz. Gruyère cheese, shredded (1 cup)
- 2 Tbsp. chopped chives
- 2 slices of yellow American cheese, each cut into 6 strips

1 Preheat the oven to 400°. Grease a 1-quart gratin dish (see Note) with butter and dust with the Parmigiano-Reggiano cheese; refrigerate. In a saucepan, melt the 3 tablespoons of butter over moderate heat. Whisk in the flour and cook, whisking, for 1 minute **(A)**. Whisk in the milk, bring to a boil and cook, whisking, until thickened, 1 minute. Remove the béchamel from the heat, then whisk in 4 egg yolks along with the salt and pepper **(B)**. Reserve the remaining yolk for another use.

2 In a clean bowl, beat the whites until firm peaks form **(C)**. Whisk one-third of the whites into the béchamel, then fold in the remaining beaten whites. Fold in the Gruyère and chives; scrape into the prepared dish. Arrange the American cheese strips on top in a crisscross pattern. Bake for 25 minutes, until puffed and golden. Serve.

NOTE To get the most crust with the cheesiest flavor, Pépin uses a wide, shallow gratin dish, then creates a lattice on top with thin slices of American cheese. A soufflé ramekin would work too.

WINE Toasty, full-bodied Champagne.

(continued on next page)

Rothschild Soufflé (Sweet)

Time	25 min active
	1 hr total
Makes	4 servings

½ cup candied and dried fruits, chopped into ¼-inch pieces

3 Tbsp. kirsch (cherry brandy)

3 Tbsp. unsalted butter, plus more for greasing

⅓ cup plus 2 Tbsp. granulated sugar

3½ Tbsp. all-purpose flour

1 cup cold whole milk

1 tsp. pure vanilla extract

5 large eggs, separated

Confectioners' sugar, for dusting

1 In a bowl, soak the fruits in the kirsch for 30 minutes or overnight. Preheat the oven to 400°. Grease a 1-quart soufflé dish with butter and dust with 2 tablespoons of the granulated sugar; refrigerate.

2 In a saucepan, melt the 3 tablespoons of butter over moderate heat. Whisk in the flour to form a paste and cook, whisking, for 1 minute. Whisk in the milk, bring to a boil and cook, whisking constantly, until thickened, 1 minute. Remove the béchamel from the heat, then whisk in the vanilla and remaining ⅓ cup of granulated sugar. Whisk in 4 egg yolks; reserve the remaining yolk for another use.

3 In a clean bowl, beat the whites until firm peaks form; whisk one-third into the béchamel, then fold in the remaining whites. Fold in the fruit and kirsch; scrape into the prepared soufflé dish. Bake for 25 minutes, until puffed and lightly golden. Dust with confectioners' sugar and serve.

WINE Fruit-forward, off-dry Champagne.

SIZE DOESN'T MATTER

Egg whites can yield different volumes when beaten. "Sometimes there's extra that won't fit in the dish—that's OK," says Pépin.

RUNNY OR NOT?

"Some people like a soufflé that's wet in the center, others do not," says Pépin. "Both are perfectly fine."

Yogurt

Yogurt is one of the healthiest things a home cook can make. Plus, it's simple—no chemistry PhD needed. It's all about adding live, active bacteria to milk. Ron Marks, founder of AtlantaFresh Artisan Creamery, shares two methods: using a bit of store-bought yogurt as a starter or, for the best result, powdered yogurt culture. Read on for the recipe and Marks's favorite yogurt add-ins.

Greek-Style Yogurt

Time	1 hr plus up to 18 hr culturing and 6 hr draining
Makes	about 2 qts

1 gal. skim or 2 percent milk, preferably not ultra-pasteurized

2 cups nonfat or 2 percent Greek-style plain yogurt with active cultures, at room temperature, or ¼ tsp. powdered yogurt culture (see Note)

1 In a large saucepan, bring 1½ inches of water to a boil. Set a large stainless steel bowl over the saucepan and add the milk; do not let the bowl touch the water. Turn the heat to low and gradually heat the milk, whisking, until it registers 180° on a candy thermometer. Keep the milk at 180° for 30 minutes, adjusting the heat as necessary.

2 Remove the bowl from the saucepan and let the milk cool down to 106°, stirring often. Meanwhile, preheat the oven to 110°.

If using yogurt, whisk it with 2 cups of the warm milk in a bowl until smooth, then add it back to the warm milk.

If using powdered yogurt culture, sprinkle the powder all over the warm milk.

3 Whisk the cultured warm milk for 3 minutes. Fill several clean jars to 1 inch below the rim with the cultured milk. Cap the jars and place in the warmed oven (or a yogurt maker or other gently heated spot); the cultured milk should stay between 105° and 110° during the entire process. Begin checking the yogurt after 4½ hours; it's ready when it is thick, tangy and surrounded by a small amount of clear whey. If using a pH meter (see Handy Tool on p. 114), the yogurt is ready when it registers 4.5. Depending on how active the cultures are, it can take up to 18 hours for the yogurt to set and develop its characteristic tang. Refrigerate until thoroughly chilled or overnight.

4 Line a large mesh colander or strainer with a moistened cotton cloth or several layers of cheesecloth and set it over a large bowl. Scoop the yogurt into the colander. Cover with plastic wrap and refrigerate for about 6 hours, or until it reaches the desired thickness.

SERVE WITH One of the following add-ins.

NOTE Powdered yogurt culture can be ordered from culturesforhealth.com.

MAKE AHEAD The strained yogurt can be refrigerated for up to 3 weeks.

(continued on next page)

BRING OUT THE BEST

"High-quality milk that isn't ultra-pasteurized will produce a better, more complex-tasting yogurt," Marks says.

GINGER-PEACH CONSERVE

In a saucepan, combine 2 cups sliced peeled peaches, ³/₄ cup plus 2 Tbsp. granulated sugar, ¹/₄ cup orange juice, 6 Tbsp. dark brown sugar and a pinch of salt; simmer for 5 minutes, stirring. Add 2 Tbsp. finely grated ginger and ¹/₈ tsp. cinnamon; simmer for 2 minutes. Add ¹/₂ tsp. cornstarch dissolved in ¹/₂ tsp. water and simmer until slightly thickened. Using an immersion blender, gently pulse until a chunky sauce forms. Serve chilled.

MIXED-BERRY CONSERVE

In a medium saucepan, combine 6 oz. raspberries, ¹/₄ cup orange juice, 2 oz. blueberries, ³/₄ cup plus 2 Tbsp. sugar and a pinch of salt; simmer over moderate heat for 5 minutes, stirring occasionally. Stir in ¹/₂ tsp. cornstarch dissolved in ¹/₂ tsp. water and simmer until the liquid is slightly thickened, 30 seconds. Using an immersion blender, gently blend until a thick sauce forms. Serve chilled.

HONEY

In a bowl, stir together 1 cup yogurt with 4 Tbsp. warmed wildflower honey.

CUCUMBER-DILL (TZATZIKI)

In a bowl, stir together 1 cup Greek-Style Yogurt; ¹/₂ large cucumber that has been peeled, halved lengthwise, seeded and cut into ¹/₂-inch dice; 2 Tbsp. chopped dill; 1 Tbsp. fresh lemon juice; and ¹/₂ minced garlic clove. Season the tzatziki with salt and pepper.

HANDY TOOL

"A pH meter can be your best friend," says Marks. Use it to gauge the acid development in your yogurt. He suggests one from Hanna Instruments; $37 at amazon.com.

Layer Cake

At Seattle's Dahlia Bakery, Tom Douglas offers an ingenious mix-and-match menu of cakes (such as chocolate or brown-butter), fillings (like dark, milk or white chocolate mousse) and frostings (including rich chocolate, hazelnut and white chocolate buttercream). Go ahead and pick your favorite combo. We've tried them all, and you can't go wrong.

Brown-Butter Layer Cake

Time	50 min active
	2 hr 10 min total
Makes	two 9-inch layers

- 3 sticks unsalted butter (12 oz.), plus more for greasing the pans
- 2¼ cups all-purpose flour, plus more for dusting
- 2¼ tsp. baking powder
- 1 tsp. kosher salt
- 1⅔ cups sugar
- 1 vanilla bean, split and seeds scraped
- 3 large egg yolks
- 2 large eggs
- 1¼ cups milk, at room temperature
- Mousse filling and buttercream frosting (recipes follow)

1 Make the cake Preheat the oven to 325°. Butter two 9-inch cake pans and line the bottoms of the pans with parchment paper. Butter the paper and dust the pans with flour, tapping out the excess.

2 In a medium saucepan, melt the 3 sticks of butter. Cook over low heat, stirring occasionally, until foamy, about 5 minutes. Continue to cook, stirring frequently, until the milk solids turn brown and the butter smells nutty, about 4 minutes longer. Scrape the melted butter and browned bits into a large heatproof bowl. Set the bowl in an ice water bath until the butter begins to set around the edge, about 8 minutes.

3 Meanwhile, in a medium bowl, whisk the 2¼ cups of flour with the baking powder and salt.

4 Remove the bowl from the ice water and scrape up the hardened butter. Transfer the butter to a stand mixer fitted with the paddle and beat until creamy. Add the sugar and vanilla seeds and beat at medium-high speed until fluffy, about 3 minutes. Beat in the egg yolks followed by the whole eggs. Beat in the dry ingredients and milk in 3 alternating additions, scraping down the side and bottom of the bowl as necessary.

5 Pour the cake batter into the prepared pans and bake in the center of the oven for about 40 minutes, rotating the pans halfway through baking, until the cakes are golden and a toothpick inserted in the centers comes out clean. Cool the cakes in the pans for 20 minutes, then invert them onto a rack to let them cool completely. Peel off the parchment paper.

6 Layer the cake Set one cake layer on a platter. Spread the mousse filling on top and cover with the second cake layer. Frost the cake all over with a thin layer of buttercream and refrigerate until set, about 5 minutes. Frost the cake with the remaining buttercream. Refrigerate the cake until the frosting is firm, at least 15 minutes, before serving.

(continued on next page)

Double-Chocolate Layer Cake

Time	40 min active 1 hr 45 min total
Makes	two 9-inch layers

2 cups plus 2 Tbsp. all-purpose flour

¼ cup plus 2 Tbsp. unsweetened cocoa powder

Unsalted butter, for greasing the pans

1 cup plus 1 Tbsp. granulated sugar

½ tsp. baking powder

½ tsp. baking soda

½ tsp. kosher salt

2 large eggs, at room temperature

⅓ cup dark brown sugar

1 cup canola oil

2½ oz. bittersweet chocolate, melted

1 cup buttermilk

2 tsp. pure vanilla extract

Mousse filling and buttercream frosting (recipes follow)

1 Make the cake Preheat the oven to 350°. In a small bowl, whisk together 2 tablespoons each of flour and cocoa powder. Butter two 9-inch round cake pans and line the bottoms with parchment paper. Butter the paper and dust the pans with the cocoa-flour mixture, tapping out the excess.

2 In a medium bowl, whisk the 2 cups of flour and ¼ cup of cocoa powder with ½ cup of the granulated sugar, the baking powder, baking soda and salt.

3 In the bowl of a stand mixer fitted with the whisk, beat the eggs with the brown sugar and the remaining ½ cup plus 1 tablespoon of granulated sugar at medium-high speed until thickened, about 5 minutes. At medium speed, gradually add ½ cup of the oil and beat for 3 minutes. Beat in the melted chocolate, then add the remaining oil in a thin stream until thoroughly blended, scraping the side and bottom of the bowl. At low speed, beat in the buttermilk and vanilla. Remove the bowl from the mixer and gently mix in the dry ingredients by hand.

4 Pour the cake batter into the prepared pans and bake in the center of the oven for about 25 minutes, until a toothpick inserted in the centers of the cakes comes out with a few moist crumbs attached. Cool the cakes in the pans for 20 minutes, then invert them onto a rack to cool completely. Peel off the parchment paper.

5 Layer the cake Set one cake layer on a platter. Spread the mousse filling on top and cover with the second cake layer. Frost the cake all over with a thin layer of buttercream and refrigerate until set, about 5 minutes. Frost the cake with the remaining buttercream. Refrigerate the cake until the frosting is firm, at least 15 minutes, before serving.

ON THE EDGE

"I love the crusty caramelized edge on a cake that's just out of a hot oven," says Douglas. "A lot of bakeries trim that edge, but I keep it."

Dark Chocolate Mousse Filling

Time	30 min plus 4 hr chilling
Makes	1½ cups, enough for one 9-inch 2-layer cake

½ tsp. unflavored gelatin
½ cup chilled heavy cream
2 Tbsp. coffee liqueur
2 large egg yolks
2 Tbsp. sugar
   Pinch of kosher salt
4 oz. bittersweet chocolate, melted and cooled

1 In a small bowl, sprinkle the gelatin over ½ tablespoon of water and let stand until softened.

2 Meanwhile, in a medium bowl, using a hand mixer, beat the cream until softly whipped. Refrigerate until chilled, about 10 minutes.

3 In a small, microwave-safe bowl, heat the coffee liqueur at high power until hot, about 45 seconds. Stir in the softened gelatin until dissolved.

4 In another medium bowl, beat the egg yolks with the sugar and salt at high speed until pale and thickened, about 5 minutes. While beating the yolks, beat in the coffee-gelatin liquid; scrape the side and bottom of the bowl. Beat in the melted chocolate. Using a rubber spatula, fold in the whipped cream in 2 additions. Scrape the mousse into a bowl, cover with plastic wrap and refrigerate until firm, at least 4 hours or overnight.

MILK CHOCOLATE VARIATION Substitute milk chocolate for the bittersweet chocolate.

WHITE CHOCOLATE VARIATION Substitute white chocolate for the bittersweet chocolate, and substitute orange liqueur for the coffee liqueur.

Rich Chocolate Buttercream

Time	30 min
Makes	3 cups, enough for one 9-inch 2-layer cake

1 cup sugar
3 large egg whites
¼ tsp. kosher salt
½ tsp. pure vanilla extract
2 sticks plus 2 Tbsp. unsalted butter (9 oz.), cut into tablespoons, at room temperature
4 oz. extra-bittersweet chocolate, melted and cooled

1 In a blender or food processor, pulse the sugar until powdery. Transfer the sugar to a medium heatproof bowl and whisk in the egg whites and salt. Set the bowl over a saucepan of simmering water and whisk gently until the sugar is completely dissolved, 5 minutes.

2 Transfer the warm egg-white mixture to the bowl of a stand mixer fitted with the whisk. Add the vanilla and beat at medium-high speed until stiff and glossy, about 8 minutes. Beat in the butter a few pieces at a time, making sure it is fully incorporated before adding more. The buttercream should be light and fluffy; if it appears runny at any time, transfer the bowl to the freezer for 5 to 10 minutes, then return it to the mixer and continue.

3 Beat in the melted chocolate until fully incorporated, scraping down the side and bottom of the bowl. Remove the bowl from the mixer and beat with a wooden spoon to remove any air bubbles.

HAZELNUT VARIATION Substitute 2 Tbsp. hazelnut-praline paste (available from kingarthurflour.com) for the extra-bittersweet chocolate.

WHITE CHOCOLATE VARIATION Substitute 4 oz. white chocolate for the extra-bittersweet chocolate.

A LAVISH SPREAD

Filling "Using a filling different from the frosting means less buttercream in the cake," Douglas says. "Otherwise, there's just too much of it."

Frosting These classic buttercream frostings are rich and luxurious. Douglas sometimes folds in whipped cream for a lighter touch.

Pie Crust

Master baker Alice Medrich is legendary for her precise, can't-go-wrong recipes. Here, she dispenses her pie wisdom. For instance: "All the ingredients need to be cold, so the butter remains in pieces," says Medrich. "That's what creates the flakes in the crust." Read on to learn how to make her double-crust fruit pie and single-crust pecan pie, plus two ways to crimp.

Perfectly Flaky Yogurt-Butter Pie Dough

Time	20 min plus 2 hr chilling
Makes	one 9-inch crust

- 6 oz. bleached all-purpose flour (1¼ cups)
- 1 stick cold unsalted butter— 5 Tbsp. cut into ¼-inch dice, the rest left whole
- ¼ cup cold plain whole yogurt (not Greek-style)
- ½ tsp. kosher salt

1 Measure the flour into a glass or ceramic bowl and freeze for 15 minutes. Freeze the 3-tablespoon-size chunk of butter for 15 minutes. Put the 5 tablespoons of diced butter on a plate and refrigerate for 15 minutes **(A)**. In a glass measuring cup, combine the yogurt and salt with 1 tablespoon of cold water and refrigerate for 15 minutes.

2 Using a pastry blender or two butter knives, cut the diced butter into the flour until the mixture resembles coarse meal. Rub the mixture between your hands until all of the fat is evenly distributed and the mixture resembles fine oat flakes **(B)**. Using a sharp knife or a cheese plane, very thinly slice the remaining butter and freeze the slices for 5 minutes.

3 Add the butter slices to the bowl. Toss gently to separate the slices and cut once or twice to combine them with the flour; the slices should remain cold and intact **(C)**. Drizzle the cold yogurt into the bowl, using a rubber spatula to stir and toss as you drizzle **(D)**. Continue tossing the dough, scraping any off the spatula and the side of the bowl, until it is crumbly and evenly moistened **(E)**. Press the dough into a 6-inch disk and wrap in plastic **(F)**. Refrigerate the dough for at least 2 hours or freeze for 1 month. (For steps G through I, see p. 123.)

Double-Crust Apple-Apricot Pie

Time	1 hr active; 3 hr total
Makes	one 9-inch pie

- 1 Tbsp. all-purpose flour, plus more for rolling
- Perfectly Flaky Yogurt-Butter Pie Dough (double the recipe above and divide the dough into two disks, one slightly larger than the other)
- 1 egg white, beaten
- 5 large apples (2½ lbs.), such as Granny Smith—peeled, cored, quartered and thickly sliced
- ½ cup sugar, plus more for sprinkling
- ½ cup diced dried apricots (2½ oz.)
- 1 tsp. finely grated orange zest
- 1 tsp. ground cinnamon
- 1 Tbsp. cold unsalted butter, cut into small dice
- 2 Tbsp. milk

1 On a floured work surface, roll out the larger disk of dough to a 13-inch round. Fold the round in quarters and transfer to a 9-inch glass pie dish; unfold the pastry and gently press it into the pie plate. Lightly brush the bottom of the dough with some of the egg white. Roll out the smaller disk of pie dough to a 12-inch round. Fold the round in quarters, transfer it to a wax paper–lined baking sheet and unfold. Freeze the pie shell and the 12-inch round of dough for 15 minutes.

2 Preheat the oven to 400°. In a bowl, toss the apples with the ½ cup of sugar and the apricots, zest, cinnamon and 1 tablespoon of flour. Scrape the apples into the pie shell and dot with the butter. Brush the edge with some of the egg white and top with the second round of dough. Press the edges together and, using scissors, trim the overhang to ½ inch. Fold the edge under itself and crimp decoratively. Brush the pie with the milk and sprinkle with sugar. Cut slashes in the top of the pie to vent steam.

3 Bake the pie in the lower third of the oven for 1 hour, until the crust is deep golden and the filling is bubbling through the vents; tent with foil during the last 20 minutes of baking. Let cool completely before serving.

(continued on page 123)

A

B

C

D

E

F

G

H

I

Pecan Pie with Candied Ginger and Rum

Time	1 hr active
	3 hr total
Makes	one 9-inch pie

- 2 cups pecan halves (7 oz.)
- All-purpose flour, for dusting
- Perfectly Flaky Yogurt-Butter Pie Dough (p. 120)
- 1 cup lightly packed light brown sugar
- ¼ cup light corn syrup
- 1 Tbsp. unsalted butter
- ½ tsp. kosher salt
- 3 large eggs
- 2 Tbsp. rum
- ¼ cup finely chopped candied ginger

1 Preheat the oven to 350°. Spread the pecans in a pie plate and toast for about 8 minutes, until fragrant. Let cool.

2 Increase the oven temperature to 400°. On a floured work surface, roll out the dough to a 13-inch round; patch any cracks **(G)**. Fold the round in quarters and transfer to a 9-inch glass pie dish; unfold the pastry and gently press it into the pie plate **(H)**. Using scissors, trim the overhanging dough to ½ inch **(I)**. Tuck the edge of the dough under itself and crimp decoratively. Line the dough with foil, shiny side down, and prick all over with a fork, piercing the foil and pie dough. Freeze for 15 minutes.

3 Fill the pie with pie weights or dried beans and bake in the lower third of the oven for 30 minutes. Remove the foil and weights. Return the crust to the oven and bake until lightly browned, about 12 minutes.

4 Meanwhile, in a heatproof bowl, combine the brown sugar, corn syrup, butter and salt. Set the bowl over a saucepan filled with 1 inch of simmering water and whisk in the eggs 1 at a time. Cook, whisking gently, until the filling is warm to the touch. Remove from the heat and whisk in the rum.

5 Arrange the pecans in the pie shell and scatter the candied ginger on top. Pour the filling over the pecans. Bake for about 25 minutes, until the filling is jiggly but not cracked; cover the edge of the crust with strips of foil halfway through baking to prevent over-browning. Let the pie cool on a wire rack. Cut into wedges and serve.

TWO WAYS TO CRIMP

The thumb crimp To create an angled, wave-like edge, work on the bias, pinching the pie dough between your thumb and bent forefinger at even intervals.

Traditional fluting To create an even, triangular crimp, form a V with your thumb and forefinger, pressing the edge of the dough into the V with your other forefinger.

A

B

C

D

E

F

G

H

I

Baklava

At Oleana and Sofra in Cambridge, Massachusetts, chef Ana Sortun serves an outrageously good baklava with chocolate and hazelnuts layered between crisp sheets of honey-soaked phyllo. Here's a step-by-step guide to re-creating this decadent dessert at home.

Chocolate-Hazelnut Baklava

Time	1 hr active; 2 hr 15 min total plus 4 hr cooling
Makes	24 pieces

- 1 lb. hazelnuts
- 12 oz. bittersweet chocolate, coarsely chopped
- 2⅔ cups sugar
- 1½ Tbsp. ground cinnamon
- 1 lb. phyllo dough
- 2 sticks unsalted butter, melted
- 1½ cups honey

1 Preheat the oven to 350°. Spread the nuts on a baking sheet and bake for 12 minutes, until the skins are blistered; let cool. Leave the oven on. Transfer the nuts to a kitchen towel and rub off the skins, then transfer to a food processor and pulse until coarsely chopped **(A)**.

2 Add the chocolate, ⅔ cup of the sugar and the cinnamon to the food processor and pulse until the chocolate and nuts are finely chopped and the same size. Transfer to a bowl **(B)**.

3 Unwrap the phyllo and cover with a sheet of plastic wrap. Generously butter a 9-by-13-inch metal baking pan. Butter and stack 8 sheets of phyllo **(C)**. Trim the edges. Ease the stack into the pan. Sprinkle about 2 cups of the filling over the phyllo **(D)**. Butter and stack 2 more phyllo sheets; fold them in half crosswise and place over the filling **(E)**. Sprinkle on another 2 cups of the filling **(F)**. Top with 2 more buttered, folded sheets and 2 cups of filling. Butter and stack 3 more phyllo sheets, fold them in half and place over the filling. Fold in the overhanging phyllo on top and brush generously with butter. Using a ruler and a sharp knife, cut the baklava (through the top and bottom) into 3-inch squares (there will be a bit left on one long side). Cut each square in half to make triangles **(G)**.

4 Bake the baklava for 25 minutes, then lower the oven temperature to 300° and bake for 50 minutes longer, until golden.

5 In a saucepan, bring the honey, 2 cups of water and the remaining 2 cups of sugar to a boil. Simmer over moderate heat for 10 minutes. Immediately ladle the hot syrup over the hot baklava **(H)**. Let stand until completely cool, at least 4 hours and preferably overnight, then serve **(I)**.

A SIMPLER SYRUP

At Sofra, pastry chef Maura Kilpatrick adds cinnamon and cocoa nibs to the syrup that soaks the baklava. Our Test Kitchen notes that the pastry is fabulous even with a basic honey syrup.

Pastry Puffs

Chances are, your favorite French treats—éclairs, profiteroles, cream puffs and cheesy gougères—are made with a *pâte à choux* base. Master baker Eric Kayser of Maison Kayser bakeries worldwide offers a tutorial to perfecting the eggy dough, plus three delicious applications.

Pâte à Choux

Time	20 min active 1 hr 15 min total
Makes	about 3 dozen choux puffs

1	stick plus 1 Tbsp. unsalted butter, cut into cubes
1	tsp. sugar
½	tsp. kosher salt
200	g. all-purpose flour (about 1½ cups)
8	large eggs

1 Preheat the oven to 400°. Line 2 large baking sheets with parchment paper. In a large saucepan, combine 1½ cups of water with the butter, sugar and salt and bring to a boil. Reduce the heat to moderate. Add the flour all at once and stir vigorously with a wooden spoon until a tight dough forms and pulls away from the side of the pan, 2 minutes. Remove the pan from the heat.

2 In a bowl, beat 7 eggs and add to the dough in four batches, stirring vigorously between additions until the eggs are completely incorporated and the pastry is smooth. The dough should be glossy and very slowly hang, stretch and fall from the spoon in thick ribbons. If necessary, beat in the remaining egg.

3 Transfer the dough to a piping bag fitted with a ½-inch plain tip. Pipe 1½-inch mounds onto the baking sheets, leaving 1 inch between them. Proceed as directed below.

3 GREAT CHOUX RECIPES

CHOUQUETTES Sprinkle each mound with ½ tsp. pearl sugar (decorating sugar). Bake for 30 minutes, until browned and puffed.

GOUGÈRES Sprinkle the mounds with 1 cup shredded Gruyère cheese. Bake for 30 minutes, until browned and puffed.

CREAM PUFFS WITH CHOCOLATE PASTRY CREAM Bake the mounds for 30 minutes, until browned and puffed. Let the puffs cool completely.

Meanwhile, in a bowl, whisk 6 egg yolks, 9 Tbsp. granulated sugar, 1½ Tbsp. all-purpose flour and 1½ tsp. cornstarch. In a saucepan, bring 2⅔ cups milk and 1⅓ cups heavy cream to a simmer; whisk ½ cup into the eggs, then whisk the mixture into the saucepan. Cook over low heat, whisking, until thick. Off the heat, whisk in 1¼ cups chopped dark chocolate until melted. Transfer to a bowl, cover the chocolate pastry cream with plastic and refrigerate until cool.

Using a serrated knife, halve the puffs horizontally. Fill each one with 2 Tbsp. of the chocolate pastry cream. Replace the tops and dust with confectioners' sugar. (Alternatively, fill each choux with 2 Tbsp. sweetened whipped cream and 3 fresh raspberries.)

DON'T WAIT

"Eat your choux the same day, the sooner the better," advises Kayser.

Caramel Sauce

You could buy caramel sauce in a jar, but it's incredibly easy to make at home—plus, it'll be free of the additives and preservatives found in most store-bought versions. This dark, luscious sauce uses only a handful of ingredients but packs a major punch with vanilla bean and fleur de sel. Cookbook author Grace Parisi shares her deeply indulgent recipe.

Vanilla Bean and Fleur de Sel Caramel Sauce

Time	15 min
Makes	2 cups

- 2   cups sugar
- 1   vanilla bean, split lengthwise and seeds scraped
- 1   cup heavy cream
- ½   tsp. fleur de sel

1 Put the sugar in a large saucepan and pour ½ cup of water all around **(A)**. Add the vanilla bean and seeds and cook over moderately high heat, stirring, until the sugar is dissolved **(B)**. Using a wet pastry brush, wash down any crystals from the side of the pan **(C)**. Cook without stirring until a deep-amber caramel forms, about 5 minutes **(D)**. Gently swirl the pan to color the caramel evenly.

2 Remove the pan from the heat and add the cream **(E)**. When the bubbling subsides, bring the sauce to a boil and cook over moderate heat, stirring, until the hardened caramel is dissolved **(F)**. Discard the vanilla bean; stir in the fleur de sel **(G)**. Let the caramel sauce cool before serving **(H)**.

POUR IT ON

This silky, dark sauce would be delicious on ice cream, cheesecake or pound cake with fresh strawberries.

Ice Cream

Molly Neitzel loves the pure taste of the American-style ice cream she sells at her Molly Moon's shops in Seattle. But she and pastry chef Christina Spittler also enjoy the lush texture of the French-style confection, too. (Egg yolks help prevent ice crystals.) "Nuts, butterscotch and caramel go great with that custardy flavor profile," says Spittler. Read on for their best recipes.

French-Style Ice Cream

Time	25 min active 5 hr total
Makes	about 1 qt

6 large egg yolks
¾ cup sugar
1¾ cups heavy cream
1¼ cups whole milk
Pinch of kosher salt

1 Set a medium bowl in a large bowl of ice water. In another medium bowl, whisk the egg yolks with ½ cup of the sugar until pale, about 3 minutes.

2 In a medium saucepan, combine the cream, milk, salt and remaining ¼ cup of sugar and bring to a simmer, whisking until the sugar is completely dissolved. Whisk the hot cream mixture into the beaten egg yolks in a thin stream.

3 Transfer the mixture to the saucepan and cook over moderately low heat, stirring constantly with a wooden spoon, until the custard is thick enough to lightly coat the back of the spoon, about 4 minutes; don't let it boil. Pour the custard through a fine-mesh strainer into the bowl in the ice water. Let cool completely, stirring frequently. Refrigerate the custard until very cold, at least 1 hour.

4 Pour the custard into an ice cream maker with flavorings, if using (see Variations), and freeze according to the manufacturer's instructions. Transfer the frozen custard to a plastic container, cover and freeze until firm, at least 3 hours.

CHOCOLATE-TOFFEE VARIATION Add 1 cup broken chocolate-and-toffee-covered saltines or pretzels in Step 4.

SALTED CARAMEL VARIATION Add ¾ cup pourable salted-caramel sauce in Step 4.

American-Style Ice Cream

Time	15 min active 5 hr total
Makes	about 1 qt

2 cups heavy cream
1 cup whole milk
¾ cup sugar
Pinch of kosher salt

1 Set a medium bowl in a large bowl of ice water. In a small saucepan, combine the cream, milk, sugar and salt and bring to a simmer, stirring to dissolve the sugar completely. Pour the ice cream base into the medium bowl and let cool completely, stirring occasionally. Refrigerate until very cold, at least 1 hour or overnight.

2 Pour the base into an ice cream maker with flavorings, if using (see Variations), and freeze according to the manufacturer's instructions. Transfer to a plastic container, cover and freeze until firm, at least 3 hours.

BLACKBERRY-SAGE VARIATION Add ¾ cup blackberry preserves mixed with 1 Tbsp. minced fresh sage in Step 2.

STRAWBERRY-JALAPEÑO VARIATION Add 1 cup strawberries macerated in 3 Tbsp. sugar with 1 tsp. minced jalapeño in Step 2.

MAKE AHEAD The ice cream can be made up to 3 days in advance.

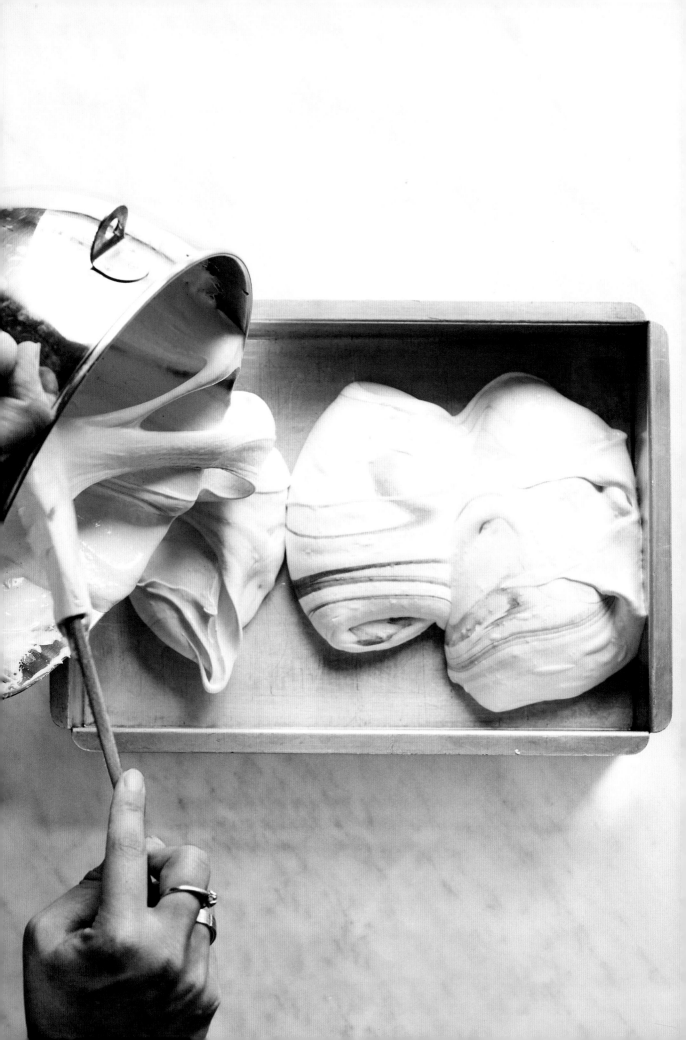

Candy

"Candy is magic," says Jami Curl, the mastermind behind Quin, the cult sweets shop in Portland, Oregon. "I remember holding the first lollipop I made up to the light and thinking, I'm a wizard!" But more than magic, making candy is all about precision: Follow Curl's recipes for marshmallows, lollipops and caramels for sweet success.

Vanilla-Mint Marshmallows

| Time | 1 hr plus 3 hr setting |
| Makes | about 50 marshmallows |

Canola oil, for greasing

98	g. (¼ cup plus 1 Tbsp.) light corn syrup
12	g. (1 Tbsp.) pure peppermint extract
1	vanilla bean, split lengthwise and seeds scraped
57	g. (20 sheets) silver leaf gelatin (see Note)
108	g. (⅓ cup plus 2 Tbsp.) ice water
600	g. (3 cups) granulated sugar
255	g. (1 cup plus 1 Tbsp.) water
15	drops natural red food coloring
114	g. (1 cup plus 1 Tbsp.) confectioners' sugar
114	g. (1 cup) cornstarch

1 Lightly grease a 9-by-13-inch metal baking pan with canola oil. In a stand mixer fitted with the whisk attachment, beat the corn syrup with the peppermint extract and vanilla seeds at low speed until combined. Reserve the vanilla bean pod for another use.

2 In a heatproof medium bowl, cover the gelatin sheets with the ice water and let stand, stirring occasionally, until the gelatin is evenly moistened and all of the water is absorbed, about 5 minutes. In a medium saucepan, bring 2 inches of water to a simmer. Set the bowl with the gelatin over the simmering water and cook, stirring once or twice, until melted, about 5 minutes. Do not let the bowl touch the water. Carefully remove the saucepan from the heat.

3 In a small, heavy-bottomed saucepan, bring the granulated sugar and water to a boil. Cook, without stirring, until the sugar syrup registers 225° on a candy thermometer, 8 to 10 minutes. Use a wet pastry brush to wash down the side of the pan.

4 With the stand mixer at low speed, slowly stream the hot sugar syrup into the corn syrup. Add the warm gelatin and continue beating until slightly thickened and opaque, about 2 minutes. Increase the speed to moderately high and beat until the marshmallow is thick and glossy and registers 105°, about 12 minutes.

5 Lightly grease a rubber spatula. Scatter the food coloring over the marshmallow, then, using the spatula, quickly scrape the marshmallow into the prepared pan, swirling the food coloring as you go. Let stand at room temperature until set, at least 3 hours or overnight.

6 Sift the confectioners' sugar and cornstarch into a shallow bowl. Invert the marshmallow onto a work surface and cut into 2-inch squares. Toss in the sugar mixture, shaking off any excess, then serve.

NOTE Silver leaf gelatin is available at most baking supply shops and from amazon.com.

MAKE AHEAD The vanilla-mint marshmallows can be stored in an airtight container at room temperature for up to 1 month.

(continued on next page)

WEIGH OUT

Perfect candy is about being exact: Use a scale to weigh ingredients in grams.

Citrus Lollipops

Time	40 min active
	1 hr 30 min total
Makes	30 lollipops

Canola oil, for greasing

Thirty 4-inch lollipop sticks

134 g. (⅓ cup plus 1 Tbsp.) light corn syrup

200 g. (1 cup) sugar

75 g. (¼ cup plus 4 tsp.) water

7 g. (1 Tbsp. plus 1 tsp.) finely grated lemon, lime, tangerine or grapefruit zest

2 g. (½ tsp.) citric acid

2 to 3 drops of natural food coloring, plus more as needed

Thirty 5-inch squares of cellophane and twist ties, for wrapping

1 Lightly grease thirty 1½-inch plastic or silicone lollipop molds with canola oil. Place a lollipop stick in each indentation, with ¾ inch of the stick inside the round mold. Alternatively, line a large baking sheet with a silicone baking mat.

2 In a small saucepan, bring the corn syrup, sugar and water to a boil. Do not stir **(A)**. Continue to cook, without stirring, until the syrup reaches 300° on a candy thermometer, 7 minutes. Remove from the heat and stir in the citrus zest, citric acid and food coloring. Spoon some of the syrup onto a white plate to check the color **(B)**. Add more food coloring if needed.

3 Working quickly, spoon 1 teaspoon of the syrup into each mold **(C)**. Alternatively, spoon teaspoonfuls of the syrup onto the prepared baking sheet, 2 inches apart, and place a stick in each lollipop, turning it to cover with syrup. Let the lollipops harden at room temperature for 30 minutes. Wrap in cellophane and secure with a twist tie.

(continued on page 137)

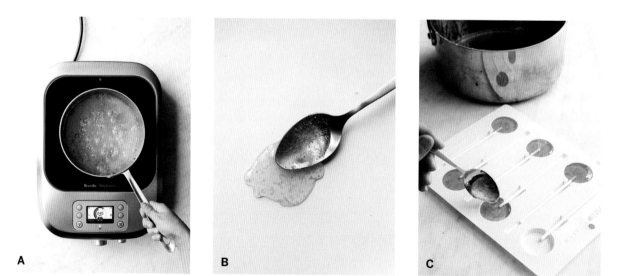

A

B

C

Chai Caramels with Salted Pepitas

Time	1 hr plus overnight setting
Makes	about 115 caramels

300 g. (2 sticks plus 5 Tbsp.) room-temperature unsalted butter, cut into 1-inch pieces, plus more for greasing

235 g. (1 cup) heavy cream

3 chai tea bags (8 g.)

18 g. (1 Tbsp. plus 1½ tsp.) pure vanilla extract

9 g. (1 Tbsp.) kosher salt

438 g. (1¼ cups plus 1 Tbsp.) light corn syrup

800 g. (4 cups) sugar

100 g. (¾ cup) roasted salted pepitas (hulled pumpkin seeds)

5-inch squares of cellophane or wax paper, for wrapping

1 Lightly butter a 9-by-13-inch metal baking pan and line with parchment paper, leaving a 1-inch overhang on all 4 sides.

2 In a small saucepan, bring the cream to a boil; remove from the heat. Add the tea bags, cover and let stand for 12 minutes. Gently squeeze the tea bags to release any cream, then discard. Stir in the vanilla and salt; keep warm.

3 In a medium, heavy-bottomed saucepan, cook the corn syrup over moderately high heat, swirling the pan occasionally, until it begins to bubble, 2 minutes. Sprinkle one-third of the sugar over the corn syrup and, using a small heatproof spatula, poke the sugar into the hot syrup until incorporated. Do not stir. Repeat with the remaining sugar in 2 batches, using a wet pastry brush to wash down any crystals on the side of the pan. Continue cooking over moderately high heat, swirling the pan occasionally, until a dark amber caramel forms and the temperature reaches 330° on a candy thermometer, about 15 minutes.

4 Remove the saucepan from the heat and gradually add the warm cream, whisking constantly, until incorporated **(A)**. Add the 300 grams of butter in 2 batches, whisking until melted before adding more. Continue whisking the caramel vigorously until it is glossy and registers 190° on a candy thermometer, about 5 minutes **(B)**. Fold in the pepitas.

5 Scrape the caramel into the prepared baking pan, then gently tap it on a work surface to release any air bubbles. Let stand at room temperature for at least 3 hours, cover loosely with foil and let stand overnight.

6 Invert the caramel onto a work surface, peel off the parchment paper and cut into 1-inch squares **(C)**. Wrap each caramel in a square of cellophane and twist the ends to seal.

MAKE AHEAD The wrapped caramels can be stored in an airtight container at room temperature for up to 6 months.

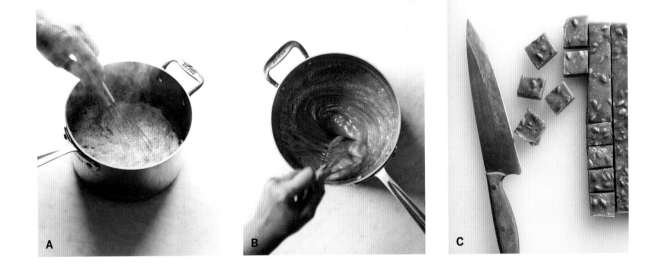

A   B   C

Barrel-Aged Cocktails

Aging cocktails in wooden barrels rounds out harsh edges and adds layers of flavor. You can offer up a mini barrel with a spigot in place of the usual punch bowl at parties, pour aged cocktails into glass bottles as gifts or give a whole barrel to a drinks-obsessed friend. Star mixologist Jeffrey Morgenthaler of Clyde Common and Pépé Le Moko in Portland, Oregon, shows how to get started.

Aged White Manhattan

Time	20 min active
	about 1 month total
Makes	about 1 liter

One 1-liter oak barrel
16 oz. unaged white whiskey, such as Trybox Series New Make
16 oz. white vermouth, such as Dolin Blanc
½ oz. orange bitters
Ice
Lemon twists, for serving

1 Age the cocktail If the barrel is new and dry inside, fill it with water and let stand until watertight, about 24 hours. Drain.

2 Using a funnel, fill the barrel with the whiskey, vermouth and bitters. Let age, tasting a sample once a week, until the cocktail has taken on a rounded but not overly oaky flavor, about 1 month.

3 Strain the cocktail through a coffee filter–lined funnel into a glass container and store indefinitely.

4 Serve the cocktail Pour 3 ounces of the cocktail into an ice-filled mixing glass and stir until chilled. Strain the drink into a chilled cocktail glass. Garnish with a twist.

Aged Martini

Time	20 min active
	about 3 weeks total
Makes	about 1 liter

One 1-liter oak barrel
22 oz. gin
11 oz. dry vermouth
Ice
Lemon twists, for serving

1 Age the cocktail If the barrel is new and dry inside, fill it with water and let stand until watertight, about 24 hours. Drain.

2 Using a funnel, fill the barrel with the gin and vermouth. Let age, tasting a sample once a week, until the cocktail has taken on a rounded but not overly oaky flavor, about 3 weeks.

3 Strain the cocktail through a coffee filter–lined funnel into a glass container and store indefinitely.

4 Serve the cocktail Pour 3 ounces of the cocktail into an ice-filled mixing glass and stir until chilled. Strain the drink into a chilled cocktail glass. Garnish with a twist.

BUYING BARRELS

You can find 1-, 2-, 3- and 5-liter barrels at tuthilltown.com ($60 to $96). For barrels larger than 1 liter, multiply each aged cocktail recipe proportionately.

Aged Negroni

Time	20 min active about 1 month total
Makes	about 1 liter

One 1-liter oak barrel
11 oz. gin
11 oz. sweet vermouth
11 oz. Campari
Ice
Orange twists, for serving

1 Age the cocktail If the barrel is new and dry inside, fill it with water and let stand until watertight, about 24 hours. Drain.

2 Using a funnel, fill the barrel with the gin, vermouth and Campari. Let age, tasting a sample once a week, until the cocktail has taken on a rounded but not overly oaky flavor, about 1 month.

3 Strain the cocktail through a coffee filter–lined funnel into a glass container and store indefinitely.

4 Serve the cocktail Pour 3 ounces of the cocktail into an ice-filled rocks glass and stir well, then garnish with a twist.

Aged Chrysanthemum

Time	20 min active about 1 month total
Makes	about 1 liter

One 1-liter oak barrel
10½ oz. Bénédictine
21 oz. dry vermouth
1¾ oz. absinthe
Ice
Orange twists, for serving

1 Age the cocktail If the barrel is new and dry inside, fill it with water and let stand until watertight, about 24 hours. Drain.

2 Using a funnel, fill the barrel with the Bénédictine, vermouth and absinthe. Let age, tasting a sample once a week, until the cocktail has taken on a rounded but not overly oaky flavor, about 1 month.

3 Strain the cocktail through a coffee filter–lined funnel into a glass container and store indefinitely.

4 Serve the cocktail Pour 3 ounces of the cocktail into an ice-filled mixing glass and stir until chilled. Strain the drink into a chilled cocktail glass. Garnish with a twist.

TASTING TIP

When aging cocktails, remember that smaller, newer barrels work faster than larger, used ones. Taste every week until you get the gently oaked flavor you want. "There's definitely a sweet spot," says Morgenthaler.

Aged El Presidente

Time	20 min active
	about 1 month total
Makes	about 1 liter

One 1-liter oak barrel

18½ oz. gold rum, such as Flor de Caña

9 oz. dry vermouth

3 oz. Grand Marnier

2 oz. grenadine, such as Small Hand Foods from caskstore.com

Ice

Orange twists, for serving

1 Age the cocktail If the barrel is new and dry inside, fill it with water and let stand until watertight, about 24 hours. Drain.

2 Using a funnel, fill the barrel with the rum, vermouth, Grand Marnier and grenadine. Let age, tasting a sample once a week, until the cocktail has taken on a rounded but not overly oaky flavor, about 1 month.

3 Strain the cocktail through a coffee filter–lined funnel into a glass container and store indefinitely.

4 Serve the cocktail Pour 3 ounces of the cocktail into an ice-filled mixing glass and stir until chilled. Strain the drink into a chilled cocktail glass. Garnish with a twist.

Aged Bamboo

Time	20 min active
	about 1 month total
Makes	about 1 liter

One 1-liter oak barrel

16 oz. amontillado sherry

16 oz. dry vermouth

½ oz. orange bitters

1 tsp. Angostura bitters

Ice

Lemon twists, for serving

1 Age the cocktail If the barrel is new and dry inside, fill it with water and let stand until watertight, about 24 hours. Drain.

2 Using a funnel, fill the barrel with the sherry, vermouth and both bitters. Let age, tasting a sample once a week, until the cocktail has taken on a rounded but not overly oaky flavor, about 1 month.

3 Strain the cocktail through a coffee filter–lined funnel into a glass container and store indefinitely.

4 Serve the cocktail Pour 3 ounces of the cocktail into an ice-filled mixing glass and stir until chilled. Strain the drink into a chilled cocktail glass. Garnish with a twist.

PAY IT FORWARD

"You can get a lot of use out of one barrel," says Morgenthaler. "For example, if you age a Manhattan and then immediately use the same barrel for a Negroni, the Negroni will pick up some of the Manhattan's flavor—and that can be a cool thing."

Level Three

144 French Onion Soup

146 Chinese Dumplings

150 Gnocchi

152 Ravioli

156 Pad Thai

160 Bouillabaisse

164 Roast Duck

166 Sausage

170 Barbacoa Beef

172 Tamales

176 Lamb Biryani

180 Dinner Rolls

182 Shortcut Bread

184 Challah

186 Pretzels

188 Doughnuts

192 Meringue Pie

196 Marshmallows

198 Mousse Cake

202 Meringues

204 Peanut Butter Candy

206 Nut Milks

210 Vermouth

French Onion Soup

At his M. Wells restaurants in New York City, Quebec native Hugue Dufour espouses a more-is-more approach to food. For instance, he amps up his French onion soup with brown ale and slab bacon. One thing he keeps traditional: The blanket of molten, gooey Gruyère cheese on top. Here, Dufour's recipe and key steps for re-creating his French Canadian spin on the bistro classic.

French (Canadian) Onion Soup

Time	40 min active
	5 hr total
Makes	10 servings

- 2 lbs. lean slab bacon, in one piece
- 1 whole pig's foot or 2 halves
- 8 large yellow onions—1 whole, 7 sliced ¼ inch thick
- ¼ cup rendered pork fat or vegetable oil
  Kosher salt and pepper
- ½ cup all-purpose flour
  Two 12-oz. bottles brown ale
- 6 rosemary sprigs
- 12 oz. rustic bread, cubed
- 6 Tbsp. unsalted butter, melted
- 6 garlic cloves, peeled
- 4 cups shredded Gruyère cheese (about ½ lb.)

1 In a large pot, cover the bacon, pig's foot and whole onion with 2 gallons of water **(A)**. Bring to a boil, then simmer over moderately low heat until the foot is tender, 3½ hours. Strain the broth and return it to the pot, reserving the bacon and pig's foot **(B)**.

2 Boil the broth until reduced to 2 quarts, about 25 minutes; skim off the fat or refrigerate overnight and then skim off the fat **(C)**. Remove all the lean meat from the bacon and pig's foot, cut into bite-size pieces and reserve **(D)**.

3 Meanwhile, in another large pot, heat the rendered pork fat. Add the sliced onions and season with salt. Cover and cook over high heat, stirring, until the onions are wilted, 15 minutes. Reduce the heat to moderate and cook until the onions are very soft, 30 minutes. Uncover and cook over moderately high heat, stirring, until the onions are lightly browned, 10 minutes. Remove from the heat and stir in the flour until smooth.

4 Return the pot to the burner. Add the strained broth, the ale and 4 of the rosemary sprigs and cook over moderately low heat, stirring, until the soup thickens **(E)**. Simmer the soup for about 15 minutes, until no floury taste remains. Add the reserved meat and season the soup with salt and pepper. Discard the rosemary sprigs.

5 Preheat the oven to 350°. On a rimmed baking sheet, toss the bread cubes, melted butter, garlic and the remaining 2 rosemary sprigs; season with salt and pepper **(F)**. Bake for 30 minutes, until the croutons are crisp. Discard the rosemary and garlic.

6 Preheat the broiler. Ladle the soup into heatproof bowls on a baking sheet and top with the croutons and cheese **(G)**. Broil for about 2 minutes, until bubbling, and serve **(H)**.

WINE Rich, aromatic Alsace Pinot Gris.

SOUPED-UP

Dufour makes a pork broth for his French onion soup using bacon for smokiness and a pig's foot for richness. Skip the pig's foot for a lighter broth.

A

B

C

D

E

F

G

H

Chinese Dumplings

Cara Stadler is a whiz at packing as much flavor as possible into a single bite. At Bao Bao Dumpling House in Portland, Maine, she does just that with her juicy dumplings, which she stuffs with traditional fillings as well as unconventional ones, like spicy mapo tofu.

Pork and Shrimp Dumplings

Time	1 hr 30 min active
	3 hr total
Makes	about 3 dozen dumplings

WRAPPERS

- ¾ cup boiling water
- 1¼ cups all-purpose flour, plus more for dusting

FILLING

- ¾ oz. dried shiitake mushroom caps
- ½ lb. fatty ground pork, preferably pork butt
- ½ lb. shelled and deveined large shrimp, finely chopped
- 2 scallions, thinly sliced
- ⅓ cup finely chopped canned water chestnuts (about 5)
- 2 Tbsp. minced peeled fresh ginger
- 1½ Tbsp. soy sauce
- 1½ Tbsp. Shaoxing wine
- ½ Tbsp. toasted sesame oil
- ½ Tbsp. sugar
- 1½ tsp. kosher salt
- 1 large egg white
- 1 Tbsp. cornstarch
- Canola oil, for frying

ROLLING IN DOUGH

A small rolling pin (available from amazon.com) makes it easier to prep the dumpling wrappers.

1 Make the wrappers In a medium bowl, slowly drizzle the boiling water into the 1¼ cups of flour and mix with a wooden spoon until the mixture just comes together. Turn it out onto a lightly floured surface and knead until a smooth dough forms, about 5 minutes. Return the dough to the bowl and cover with plastic wrap. Let rest at room temperature for at least 1 hour or up to 4 hours.

2 Turn the dough out onto a lightly floured work surface and, using a sharp knife, cut it into 36 equal pieces (9 to 10 grams each). Roll each piece into a ball. Using a small, lightly floured rolling pin, roll out 1 ball of dough to a ⅛-inch-thick round, then roll out just the outer edge until it is 1/16 inch thick and the wrapper is 3½ inches in diameter. (To hold the filling properly, the wrapper should be slightly thicker in the center than at the edge.) Transfer the wrapper to a parchment paper–lined baking sheet and cover with a damp kitchen towel. Repeat with the remaining balls of dough.

3 Make the filling In a medium bowl, cover the mushrooms with boiling water and let stand, stirring occasionally, until softened, about 15 minutes. Drain well, then squeeze out any excess water. Finely chop the mushrooms and transfer to a large bowl. Add all of the remaining ingredients except the cornstarch and canola oil and fold gently until well blended. Fold in the cornstarch just until incorporated.

4 Fill the dumplings Lay a wrapper in the palm of one hand. Using your finger, brush the outer edge of the wrapper with water. Spoon 1 heaping tablespoon of filling in the center. Fold the wrapper over the filling to form a half-moon; pinch at the top to adhere. Fold a pleat in the dough on the top left, angling back toward the center. Press with your fingers to adhere. Make a second pleat on the top right to meet the first pleat in the center. Transfer the dumpling to a parchment-lined baking sheet and cover with plastic wrap; repeat with the rest of the wrappers and filling.

5 Cook the dumplings Pour enough canola oil into a large nonstick skillet to cover the bottom. Arrange some of the dumplings in the skillet with a non-pleated side down (you will need to work in batches). Cook over low heat until golden on the bottom, about 3 minutes.

6 Carefully pour in enough water to reach halfway up the dumplings. Cover and cook until almost all of the water is absorbed and the filling is cooked through, 4 minutes. Uncover and cook until all of the liquid has evaporated and the dumplings are crispy on the bottom, 2 minutes. Invert onto a plate. Repeat the process with the remaining dumplings. Serve.

(continued on next page)

Spicy Mapo Tofu Dumplings

Time	1 hr 30 min active
	3 hr total
Makes	about 3 dozen dumplings

WRAPPERS

¾ cup boiling water

1¼ cups all-purpose flour, plus more
for dusting

FILLING

7 oz. firm tofu, drained

4 dried chiles de árbol, stemmed

1 tsp. Sichuan peppercorns

½ lb. fatty ground pork, preferably
pork butt

2 garlic cloves, minced

1 scallion, thinly sliced

½ cup finely chopped flowering
chives

¼ cup minced peeled fresh ginger

¼ cup black bean paste with chile

3 Tbsp. Shaoxing wine

1 Tbsp. ground bean sauce
(see Note)

1 Tbsp. tobanjan (fermented
broad-bean paste; see Note)

1 large egg white

½ tsp. kosher salt

2 Tbsp. cornstarch

Canola oil, for frying

WRAPPER SHORTCUT

Stadler's recipe results in
exceptionally delicate and chewy
dumpling skins. If you're
pressed for time, you could also use
store-bought gyoza wrappers.

1 Make the wrappers In a medium bowl, slowly drizzle the boiling water into the 1¼ cups of flour and mix with a wooden spoon until the mixture just comes together. Turn it out onto a lightly floured surface and knead until a smooth dough forms, about 5 minutes. Return the dough to the bowl and cover with plastic wrap. Let rest at room temperature for at least 1 hour or up to 4 hours.

2 Turn the dough out onto a lightly floured surface; using a sharp knife, cut it into 36 equal pieces (9 to 10 grams each). Roll each piece into a ball **(A)**. Using a small, lightly floured rolling pin, roll out 1 ball of dough to a ⅛-inch-thick round, then roll out just the outer edge until it is 1/16 inch thick and the wrapper is 3½ inches in diameter **(B)**. (To hold the filling properly, the wrapper should be slightly thicker in the center than at the edge.) Transfer the wrapper to a parchment paper–lined baking sheet and cover with a damp kitchen towel. Repeat with the remaining balls of dough **(C)**.

3 Make the filling Cut the tofu into ¼-inch-thick slices; put them on a paper towel–lined plate and press dry with paper towels. Finely chop the tofu and transfer to a large bowl. In a spice grinder, combine the chiles and Sichuan peppercorns and finely grind. Add to the tofu in the bowl along with all of the remaining ingredients except the cornstarch and canola oil. Fold gently until well blended. Fold in the cornstarch just until incorporated.

4 Fill the dumplings Lay a wrapper in the palm of one hand. Using your finger, brush the outer edge of the wrapper with water. Spoon 1 heaping tablespoon of filling in the center **(D)**. Fold the wrapper over the filling to form a half-moon; pinch at the top to adhere **(E)**. Fold a pleat in the dough on the top left, angling back toward the center. Press with your fingers to adhere **(F)**. Make a second pleat on the top right to meet the first pleat in the center **(G)**. Transfer the dumpling to a parchment-lined baking sheet and cover with plastic wrap; repeat with the rest of the wrappers and filling.

5 Cook the dumplings Pour enough canola oil into a large nonstick skillet to cover the bottom. Arrange some of the dumplings in the skillet with a non-pleated side down (you will need to work in batches). Cook over low heat until golden on the bottom, about 3 minutes.

6 Carefully pour in enough water to reach halfway up the dumplings **(H)**. Cover and cook until almost all of the water is absorbed and the filling is cooked through, about 4 minutes. Uncover and cook until all of the liquid has evaporated and the dumplings are crispy on the bottom, about 2 minutes longer **(I)**. Carefully invert onto a plate. Repeat the process with the remaining dumplings. Serve warm.

NOTE Ground bean sauce and tobanjan are jarred condiments available at Chinese markets and online from amazon.com.

MAKE AHEAD The wrapper dough can be refrigerated for 2 days. Bring to room temperature before rolling out. The fillings can be refrigerated overnight. The assembled, uncooked dumplings can be frozen for up to 1 month and cooked from frozen. Just add 2 minutes to the covered cooking time in Step 6. Alternatively, you can boil or steam the frozen dumplings for about 8 minutes.

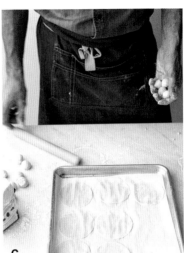

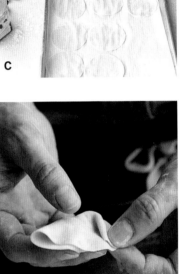

A

B

C

D

E

F

G

H

I

Gnocchi

Cookbook author Grace Parisi makes light-as-air gnocchi that are like divine little pillows of pasta. A potato ricer helps make them fluffy and tender, without overworking the dough. She shares her recipe and two tasty variations—roasted garlic and rye flour—along with two ultraquick sauces.

Potato Gnocchi with Butter and Cheese

Time	30 min active
	1 hr 30 min total
Makes	4 to 6 servings

2 lbs. baking potatoes (about 4)

2 large egg yolks

Kosher salt and pepper

½ cup all-purpose flour, plus more for dusting

4 Tbsp. unsalted butter

Freshly grated Parmigiano-Reggiano cheese

1 Preheat the oven to 400°. Pierce the potatoes all over with a fork **(A)**. Bake in a microwave oven at high power for 10 minutes, then flip the potatoes and microwave for 5 minutes longer. Transfer the potatoes to the oven and bake for 15 minutes. Alternatively, bake the potatoes in the oven for about 1 hour, until tender.

2 Halve the potatoes. Scoop the flesh into a ricer and rice the potatoes **(B)**. Transfer 2 slightly packed cups of riced potatoes to a bowl. Stir in the egg yolks and 1 teaspoon of salt **(C)**. Add the ½ cup of flour; stir until a stiff dough forms **(D)**. Knead the dough gently until smooth but slightly sticky **(E)**.

3 Line a baking sheet with wax paper and dust with flour. On a floured surface, cut the dough into 4 pieces, rolling each into a ¾-inch-thick rope **(F)**. Cut the ropes into ¾-inch pieces **(G)**. Roll each piece against the tines of a fork to make ridges **(H)**. Transfer to the prepared baking sheet.

4 In a large, deep skillet of simmering salted water, cook the gnocchi until they rise to the surface, then simmer for 2 minutes longer. In a large nonstick skillet, melt the butter. Using a slotted spoon, add the gnocchi to the butter. Season with salt and pepper and cook over high heat for 1 minute. Sprinkle with cheese and serve **(I)**.

RYE-POTATO VARIATION Substitute ½ cup plus 2 Tbsp. dark rye flour for the all-purpose flour.

ROASTED GARLIC–POTATO VARIATION On a sheet of foil, drizzle 10 unpeeled garlic cloves with olive oil. Wrap up the garlic and roast at 450° for 30 minutes, until tender. Squeeze out the garlic and add to the dough along with 2 additional Tbsp. flour in Step 2.

WINE Lively, berry-inflected Dolcetto d'Alba.

TWO GNOCCHI SAUCES

PARMIGIANO-REGGIANO CREAM In a large skillet, simmer ¾ cup heavy cream for 2 minutes. Add the simmered gnocchi and ¼ cup grated Parmigiano-Reggiano and cook until the cheese is melted, about 1 minute.

BROWN BUTTER AND SAGE In a medium skillet, cook 4 Tbsp. unsalted butter with 10 small sage leaves until the butter is fragrant and nutty, about 3 minutes. Add the simmered gnocchi and cook for 1 minute. Sprinkle with grated Parmigiano-Reggiano and freshly ground pepper.

FREEZE A BATCH

Uncooked gnocchi can be frozen on the prepared baking sheet (Step 3), then transferred to a resealable plastic bag and kept for up to 1 month. Boil without defrosting.

Ravioli

"Ravioli should be tender, but not wimpy," says Domenica Marchetti. In her definitive book *The Glorious Pasta of Italy,* she offers a dozen ravioli variations made with the fail-safe dough she uses here. We've got three of her favorite fillings, plus expert advice that would impress an Italian nonna.

Meat Ravioli

Time	1 hr 40 min active 2 hr 15 min total
Makes	40 ravioli

FILLING

- 2 tsp. unsalted butter
- 2 tsp. extra-virgin olive oil
- ½ lb. ground pork, veal, turkey or chicken (or a mixture of all four)
- ½ small onion, minced
- 1 garlic clove, minced
  Kosher salt and pepper
- ¼ cup dry white wine
- ¼ cup freshly grated Parmigiano-Reggiano cheese
- 1 oz. mortadella, finely chopped
- 1 oz. prosciutto, finely chopped
  Pinch of freshly grated nutmeg
- 1 large egg, lightly beaten

DOUGH

- 2 cups all-purpose flour
- ½ tsp. fine sea salt
  Pinch of freshly grated nutmeg
- 1 Tbsp. semolina flour, plus more for dusting
- 3 extra-large eggs
- 1 Tbsp. extra-virgin olive oil

KNEAD-TO-KNOW

"Always err on the side of making ravioli dough a little bit sticky," Marchetti says. "You can sprinkle on more flour as you roll it out."

1 Make the filling In a skillet, melt the butter in the oil. Add the ground meat, onion and garlic and season with salt and pepper. Cook over moderate heat, stirring to break up lumps, until the meat is cooked and the onion is tender, about 10 minutes. Add the wine and cook over moderately high heat until evaporated, about 4 minutes.

2 Scrape the mixture into a food processor and pulse until the meat is finely chopped. Scrape the filling into a large bowl and let cool. Stir in the Parmigiano, mortadella, prosciutto and nutmeg and season with salt and pepper. Stir in the beaten egg.

3 Make the dough In a food processor, pulse the all-purpose flour with the salt, nutmeg and the 1 tablespoon of semolina. Add the eggs and pulse until incorporated. With the machine on, add the olive oil in a thin stream and process just until moistened crumbs form (do not let a ball form). Turn the crumbs out onto a semolina-dusted work surface and knead just until a smooth dough forms. Wrap the dough in plastic and let stand at room temperature for 30 minutes.

4 Cut the dough into 4 equal pieces and cover with plastic wrap. Work with 1 piece at a time: Using a rolling pin or your palm, flatten the dough into a 5-by-4-inch oval, about ½ inch thick. Dust lightly with semolina. Roll the dough through a hand-cranked pasta machine at the widest setting. Fold the dough in thirds (like a letter), then run it through the machine at the same setting, folded edge first. Repeat the folding and rolling once more. Roll the dough through at successively narrower settings, two times per setting, until it is thin enough for you to see the outline of your hand through it. Lay the dough out on a work surface lightly dusted with semolina.

5 Fill, shape and cook the ravioli Brush any semolina off the dough. Cut a sheet of dough in half crosswise. On one half, spoon 10 mounded teaspoons of filling in 2 rows of 5, about 3 inches apart; cover with the second half. Press out any air around the filling. Using a fluted pastry cutter or a sharp knife, cut between the mounds to form squares; transfer to a large rimmed baking sheet lightly dusted with semolina. Repeat with the remaining pasta dough and filling. (For alternative shapes, see sun and half-moon variations on p. 155.)

6 In a large pot of salted boiling water, cook half of the ravioli over high heat until al dente, about 3 minutes. Using a slotted spoon, transfer the ravioli to a platter. Repeat with the remaining ravioli and serve.

WINE Berry-rich Sangiovese.

(continued on page 155)

Carrot and Ricotta Ravioli

Time	1 hr 45 min active
	2 hr 15 min total
Makes	40 ravioli

FILLING

- 3 large carrots, peeled and cut into 1-inch chunks (¾ lb.)
- 1 Tbsp. extra-virgin olive oil
  Kosher salt and pepper
- 2 tsp. unsalted butter
- 1 Tbsp. minced shallot
- 1 Tbsp. heavy cream
- 5 oz. sheep-milk ricotta or well-drained fresh cow-milk ricotta (½ cup firmly packed)
- 6 Tbsp. freshly grated Parmigiano-Reggiano cheese
  Pinch of freshly grated nutmeg
- 1 large egg yolk

DOUGH

- 2 cups all-purpose flour
- ½ tsp. fine sea salt
  Pinch of freshly grated nutmeg
- 1 Tbsp. semolina flour, plus more for dusting
- 3 extra-large eggs
- 1 Tbsp. extra-virgin olive oil

MAKE-AHEAD TIP

Ravioli can be prepared over two days. Mix the filling on day one, store it in the fridge overnight, then make the dough and assemble the ravioli the next day. You can keep them frozen for up to one month.

1 Make the filling Preheat the oven to 400°. In a baking dish, toss the carrots with the olive oil and season with salt and pepper. Cover with foil and bake until tender and lightly browned, 30 minutes. Let cool slightly.

2 In a small skillet, melt the butter. Add the shallot and cook over moderate heat until softened, about 3 minutes.

3 In a food processor, combine the carrots, shallot and cream and puree until smooth. Transfer the puree to a bowl. Stir in the ricotta, Parmigiano and nutmeg and season with salt and pepper. Stir in the egg yolk.

4 Make the dough In a food processor, pulse the all-purpose flour with the salt, nutmeg and the 1 tablespoon of semolina. Add the eggs and pulse until incorporated. With the machine on, add the oil in a thin stream and process just until moistened crumbs form. Turn the crumbs out onto a semolina-dusted work surface and knead just until a smooth dough forms. Wrap the dough in plastic; let stand at room temperature for 30 minutes.

5 Cut the dough into 4 equal pieces and cover with plastic wrap. Work with 1 piece at a time: Flatten the dough into a 5-by-4-inch oval, about ½ inch thick. Dust lightly with semolina. Roll the dough through a hand-cranked pasta machine at the widest setting. Fold the dough in thirds (like a letter), then run it through the machine at the same setting, folded edge first. Repeat the folding and rolling once more. Roll the dough through at successively narrower settings, two times per setting, until it is thin enough for you to see the outline of your hand through it. Lay the dough out on a work surface lightly dusted with semolina.

6 Fill, shape and cook the ravioli Brush any semolina off the dough. Cut a sheet of dough in half crosswise. On one half, spoon 10 mounded teaspoons of filling in 2 rows of 5, about 3 inches apart; cover with the second half. Press out any air around the filling. Using a fluted pastry cutter or a sharp knife, cut between the mounds to form squares; transfer to a large rimmed baking sheet lightly dusted with semolina. Repeat with the remaining pasta dough and filling. (For alternative shapes, see sun and half-moon variations, below.)

7 In a large pot of boiling salted water, cook half of the ravioli over high heat until al dente, about 3 minutes. Using a slotted spoon, transfer the ravioli to a platter. Repeat with the remaining ravioli and serve.

FOUR-CHEESE VARIATION For the filling, combine ¾ cup sheep-milk ricotta or well-drained fresh whole cow-milk ricotta with ⅔ cup shredded Fontina cheese, ½ cup diced fresh mozzarella and ½ cup freshly grated Parmigiano-Reggiano cheese and season with salt and pepper. Add 1 large, lightly beaten egg and stir until incorporated.

SUN VARIATION Stamp out the ravioli with a 2½-inch round cookie cutter. Make "rays" around the edges with the tines of a fork.

HALF-MOON VARIATION Don't cut the sheet of dough in half crosswise. Spoon 10 rounded teaspoons of filling 3 inches apart in a row along the center. Fold the dough over the mounds. Press out any air around the filling, then press the edges to seal. Using a fluted pastry cutter, cut out half-moons.

WINE Creamy, nutmeg-scented Sicilian white, such as Grillo.

Pad Thai

"A good pad Thai is all about balance, but a lot of times you get goopy, overly sweet noodles," says Ann Redding. She and Matt Danzer of the Thai restaurant Uncle Boons in New York City show us how to make a killer version at home. The key: Prepare one portion at a time in a large skillet so the noodles absorb just the right amount of sauce without becoming gummy.

Shrimp Pad Thai

Time | 35 min plus 2 hr soaking
Makes | 1 serving

- 2 oz. flat rice noodles
- 1½ Tbsp. peanuts
- ¼ cup tamarind concentrate
- ¼ cup Asian fish sauce
- 1½ oz. palm sugar, grated on the large holes of a box grater (¼ cup)
- 1 Tbsp. distilled white vinegar
- ½ tsp. shrimp paste in oil
- ¼ tsp. Thai chile powder
- 3 Tbsp. canola oil
- 2 Tbsp. dried shrimp
- 7 head-on shrimp, peeled and deveined
- 2 Tbsp. diced extra-firm tofu (1 oz.)
- 1 Tbsp. minced garlic
- 1 Tbsp. finely chopped shallot
- 1 Tbsp. minced Thai preserved sweet radish (also sold as sweet-salty turnip)
- 1 large egg, beaten
- 2 Tbsp. 1-inch pieces of garlic chives
  Bean sprouts and lime wedges, for serving

1 In a large bowl, cover the noodles with cold water and let stand for 2 hours. Drain well.

2 Preheat the oven to 375°. Spread the peanuts on a baking sheet and toast for 10 minutes, until fragrant. Let cool, then coarsely chop.

3 Meanwhile, in a medium saucepan, combine the tamarind concentrate, fish sauce, palm sugar, vinegar, shrimp paste and chile powder and bring to a boil, stirring to dissolve the sugar. Let the tamarind sauce cool.

4 In a large nonstick skillet, heat 1 tablespoon of the canola oil. Add the dried shrimp and stir-fry over high heat for 1 minute. Using a slotted spoon, transfer the shrimp to a paper towel–lined plate. Let cool slightly, then coarsely chop the dried shrimp.

5 In the same skillet, cook the fresh shrimp over moderately high heat, turning once, until just white throughout, about 2 minutes **(A)**. Transfer the shrimp to a plate.

6 Add the remaining 2 tablespoons of canola oil to the skillet and heat until shimmering. Add the tofu, garlic, shallot and preserved radish and stir-fry over high heat until the garlic and shallot are golden, about 1 minute **(B)**.

(continued on next page)

SOURCE MATERIAL

Tamarind concentrate, palm sugar, shrimp paste, Thai chile powder, dried shrimp and preserved sweet radish are available online from templeofthai.com. If you can't get head-on shrimp, regular shrimp will still be delicious here.

A

B

7 Add the noodles and 3 tablespoons of the tamarind sauce to the skillet and stir-fry until the noodles are coated and most of the sauce is absorbed, about 2 minutes **(C)**. Add the egg and chives and cook, stirring and tossing, until the egg is cooked, about 1 minute **(D)**. Remove the skillet from the heat and stir in the peanuts and dried shrimp. Transfer to a plate, top with the head-on shrimp and serve with bean sprouts and lime wedges. Save the remaining tamarind sauce for subsequent batches.

MAKE AHEAD The soaked and drained rice noodles can be covered with a damp towel and refrigerated overnight. The tamarind sauce can be refrigerated for up to 1 week.

WINE Zesty, fragrant Riesling.

FINISH THE DISH

Toss the noodles and sauce in the pan until the liquid is absorbed. Then quickly stir in the beaten egg, along with the chives, until cooked through.

Bouillabaisse

Master chef Daniel Boulud of Daniel restaurant in New York City creates an elegant, Americanized version of bouillabaisse that still captures every bit of the Provençal fish soup's classic flavor. Boulud swaps in black sea bass and red snapper fillets for the traditional small whole fish, making the dish so much easier to eat (no bones or skin to deal with).

Bouillabaisse à l'Américaine

Time	1 hr 45 min active
	3 hr total
Makes	6 to 8 servings

HERB-AND-SPICE SACHET

- 2 tsp. fennel seeds
- 2 tsp. whole coriander seeds
- 1 bay leaf
- 4 thyme sprigs
- 1 head of garlic, halved crosswise, or 6 large cloves, crushed
- Three 3-inch-long strips of orange zest

BOUILLABAISSE

- Two 2-lb. whole black sea bass, cleaned and filleted, heads and bones reserved
- One 4-lb. red snapper, cleaned and filleted, head and bones reserved
- ¼ cup extra-virgin olive oil
- 2 yellow onions, chopped
- 3 celery ribs, chopped
- 1 fennel bulb, trimmed and thinly sliced
- 1 leek, white and light green parts only, coarsely chopped
- ½ tsp. saffron threads
- ¼ tsp. cayenne or crushed red pepper, plus more for seasoning
- ¼ cup pastis
- 2 Tbsp. tomato paste
- 1 lb. large shrimp, shelled and deveined, shells reserved
- 1 lb. plum tomatoes, quartered
- 1 lb. German Butterball or small Yukon Gold potatoes, quartered
- Kosher salt and white pepper
- 1 lb. mussels, scrubbed and debearded
- Garlicky Rouille (recipe follows) and crusty baguette, for serving

1 Make the herb-and-spice sachet Assemble all of the ingredients on a piece of cheesecloth, wrap into a bundle and tie with kitchen string.

2 Start the bouillabaisse Rinse all of the fish heads and bones until the water runs clear **(A)**. Cut the fillets into 2-inch pieces and transfer them to a bowl; cover and refrigerate.

3 In a large enameled cast-iron casserole or pot, heat the olive oil. Add the onions, celery, fennel, leek, saffron and cayenne and cook over moderate heat until the vegetables soften, about 8 minutes. Add the pastis and cook until evaporated. Add the tomato paste and cook, stirring, until beginning to caramelize, about 5 minutes.

4 Add the fish heads and bones, shrimp shells and herb-and-spice sachet to the casserole **(B)**. Add enough water to just cover, about 16 cups. Bring to a simmer and cook over moderately low heat for 20 minutes, skimming off the foam that rises to the surface **(C)**. Stir in the tomatoes and cook gently for 30 minutes **(D)**.

5 Meanwhile, cook the potatoes in a large saucepan of salted boiling water until tender, about 15 minutes. Drain well.

6 Pick out and discard the herb-and-spice sachet, the fish heads and any large fish bones. Working in batches, transfer the contents of the casserole to a blender and puree until smooth. Strain the soup through a fine-mesh sieve into a bowl, pressing on the solids **(E)**. Wipe out the casserole.

7 Finish the bouillabaisse Return the soup to the casserole and bring to a simmer. Add the potatoes. Season the fish fillets with salt and pepper and add to the soup **(F)**. Cook over low heat for 3 minutes. Add the shrimp and mussels, cover and cook until the mussels open and the fish and shrimp are cooked through, 2 minutes longer. Season with salt, pepper and cayenne **(G)**.

8 Stir 2 tablespoons of the hot soup into the Garlicky Rouille. Ladle the bouillabaisse into shallow bowls. Serve with the rouille and crusty bread.

(continued on next page)

MAKE AHEAD The rouille can be refrigerated for 2 days. The soup can be refrigerated for 3 days or frozen for 3 months.

WINE White wine from the Bandol region of Provence.

GARLICKY ROUILLE

Peel 1 baking potato and cut it into 1-inch pieces. Transfer to a medium saucepan and add a pinch each of saffron threads and kosher salt and 2 cups of water. Bring to a boil and cook until the saffron water is reduced by half and the potato is cooked through, about 20 minutes **(H)**. Let cool completely, then transfer the potato and saffron water to a blender. Add a pinch of cayenne, 6 superfresh garlic cloves and 2 large egg yolks and pulse to combine. With the machine on, slowly drizzle in 1 cup extra-virgin olive oil until well blended. Season with salt. Transfer the rouille to a serving bowl **(I)**. Refrigerate until ready to use.

SEAFOOD SWAP

This recipe is very forgiving. For the soup, you can use the bones of any mild, nonoily white fish. And you can replace the bass, snapper, shrimp and mussels listed here with any local seafood.

AWESOME SAUCE

Rouille, a zesty, aioli-like condiment flavored with saffron, is a traditional accompaniment to bouillabaisse. Boulud adds a bit of the hot bouillabaisse broth to the rouille before serving to warm it and build a flavor bridge to the soup.

A

B

C

D

E

F

G

H

I

Roast Duck

Legendary cookbook author Paula Wolfert roasts a phenomenal duck in a way that defies all convention: She halves the bird, never turns it or removes the fat during cooking and forgoes the rack. Instead, Wolfert nestles the duck in a bed of chopped vegetables, which, together with the rendered fat, make the meat as tender as confit while keeping the skin shatter-crisp.

Slow-Cooked Duck with Green Olives and Herbes de Provence

Time	45 min active 3 hr 45 min total
Makes	2 to 4 servings

- 2   medium onions, coarsely chopped
- ¼   cup plus 2 tsp. coarsely chopped flat-leaf parsley
- 1   Tbsp. plus 1 tsp. chopped thyme
- 8   garlic cloves, halved
- 2   bay leaves
- 1   large celery rib, sliced ¼ inch thick
-     One 5½-lb. duck, halved, with backbone, neck and wing tips removed and reserved
-     Kosher salt and pepper
-     Herbes de Provence
- 1   Tbsp. tomato paste
- ½   cup dry white wine
- 1   cup chicken stock, preferably homemade
-     Pinch of sugar
- 1½ cups French green olives, rinsed and pitted

1 Preheat the oven to 475°. In a small roasting pan, spread half of the onions, ¼ cup of the parsley, 1 tablespoon of the thyme and the garlic, bay leaves and celery. Prick the duck skin all over with a fork and rub the duck with 2 teaspoons of salt, 1 teaspoon of pepper and 1 teaspoon of herbes de Provence. Set the duck halves on the vegetables, cut side down, and roast for 10 minutes. Prick the duck skin again, cover the pan with foil and reduce the oven temperature to 275°. Roast the duck for about 3 hours longer, until the meat is very tender and most of the fat has rendered.

2 Meanwhile, in a large skillet, cook the backbone, neck and wing tips over low heat until well browned all over. Add the remaining onions and cook over moderate heat until browned, about 4 minutes. Pour off the fat from the skillet and add the tomato paste. Cook, stirring, until it begins to brown, about 3 minutes. Add the wine and bring to a boil. Add 3 cups of water, the chicken stock and sugar and simmer until reduced to 1 cup, about 1 hour. Strain the stock and skim the fat from the surface.

3 When the duck is tender, transfer the halves to a work surface. Remove and discard any vegetables, pockets of fat and loose bones. Halve each duck half and transfer the pieces to a rimmed baking sheet, skin side up.

4 Strain the juices from the roasting pan into a saucepan and skim off the fat; boil the strained juices until reduced to ¼ cup. Add the strained stock and the olives to the saucepan and simmer for 10 minutes. Season the sauce with salt, pepper and herbes de Provence.

5 Preheat the broiler. Season the duck with herbes de Provence, salt and pepper. Broil 10 inches from the heat for about 5 minutes, or until the duck is hot and the skin is crisp. Spoon the sauce onto a platter and set the duck on top. Sprinkle with the remaining 2 teaspoons of chopped parsley and 1 teaspoon of thyme and serve.

MAKE AHEAD The recipe can be prepared through Step 4 up to 2 days ahead. Cover and refrigerate the duck and sauce separately. Allow the duck to come to room temperature before broiling it.

WINE Herbal, dense Provençal red.

WANT FEWER STEPS?

Simply serve the duck with the strained pan juices and skip the olive sauce altogether.

THREE'S A CROWD

Cook three ducks in a large roasting pan, increasing the onions and aromatics slightly and allowing just a little more cooking time.

Sausage

Making sausage at home is a fantastic project well worth the effort, and you can get started without committing to a houseful of gear. In fact, Hank Shaw, author of *Hunt, Gather, Cook*, spent years forming sausage meat into patties before purchasing a stuffing device, and his recipes work great with or without the casings. While Shaw recommends grinding the meat at home, a trusted butcher who understands sausage-making can do it too.

Fiery Moroccan Lamb Merguez

Time	1 hr 30 min active; 3 hr 45 min total plus overnight rest
Makes	5 lbs

- 4 lbs. boneless lamb shoulder, cut into 3-by-1-inch strips
- 1 lb. lamb or pork fat, cut into 2-by-1-inch strips
- 4 garlic cloves, minced
- 2 Tbsp. plus 1 tsp. kosher salt
- 1 Tbsp. hot paprika
- 2 tsp. ground black pepper
- 2 tsp. ground cumin
- 2 tsp. ground coriander
- ¼ cup plus 1 Tbsp. red wine vinegar, chilled
- ¼ cup harissa
- 3 Tbsp. cold water
- 15 to 18 feet (about ½ oz.) salted pork or sheep casings (available at many good butcher shops)

TOOLS OF THE TRADE

For grinding meat and stuffing sausage at home, our Test Kitchen suggests the KitchenAid stand-mixer and its attachments as a relatively inexpensive option.

KEEP IT COOL

"Working the sausage mixture heats it up, and heat is your enemy," Shaw says. "Keep the meat's temperature below 45 degrees." At 45 degrees, the fat begins to melt, ruining the texture of the sausage.

1 Season the meat Spread the meat and fat strips on 2 large rimmed baking sheets. In a small bowl, combine the garlic, dry seasonings and spices and sprinkle the mixture all over the meat and fat. Refrigerate the meat and fat for 15 minutes. Drizzle the liquid ingredients all over the meat and fat. Freeze the seasoned meat and fat until very firm, about 45 minutes.

2 Grind the meat Chill the bowl of a stand mixer and the meat grinder's parts in the freezer. Set up the grinder with the coarse grinding plate; place the bowl below. With the machine at medium-high speed, gradually drop in the meat and fat **(A)**. Add any liquid on the baking sheets to the ground meat.

3 Work the meat Put the ground meat in the freezer again to keep it at 32° to 40°. Using clean hands or the paddle of the stand mixer, knead or beat the meat until a sticky mass forms, about 50 seconds; be careful not to let the meat get too warm. Refrigerate for up to 3 hours.

4 Soak the casings Meanwhile, soak the casings in warm water for 30 minutes. Drain the casings. Working over the sink or 2 bowls, gently run warm water through each casing. Pinch both ends and lift up the water-filled casing. Look for any spots that leak and cut out those portions **(B)**.

5 Stuff the sausages Place the sausage stuffer attachment in the freezer for 15 minutes. Set up the sausage stuffer and slip all but 6 inches of a casing onto the tube, leaving the trailing end untied **(C)**. With the machine at low speed, gradually add some of the sausage mixture until it emerges from the tube. Turn off the machine and tie a knot at the trailing end of the casing **(D)**. With the machine at low speed, gradually add the rest of the sausage mixture, using your free hand to regulate how tightly the sausage is packed in the casing; make sure not to overstuff it **(E)**. When the casing is nearly stuffed, turn off the machine and tie off the end of the casing.

6 Starting at one end, pinch off the first link by pinching your fingers around the sausage to separate the filling; 6 inches is a good average length. Then, roll the link toward you 3 to 5 times, creating a twist in the casing. Move down to form the next link, rolling 3 to 5 times in the opposite direction (this prevents unraveling) **(F)**. If the casing splits, remove the stuffing near the split and tie the casing closed before proceeding. Alternatively, the links can be formed by sectioning them off with butcher's twine. Repeat with the remaining casings and sausage.

(continued on page 169)

7 Sterilize a needle over a flame. Prick holes all over the sausages with the needle, especially where there are air pockets **(G)**. Hang the sausages on wooden or metal racks over 2 rimmed baking sheets, making sure not to crowd them so that air can circulate around them. Let the sausages hang to dry for 1 to 2 hours, then wrap in butcher's paper and refrigerate overnight before cooking **(H)**.

HMONG SPICY PORK SAUSAGE VARIATION For the meat filling, use 4 lbs. marbled pork shoulder cut into 3-by-1-inch strips, 1 lb. pork fat cut into 2-by-1-inch strips, 4 minced garlic cloves, 3 minced Thai chiles, ½ cup chopped Thai basil, ¼ cup finely grated fresh ginger, 2 Tbsp. plus 1 tsp. kosher salt, 1 Tbsp. ground ginger, 2 tsp. ground black pepper and ½ cup chilled fresh lime juice.

PROVENÇAL-STYLE CHICKEN SAUSAGE VARIATION For the meat filling, use 4½ lbs. skinless, boneless chicken thighs (with fat) cut into 3-by-1-inch strips, ½ lb. pork fat cut into 2-by-1-inch strips, 4 minced garlic cloves, 2 Tbsp. plus 1 tsp. kosher salt, 1 Tbsp. finely chopped basil, 1 Tbsp. finely chopped thyme, 1 Tbsp. ground black pepper, 1 Tbsp. herbes de Provence and ½ cup chilled dry white wine.

MAKE AHEAD The sausages can be refrigerated for up to 3 days or frozen for up to 2 weeks.

TEST BEFORE THE REST

Before stuffing sausages, test the filling's flavor and consistency by frying a small patty in a pan. Imperfect batches can be used for pasta sauce or chili.

Barbacoa Beef

For taco meat that's fall-apart tender yet delectably crispy, chef Roberto Santibañez of New York City's Fonda restaurants takes a "braise first, grill later" approach. He serves his tacos with both a chile sauce made from the braising liquid and a fresh salsa verde. And while traditional barbacoa calls for cooking a cow's head or a whole lamb in a pit, we opted for short ribs and a roasting pan.

Barbacoa Beef Tacos with Two Sauces

Time	40 min active
	4 hr total
Makes	6 servings

4   large ancho chiles, stemmed and seeded

4   dried chipotle chiles, stemmed

3   celery ribs, chopped

2   medium carrots, chopped

1   large onion, halved and thinly sliced

15 garlic cloves, crushed and peeled

8   bay leaves

Six 1-lb. English-cut bone-in beef short ribs

2   Tbsp. dried oregano

½   tsp. ground cumin

Kosher salt and pepper

Warm corn tortillas, cilantro sprigs, finely chopped white onion and lime wedges, for serving

Salsa Verde Cruda (recipe below), for serving

1 Braise the meat Preheat the oven to 325°. In a medium skillet, toast the ancho chiles over moderate heat, turning, until pliable and charred in spots, about 2 minutes; let cool slightly, then tear into pieces.

2 In a large roasting pan, toss the ancho and chipotle chiles with the celery, carrots, onion, garlic and bay leaves. In a large bowl, toss the short ribs with the oregano, cumin and 2 tablespoons of salt. Arrange the ribs over the vegetables in the roasting pan. Add 2 cups of water to the pan, cover tightly with foil and braise in the oven for about 3½ hours, until the meat is very tender.

3 Make the chile sauce Transfer the ribs to a baking sheet. Strain the braising liquid through a colander set over a heatproof bowl; skim off any fat. Discard the bay leaves and return the vegetables and chiles to the braising liquid. Working in batches, puree the vegetables and liquid in a blender until smooth. Season the sauce with salt and pepper.

4 Grill Light a grill or heat a grill pan. Working in batches if necessary, grill the ribs over high heat, turning occasionally, until charred and crisp, about 5 minutes. Transfer to a platter and, using two forks, shred the meat; discard the bones. Serve the barbacoa in warm corn tortillas with the chile sauce, cilantro, chopped onion, lime wedges and Salsa Verde Cruda.

MAKE AHEAD The braised short ribs and sauce can be refrigerated separately for 3 days. Warm the ribs in a low oven before grilling.

WINE Robust, spicy Zinfandel.

BEER Crisp Mexican pilsner: Pacifico.

---

3 WAYS TO USE EXTRA CHILE SAUCE

Quick breakfast Pour over fried, poached or scrambled eggs.

Fast pasta Toss with spaghetti, adding a little of the pasta cooking water if the noodles seem dry.

Ten-minute stew Brown beef, pork or chicken in a pot, stir in the sauce and simmer until the meat is just cooked through.

SALSA VERDE CRUDA

Husk, rinse and quarter ½ lb. tomatillos and transfer to a blender. Add ½ cup chopped cilantro, 1 chopped jalapeño and 1 crushed and peeled garlic clove. Puree until smooth. Season with salt and pepper. Makes 1¼ cups.

MAKE AHEAD The salsa can be refrigerated for up to 3 days.

Tamales

Alex Stupak, Mexican food guru and chef at New York City's Empellón restaurants, shows the versatility of masa dough with three recipes: tamales stuffed with spicy braised pork and wrapped in banana leaves, a variety he first tasted in Oaxaca; *tamal de cazuela*, a savory pie that's a great, easy way to feed a group; and leftover tamales fried in a skillet for a hot, crispy snack.

Tamales with Red-Chile-Braised Pork

Time	1 hr 15 min active
	6 hr 15 min total
Makes	16 to 18 tamales

MASA DOUGH

2½ cups masa harina (see Go to the Source, p. 175)

1 cup cold lard

2 tsp. baking powder

1½ tsp. kosher salt

1 cup cold chicken stock or low-sodium broth

PORK FILLING

10 guajillo chiles, stemmed and seeded

10 garlic cloves

2 canned chipotles in adobo sauce

1 tsp. black pepper

½ tsp. ground cinnamon

½ tsp. dried oregano

3 lbs. boneless pork shoulder

Kosher salt

ASSEMBLY

About 20 banana leaves (see Go to the Source, p. 175)

1 Make the masa dough In a large bowl, stir the masa harina with 1½ cups of hot water until evenly moistened; let cool. In a stand mixer fitted with the paddle, beat the lard with the baking powder and salt at medium speed until fluffy, about 3 minutes. With the machine on, add the masa in golf-ball-size lumps, then drizzle in the chicken stock and beat the masa until completely smooth. Increase the speed to high and beat until fluffy, about 3 minutes; the texture should resemble that of soft hummus.

2 Prepare the pork filling Using tongs, briefly toast the guajillo chiles over an open flame or in a cast-iron skillet until fragrant, 5 seconds per side. Transfer the guajillos to a blender. Add 2 cups of hot water and let stand for 15 minutes.

3 Add the garlic, chipotles, black pepper, cinnamon and oregano to the blender and puree. Strain the sauce into a large enameled cast-iron casserole, pressing on the solids. Add the pork and 6 cups of hot water to the casserole; bring to a boil. Cover partially and simmer over low heat until the pork is tender, 2 hours.

4 Using a slotted spoon, transfer the pork to a bowl and let cool slightly. Boil the sauce until it is reduced to 4 cups, about 20 minutes.

5 Shred the pork with two forks and return it to the sauce. Simmer uncovered until the sauce is reduced and just coats the pork, about 20 minutes. Season the pork with salt and let cool slightly.

6 Assemble the tamales Using a sharp knife, cut off the stringy tops and bottoms of each banana leaf. Carefully cut the leaves into 8-inch squares; you'll need about 18. Set aside any torn leaves to line the steamer.

7 Spread ¼ cup masa in a slightly off-center, 4-by-6-inch rectangle on a banana leaf square **(A)**. Spread 2 tablespoons of the pork filling over the masa **(B)**. Fold the bottom edge of the square up and over so that the masa encloses the filling. Fold the top edge of the leaf down, then fold in the sides to close the packet **(C)**. Tie the packet with kitchen string **(D)**. Repeat to form the remaining tamales.

(continued on next page)

8 Steam the tamales Line a large steamer with a layer of banana-leaf scraps. Add the tamales in 2 loose layers **(E)**. Steam over boiling water for 1 hour and 20 minutes; replenish the water as needed. Remove from the heat and let the tamales stand in the covered steamer for 30 minutes. Transfer the tamales to a platter and pass scissors at the table **(F)**.

TAMAL PIE VARIATION Baked in a skillet, this tamal is easy to assemble. Preheat the oven to 300° and grease a 10-inch cast-iron skillet with lard. Spoon two-thirds of the masa dough from the above recipe into the skillet, mounding it slightly up the side. Spread 2½ cups of the pork filling evenly over the masa and top with the remaining masa. Bake for 30 minutes, until nearly set. Increase the temperature to 375° and bake until firm and lightly browned, about 35 minutes longer. Let stand for 30 minutes, then cut into wedges and serve.

CRISPY FRIED TAMALES VARIATION Leftover tamales can be revived by frying them in oil. Dust unwrapped tamales with rice flour. In a large skillet, heat ½ inch vegetable oil to 350°. Add the tamales in batches and fry, turning once, until golden, 5 minutes. Drain on paper towels and serve.

BEER Dark Mexican lager: Negra Modelo.

DID SOMEONE SAY FIESTA?

"Tamales are often made by Mexican matriarchs to feed a crowd at parties or weddings," says Stupak. For your own gathering, invite friends and family to help make tamales. You'll be glad to have the extra hands for folding and tying.

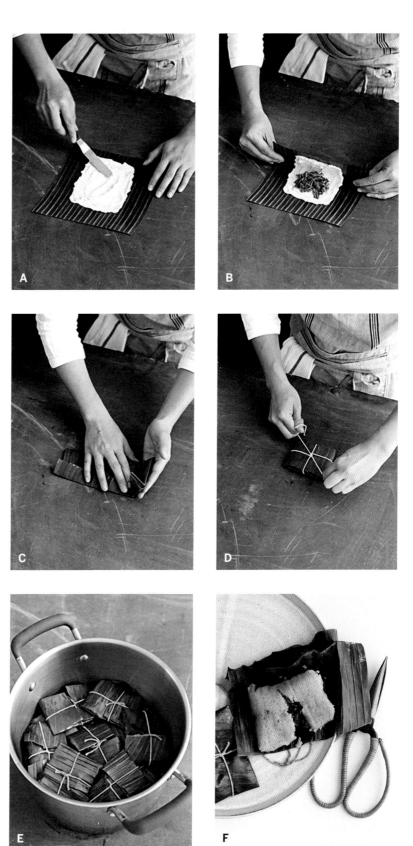

GO TO THE SOURCE

Masa harina (nixtamalized corn flour) is available at supermarkets, specialty food shops and from mexgrocer.com. Look for banana leaves at specialty food shops or store.gourmetsleuth.com.

Lamb Biryani

Maneet Chauhan hosts festivals to celebrate biryani at her Nashville restaurant, Chauhan Ale & Masala House. A favorite version of the beguiling Indian rice dish is this Hyderabadi one, in which a dough "lid" draped over the pot seals in flavor and absorbs moisture as the rice steams. Some biryanis call for goat, quail or jackfruit; this one features tender chunks of yogurt-marinated lamb.

Hyderabadi Lamb Biryani

Time	2 hr active 7 hr total
Makes	4 servings

LAMB

- ¼ cup canola oil
- 2 onions (1 lb.), thinly sliced
- ¾ cup finely chopped mint
- ½ cup finely chopped cilantro
- ¼ cup yogurt
- 3 Tbsp. fresh lemon juice
- 2 to 3 Thai chiles, minced
- 1 Tbsp. finely grated garlic
- 1 Tbsp. finely grated peeled fresh ginger
- 1 Tbsp. kosher salt
- 2 tsp. cayenne
- 1½ tsp. ground coriander
- 1½ tsp. ground cumin
- 1 tsp. Garam Masala (recipe follows)
- ¼ tsp. ground turmeric
- 1½ lbs. trimmed boneless lamb shoulder, cut into 1-inch cubes
- 2 Tbsp. ghee or clarified butter

RICE

- 4 whole black peppercorns
- 2 whole cloves
- 2 green cardamom pods
- 1 black cardamom pod
- One 2-inch cinnamon stick
- 1 bay leaf
- Pinch of freshly grated nutmeg
- Small piece of mace
- 1 Tbsp. canola oil
- 1 Tbsp. kosher salt
- 1 tsp. caraway seeds
- 2 cups basmati rice
- Pinch of saffron threads
- ½ cup whole milk

(continued on next page)

1 Prepare the lamb In a large nonstick skillet, heat the oil. Add the onions and cook over moderate heat, stirring occasionally, until golden brown, 10 to 12 minutes. Reserve one-third of the onions in a small bowl. Scrape the remaining onions into a large bowl and let cool to room temperature. Add all of the remaining ingredients except the lamb and ghee and mix well **(A)**. Stir in the lamb until evenly coated **(B)**. Cover and refrigerate for at least 3 hours or overnight.

2 In a large enameled cast-iron casserole, heat the ghee. Add the lamb mixture and cook over moderate heat, stirring occasionally, until browned, about 8 minutes **(C)**. Add ½ cup of water, cover and cook over moderately low heat until the lamb is tender, about 1 hour and 15 minutes.

3 Prepare the rice In a large saucepan, bring 4 cups of water to a boil. Wrap the peppercorns, cloves, cardamom pods, cinnamon stick, bay leaf, nutmeg and mace in a piece of cheesecloth and tie into a secure bundle. Add to the saucepan along with the oil, salt and caraway; stir in the rice. Bring to a simmer and cook over moderate heat, stirring occasionally, until the rice is cooked three-quarters of the way, 8 to 10 minutes **(D)**. Drain well, reserving ¼ cup of the cooking liquid. Discard the bundle.

4 Meanwhile, in a small saucepan, toast the saffron over moderately low heat, stirring, until fragrant, about 2 minutes. Remove from the heat and stir in the milk.

5 Assemble the biryani Preheat the oven to 350°. Drizzle 1 tablespoon of the ghee in a large enameled cast-iron casserole. Spoon half of the lamb mixture into the casserole in an even layer. Spread half of the rice over the lamb. Top with half each of the remaining cooked onions, saffron milk, ghee, cilantro, mint, rosewater and garam masala and 2 tablespoons of the reserved rice cooking water **(E)**. Repeat the layering once more.

6 Make the dough lid In a medium bowl, mix the flour and water until a rough dough forms. On a lightly floured work surface, knead the dough until it is smooth and pliable, about 5 minutes. Gather into a ball and roll out to a ⅛-inch-thick round that's a few inches larger than your casserole **(F)**.

(continued on next page)

BIRYANI

- 3 Tbsp. ghee or clarified butter, plus more for brushing
- 2 Tbsp. chopped cilantro
- 2 Tbsp. chopped mint
- ½ tsp. rosewater
- ½ tsp. Garam Masala (recipe below)

DOUGH LID

- 1½ cups whole-wheat flour
- ½ cup plus 2 Tbsp. water

TOMATO-ONION RAITA

- 1 cup yogurt
- ½ cup finely chopped tomato
- 1 small Thai chile, minced
- 1 Tbsp. minced red onion
- 2 tsp. chopped mint, plus small leaves for garnish
- 2 tsp. chopped cilantro
- 1 tsp. ground cumin
- ⅛ tsp. cayenne
- Pinch of sugar
- Kosher salt

7 Drape the dough over the top of the casserole, pressing to seal it around the edge **(G)**. Bake the biryani for 20 to 25 minutes, until the dough is golden and the rice is hot. Brush the crust with ghee and let stand for 5 minutes.

8 Make the tomato-onion raita Combine all of the ingredients in a bowl and garnish with mint leaves **(H)**.

9 Crack off and discard the dough lid and serve the lamb biryani hot, with the cooling raita **(I)**.

MAKE AHEAD The cooked lamb and cooked onions can be refrigerated separately overnight. Bring to room temperature before assembling the biryani.

WINE Juicy, herby Cabernet Franc.

GARAM MASALA

In a small skillet, combine 10 black peppercorns, 2 whole cloves, one 4-inch cinnamon stick, ¼ tsp. caraway seeds, a pinch of freshly grated nutmeg, a piece of mace and the seeds from 4 green cardamom pods. Toast over moderate heat until very fragrant. Let cool and grind to a powder. Makes 1 Tbsp.

BIRYANI GAME PLAN

Once you've gathered all the ingredients, making biryani is straightforward and can be done in stages. You can marinate the lamb overnight and cook it in advance— the onions, too. You can prepare the raita a day ahead as well. Assemble the entire dish and pop it in the oven a half-hour or so before serving.

DOUGH LID DOS AND DON'TS

The flour-and-water dough that covers the biryani while it cooks is not meant to be eaten. Instead, crack it off and discard before serving, then scoop out the fragrant, saffron-laced rice and lamb beneath.

A

B

C

D

E

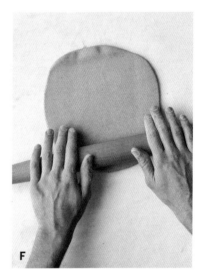

F

G

H

I

Dinner Rolls

"If you're going to serve a bread basket these days, it better be incredible," says Alex Guarnaschelli of Butter in New York City. Her Parker House rolls are so tender, buttery and sweet, with a sprinkling of crunchy salt on top, that they'll sway even the staunchest carb-phobe. This recipe makes a big batch, but the unbaked rolls can be frozen and baked straight from the freezer.

Parker House Rolls

Time	35 min active
	2 hr 55 min total
Makes	3 dozen rolls

One ¼-oz. package active dry yeast

½ cup warm water

½ cup sugar

2 sticks unsalted butter, melted and cooled (1 cup)

2 cups whole milk, at room temperature

2 large eggs, lightly beaten

1 Tbsp. kosher salt

7½ to 8 cups all-purpose flour, plus more for shaping

Flaky sea salt, for sprinkling

1 In a stand mixer fitted with the dough hook, mix the yeast with the water and 1 teaspoon of the sugar. Let stand until foamy, 10 minutes. Beat in the remaining sugar, ¾ cup of the butter and the milk, eggs and kosher salt. At low speed, stir in the 7½ cups of flour until the dough comes together; add more flour by the tablespoon, if necessary. Mix at medium speed until the dough forms a loose ball around the hook, 3 minutes. Brush a large bowl with some of the melted butter. Transfer the dough to the bowl and cover with plastic wrap. Let stand in a warm spot until doubled in bulk, 1½ hours.

2 Preheat the oven to 375° and line 2 baking sheets with parchment paper. Scrape the dough out onto a lightly floured work surface and shape it into a 9-by-16-inch rectangle **(A)**. Using a floured knife, cut the dough lengthwise into 3 strips, then cut each strip crosswise into 12 small strips. Working with 1 piece at a time, fold it unevenly so the top half slightly overlaps the bottom half **(B)**. Tuck the overhang under and place the roll seam side down on a baking sheet. Repeat with the remaining dough, forming 2 rows of 9 rolls on each baking sheet. Each roll should just touch its neighbors, but leave about 4 inches between the rows.

3 Bake the rolls for about 18 minutes, until browned; rotate the baking sheets from top to bottom and front to back halfway through baking. Immediately brush the rolls with the remaining melted butter and sprinkle with sea salt **(C)**. Transfer the rolls to a rack and let cool for 15 minutes before serving. To reheat, toast in a 350° oven for about 10 minutes.

A

B

C

Shortcut Bread

Chad Robertson of San Francisco's famed Tartine Bakery streamlines the complicated bread-making process so that anyone can make stunning loaves. His trick: Ditch the starter and use a pre-ferment—flour and water mixed with a pinch of yeast and left to develop flavor overnight.

Crusty White Bread

Time	1 hr active; 10 hr total plus overnight rising
Makes	2 large loaves

PRE-FERMENT

250	g. warm water (1 cup plus 2 Tbsp.)
¼	tsp. dry granulated yeast
300	g. organic all-purpose flour (2½ cups)

BREAD DOUGH

1.25	kg. warm water (5½ cups)
1.8	kg. organic all-purpose flour (13¾ cups)
200	g. organic whole-wheat flour (1½ cups)
5	Tbsp. kosher salt dissolved in ½ cup of warm water
	White rice flour or all-purpose flour, for dusting

1 Prepare the pre-ferment In a medium bowl, mix the water with the yeast and stir until the yeast is dissolved. Stir in the flour. Cover loosely with plastic wrap and let rise at room temperature for 10 to 14 hours.

2 Prepare the bread dough In a large bowl, combine the warm water with the pre-ferment: Using your hands, break up the pre-ferment until dissolved. In a very large bowl, whisk the all-purpose flour with the whole-wheat flour. Using your hands, mix the dissolved pre-ferment into the flours until a smooth dough forms. Cover the bowl with plastic wrap and let stand for 30 minutes.

3 Uncover the dough and add the salt water. Gently fold the dough over onto itself until the salt water is thoroughly incorporated. Loosely cover the dough and let rest for 1 hour; every 20 minutes, gently fold the dough up and over onto itself 4 times. Cover the dough and let stand for 3 to 4 hours.

4 Turn the dough out onto a floured work surface and cut it in half. Using a bench scraper and floured hands, gently shape the dough into 2 rounds, folding the dough under itself as necessary. Let the loaves stand on the work surface for 20 minutes, then gently fold the sides under again.

5 Line 2 large bowls with kitchen towels and generously dust the towels with rice flour. Transfer the loaves to the bowls, rounded side down. Cover the loaves with clean towels and let rise for 4 to 5 hours. Alternatively, let the dough rise for 1 hour at room temperature, then refrigerate the loaves overnight. Let the dough come to room temperature before baking.

6 Bake Preheat the oven to 490°. Heat 2 large enameled cast-iron casseroles or cast-iron skillets with lids for 30 minutes. Remove from the oven and dust the bottoms with rice flour. Turn the loaves into the casseroles, rounded side up, and score the tops with a sharp, thin knife. Cover the casseroles and bake the bread for 15 minutes. Reduce the oven temperature to 470° and bake for 20 minutes. Uncover and bake the loaves for 25 minutes, until richly browned. Transfer the bread to a rack; let cool before slicing.

WHEAT VARIATION Make the pre-ferment with 300 g. whole-wheat flour and 300 g. water. For the dough, use 1.4 kg. white flour, 600 g. whole-wheat flour and 1.5 kg. water.

RYE VARIATION Make the pre-ferment with 300 g. rye flour and 300 g. water. For the dough, use 1.7 kg. white flour, 300 g. rye flour and 1.5 kg. water.

FRUIT AND NUT VARIATIONS In Step 3, after folding in the salt water, fold in 2½ cups toasted sunflower seeds, 5 cups soaked and drained dried currants or 6 cups walnut halves.

IDEAL WEIGHT

Measure ingredients in grams; measuring by volume is less accurate. We love Oxo's digital scale ($50; williams-sonoma.com).

A

B

C

D

E

F

G

H

I

Challah

Jessamyn Waldman Rodriguez, founder of New York City's Hot Bread Kitchen, grew up eating the eggy challahs of Eastern Europe. In a Jewish baking class, she learned about another kind of Sabbath bread—a spice-studded version from the Sephardic Jews of the Mediterranean, who flavor their dough with caraway and anise. Instead of braiding, she twists this one into a round, turban-shaped loaf to symbolize the wheel of time for Rosh Hashanah, the Jewish New Year.

Jessamyn's Sephardic Challah

Time	25 min active
	3 hr 45 min total plus cooling
Makes	2 round loaves

- 3 Tbsp. sesame seeds
- 1½ Tbsp. caraway seeds
- 1½ Tbsp. anise seeds
- 1 envelope active dry yeast
- 2 cups lukewarm water
- 5 cups bread flour
- 2½ Tbsp. extra-virgin olive oil
- 2 Tbsp. honey
- 1 Tbsp. kosher salt
- Cornmeal, for dusting
- 2 large egg yolks

1 In a skillet, toast the sesame, caraway and anise seeds over moderate heat until fragrant, 2 minutes **(A)**. Transfer to a plate and let cool. In a small bowl, combine the yeast with 2 tablespoons of the water and let stand until thoroughly moistened, about 5 minutes **(B)**.

2 In the bowl of a stand mixer fitted with the dough hook, combine the flour with the olive oil, honey and the remaining water and mix at low speed until a very soft dough forms. Add the salt, yeast mixture and all but 1 tablespoon of the seeds and mix at medium-low speed until the dough is supple and smooth, 10 minutes **(C)**. Using oiled hands, transfer the dough to a large oiled bowl **(D)**. Cover the bowl with plastic wrap and let stand in a draft-free spot until the dough has risen, 1 hour.

3 Lightly oil 2 small cookie sheets and dust them with cornmeal. Turn the dough out onto a lightly floured work surface and press to deflate. Cut the dough in half and let rest for 5 minutes **(E)**. Roll each piece into an 18-inch-long rope and let rest for 5 minutes longer, then roll each rope into a 32-inch rope. Beginning at the center and working outward, form each rope into a coil **(F)**. Tuck the ends under the coils.

4 Transfer each coil to a baking sheet and cover each loaf with a large inverted bowl **(G)**. Let stand for 1 hour, until the loaves have nearly doubled in bulk.

5 Preheat the oven to 400°. In a bowl, whisk the egg yolks with 1 tablespoon of water. Brush the egg wash over the loaves and let stand uncovered for 30 minutes **(H)**. Brush with the egg wash once more and sprinkle with the reserved 1 tablespoon of seeds. Bake the loaves side by side in the center of the oven for 30 minutes, until they're golden and sound hollow when tapped on the bottom. Transfer the loaves to racks and let cool completely before slicing **(I)**.

MAKE AHEAD The loaves can be wrapped in foil and refrigerated for up to 1 week.

DON'T GET IT TWISTED

To shape this challah, first stretch the dough into a long rope, then coil it. If the dough resists stretching, let it rest for 5 minutes before trying again.

Pretzels

Chefs now compete with sidewalk vendors to make the best pretzels. No surprise: Chefs are winning—handily. At his eponymous bakery in L.A., German-born Hans Röckenwagner creates pretzels with a soft, chewy interior and the signature shiny crust. The key is soaking the uncooked twists in a lye solution. Don't be intimidated by this food-grade alkali; baking neutralizes the high pH, and Röckenwagner says it poses no more risk than boiling water or heating oil.

German-Style Pretzels

Time	45 min active
	4 hr total
Makes	8 pretzels

3¾   cups bread flour (20 oz.), plus more for dusting

1½   cups warm water

1¼   tsp. active dry yeast

2   tsp. kosher salt

2   Tbsp. unsalted butter, softened

10   cups lukewarm water

½   cup food-grade lye micro beads (see Note)

Coarse salt or pretzel salt, for sprinkling (see Note)

1 In the bowl of a stand mixer fitted with the dough hook, combine the 3¾ cups of bread flour with the warm water, yeast, kosher salt and butter and knead at medium speed until the flour is evenly moistened, 2 minutes. Increase the speed to high and knead until a smooth, elastic dough forms around the hook, 8 minutes.

2 Transfer the dough to a lightly floured surface. Cover loosely with a dry kitchen towel and let rest for 5 minutes. Cut the dough into 8 equal pieces and form each one into a ball. Cover the dough balls with the towel and let rest for another 5 minutes **(A)**.

3 On an unfloured surface, roll each ball of dough into an 18-inch-long rope, tapering them slightly at both ends **(B)**. To shape each pretzel, form the rope into a U shape. Cross the ends over each other twice to form the twist **(C)**. Bring the ends to the bottom of the U and press the tips onto it **(D)**. Arrange the pretzels on 2 large baking sheets lined with parchment paper and let stand uncovered in a warm place for 45 minutes, until slightly risen. Refrigerate the pretzels uncovered for at least 2 hours or overnight.

CUT THE MUSTARD

"The best way to eat one of my pretzels is with a little butter and maybe some radish slices," says Röckenwagner.

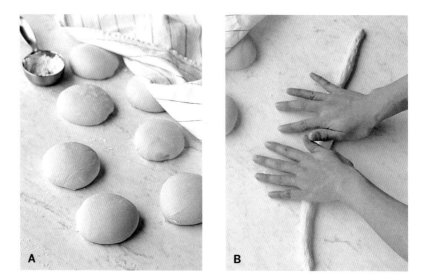

A

B

4 Preheat the oven to 400°. While wearing latex gloves, long sleeves and safety goggles, fill a large, deep ceramic, plastic or glass bowl with the lukewarm water. Carefully add the lye (always be sure to add lye to water, never the other way around) and, taking care not to splash, stir the solution occasionally until all the beads have fully dissolved, about 5 minutes. Using a slotted spatula, gently lower a pretzel into the solution for 15 seconds. Carefully turn the pretzel over and soak it for another 15 seconds. With the spatula, remove the pretzel from the lye solution and return it to the baking sheet.

5 Sprinkle the pretzels with coarse salt and bake on the top and middle racks of the oven until shiny-brown and risen, about 17 minutes; shift the pans halfway through baking. Let the pretzels cool slightly on the baking sheets before serving **(E)**.

NOTE You can order food-grade lye from essentialdepot.com. Look for coarse salt and pretzel salt at specialty food stores or online from americanspice.com.

LYE ALTERNATIVE Dissolve ½ cup baking soda in 2 qts. boiling water. Boil the pretzels for 30 seconds, then drain on wire racks before salting and baking.

MAKE AHEAD Pretzels baked without salt can be frozen for up to 1 month. Spray the frozen pretzels with water and sprinkle with salt before reheating in a 275° oven until warmed through, about 20 minutes.

C   D   E

Doughnuts

Seattle's Top Pot Doughnuts has a cult following—even drawing a visit from President Obama. Here, owners Mark and Michael Klebeck offer devotees tips for re-creating their old-fashioned recipes at home. They stress the importance of correctly proofing a yeast dough (i.e., letting it rise), and have this to say about frying: Filter the used oil and save it for another batch—doughnuts improve as the oil takes on their flavor. See below for their recipes, tips and three festive glazes.

Vanilla Raised Doughnuts

Time	1 hr active; 4 hr total
Makes	about 16 doughnuts or 4 dozen doughnut holes

1	cup skim milk
1½	vanilla beans, split and seeds scraped
½	cup plus 1 Tbsp. sugar
	Four ¼-oz. packages active dry yeast
¼	cup solid vegetable shortening
3	large egg yolks
2	tsp. table salt
½	tsp. baking powder
½	tsp. ground mace
500	g. bread flour, sifted (3⅔ cups)
	Boiling water
	Vegetable oil, for frying
	Glaze, for coating (recipes follow)

YES, WEIGH

According to Jess Thomson, who helped Top Pot's owners translate their recipes for the home cook in the *Top Pot Hand-Forged Doughnuts* cookbook, it's best to weigh flour on a kitchen scale instead of using measuring cups.

LEVEL ENTRY

Never drop the doughnuts flat into hot oil. "Insert them along their sides, like a coin into a slot, so that they don't splash," suggests Thomson.

1 Make the doughnuts In a small saucepan, warm the milk, vanilla seeds and 1 tablespoon of the sugar over moderate heat until the temperature registers 105° on a candy thermometer. Transfer to the bowl of a stand mixer fitted with the dough hook. Add the yeast and let stand until foamy, 5 minutes. Add the shortening, egg yolks and remaining ½ cup of sugar and beat at medium speed just until the shortening is broken up. Beat in the salt, baking powder and mace. At low speed, add the flour, 1 cup at a time, until the dough is firm but still tacky (you may need to add more or less flour to achieve the desired consistency).

2 Transfer the dough to a lightly floured work surface and knead a few times; pat it into a disk and transfer to a floured baking sheet. Dust with flour and cover with a towel. Place the baking sheet in the center of a turned-off oven. Set a large roasting pan on the bottom rack and fill it halfway with boiling water. Close the oven door and let the dough stand until doubled in bulk, about 1 hour.

3 Line 2 baking sheets with wax paper and dust with flour. Turn the dough out onto a floured work surface and roll out to a 12-inch round, ½ inch thick. For doughnuts, use a floured 2¾-inch doughnut cutter (or 2¾-inch and 1¼-inch cookie cutters) and stamp them out as close together as possible; alternatively, for doughnut holes, use a 1-inch cookie cutter. Transfer the doughnuts and/or holes to the baking sheets and return them to the oven. Refill the roasting pan with boiling water and close the oven door. Let stand until the dough has doubled in bulk, 45 minutes.

4 Set a rack on a baking sheet and cover with paper towels. In a large saucepan, heat 2 inches of oil to 365°. Add 3 or 4 doughnuts at a time; adjust the heat to keep the oil between 350° and 360°. Fry the doughnuts until golden brown, 1 minute per side. If frying doughnut holes, cook them in batches of 12. Using a slotted spoon, transfer the doughnuts to the paper towels.

(continued on page 191)

5 Glaze the doughnuts While the doughnuts are still warm, dip them in the glaze to coat the tops **(A)**. Invert them on a rack and let stand.

6 When the first coat of glaze is slightly hardened, dip the doughnuts a second time **(B)**. Let the glaze set again, then serve.

RICH FIVE-SPICE GLAZE

In a medium bowl, mix 3½ cups confectioners' sugar, ⅓ cup heavy cream, 1½ tsp. light corn syrup, ¾ tsp. Chinese five-spice powder, ½ tsp. pure vanilla extract and ¼ tsp. table salt. Using a hand mixer, beat at low speed until smooth; add 2 to 3 Tbsp. hot water 1 tablespoon at a time until the glaze is thin enough for dipping. Use right away, or cover with plastic wrap and refrigerate for up to 1 week.

KAFFIR LIME–COCONUT GLAZE

In a small saucepan, simmer ½ cup plus 2 Tbsp. coconut milk and 4 twisted fresh kaffir lime leaves for 2 minutes. Let cool slightly, then transfer the mixture to a bowl. Discard the lime leaves. Add 3½ cups confectioners' sugar, 1½ tsp. light corn syrup, ½ tsp. pure vanilla extract and ¼ tsp. table salt and beat at medium speed until smooth. Use the glaze right away or cover with plastic wrap and refrigerate for up to 1 week.

TART CRANBERRY GLAZE

In a small saucepan, combine 1 cup fresh or frozen cranberries, 2 Tbsp. granulated sugar and ¼ cup water and simmer, crushing the berries, until jammy, 8 minutes. Let cool slightly. Transfer to a bowl and add 3½ cups confectioners' sugar, 1½ tsp. light corn syrup, ½ tsp. pure vanilla extract and ¼ tsp. table salt. Using a hand mixer, beat at medium speed until smooth. Use the glaze right away, or cover with plastic wrap and refrigerate for up to 1 week.

Meringue Pie

At Revival in Minneapolis, guests who've gorged themselves on Thomas Boemer's Southern classics still make room for this mile-high lemon meringue pie. To give the custard a luxurious texture, Boemer makes his own sweetened condensed milk. For a spectacular finish, he tops it with a marshmallowy Italian meringue that's perfect for serious swirling.

Lemon Meringue Pie

Time	1 hr active; 4 hr total plus chilling
Makes	one 9-inch pie

SWEETENED CONDENSED MILK

- 2 cups whole milk
- ⅔ cup granulated sugar
- ½ tsp. pure vanilla extract

GRAHAM CRACKER CRUST

- 9 graham crackers
- ¼ cup lightly packed light brown sugar
- 6 Tbsp. unsalted butter, melted

LEMON CUSTARD

- 8 large egg yolks
- ¼ cup cornstarch
- 2 tsp. finely grated lemon zest plus 1 cup fresh lemon juice
- 4 Tbsp. unsalted butter

MERINGUE

- 1 cup granulated sugar
- 4 large egg whites
- ¼ tsp. cream of tartar

📷 page 194

1 Make the sweetened condensed milk In a small saucepan, combine the milk and granulated sugar and bring to a simmer, whisking constantly, until the sugar dissolves. Cook over very low heat (the mixture should not bubble), stirring occasionally, until thickened and reduced to 1¼ cups, about 2 hours and 30 minutes **(A)**. Stir in the vanilla and scrape the sweetened condensed milk into a medium bowl.

2 Meanwhile, make the crust In a food processor, pulse the graham crackers with the brown sugar until fine crumbs form. Add the butter and pulse until incorporated. Press the crumbs evenly over the bottom and up the side of a 9-inch glass pie plate to form a ½-inch-thick crust; use the bottom of a metal measuring cup to help form an even layer of crumbs **(B)**. Refrigerate the crust for at least 45 minutes.

3 Preheat the oven to 350°. Bake the crust for about 12 minutes, until fragrant and browned. Transfer to a rack and let cool completely.

4 Make the lemon custard In a medium bowl, beat the egg yolks. In a medium saucepan, whisk the sweetened condensed milk with the cornstarch until well blended. Add the lemon zest and lemon juice and bring to a simmer. Cook over moderately low heat, whisking, until thickened, 1 to 2 minutes. While whisking constantly, slowly drizzle half of the milk mixture into the egg yolks. Add the egg yolk mixture to the saucepan and cook over moderately low heat, whisking, until very thick, about 3 minutes. Whisk in the butter until smooth. Pour the custard into the crust and let cool to room temperature **(C)**.

5 Make the meringue Preheat the oven to 325°. In a medium saucepan, combine the sugar and ¼ cup of water; bring to a boil. Cook over moderate heat until the syrup reaches 243° on a candy thermometer, 8 to 10 minutes.

6 Meanwhile, in the bowl of a stand mixer fitted with the whisk, beat the egg whites with the cream of tartar at medium speed until soft peaks form. With the machine on, slowly drizzle in the hot syrup and beat the meringue at medium-high speed until stiff and glossy, about 10 minutes **(D)**. Scoop the meringue onto the pie, spreading and swirling it decoratively; make sure the meringue covers the filling completely and touches the crust all around **(E)**. Bake the pie on the middle rack of the oven for 10 minutes. Turn on the broiler; broil the meringue 6 inches from the heat until golden brown in spots, about 3 minutes (or use a blowtorch) **(F)**. Transfer the pie to a wire rack to cool completely. Refrigerate until chilled, 3 hours.

MAKE AHEAD The pie can be made up to 8 hours ahead.

A

B

C

D

DON'T LET IT SLIDE

The billowy Italian meringue
is made by beating egg whites with
a hot sugar syrup. This type of
meringue is more stable than the
simple egg-white-and-sugar
kind, and much less likely to weep
(dissolve) or slide off.

E

F

Lemon Meringue Pie
page 192

Coconut-Lime, Hazelnut and
Cinnamon Marshmallows, next page

Marshmallows

"I don't really like sweets," says Dominique Ansel, whose amazing marshmallows are remarkably less sweet than most. "Just like salt, too much sugar can kill flavor." At his eponymous NYC bakery, Ansel makes two kinds of marshmallows: a French variety made fluffy with whipped egg whites and a chewier, egg-free American version. Read on for both recipes and his three favorite add-ins.

Light and Fluffy Marshmallows

Time	40 min plus 3 hr setting
Makes	about 25 marshmallows

- 1 Tbsp. plus 2 tsp. unflavored powdered gelatin
  Canola oil, for greasing
  Cornstarch, for dusting
- 1 cup sugar
- 2 Tbsp. light corn syrup
- 3 large egg whites

1 In a small bowl, mix the gelatin with ⅓ cup of water and let stand for 15 minutes. Meanwhile, grease an 8-inch square cake pan with oil and dust lightly with cornstarch, tapping out the excess.

2 In a small saucepan, mix the sugar with ⅓ cup of water and bring to a boil, stirring to dissolve the sugar. Add the corn syrup and cook over moderately high heat, without stirring, until the syrup registers 260° on a candy thermometer **(A)**. Off the heat, stir in the gelatin mixture until dissolved.

3 In a stand mixer fitted with the whisk, beat the egg whites at moderately high speed until soft peaks form **(B)**. With the machine on, drizzle the hot syrup into the egg whites in a very thin stream down the side of the bowl. Scrape the marshmallow into the prepared pan, smoothing the surface. Let stand until set, at least 3 hours.

4 Run a sharp knife around the marshmallow. Very lightly dust a work surface with cornstarch and invert the cake pan onto it, tapping to release the marshmallow. Using a lightly greased sharp knife, cut the marshmallow into 1½-inch pieces **(C)**.

VARIATIONS See the opposite page for three add-ins.

Soft and Chewy Marshmallows

Time | 40 min plus overnight setting
Makes | about 25 marshmallows

Canola oil, for greasing

2 Tbsp. unflavored powdered gelatin

2 cups sugar

2/3 cup plus 3 Tbsp. light corn syrup

3 Tbsp. honey

Cornstarch, for dusting

📷 page 195

1 Line an 8-inch square cake pan with foil, allowing 2 inches of overhang on 2 sides; grease the foil with canola oil. In a medium heatproof bowl, mix the gelatin with ½ cup plus 2 tablespoons of cold water; let stand for 15 minutes. Set the bowl over a saucepan of simmering water and cook, stirring occasionally, until the gelatin dissolves and the mixture is smooth, about 2 minutes.

2 Meanwhile, in a medium saucepan, combine the sugar, corn syrup, honey and ⅓ cup plus 2 tablespoons of water and bring to a boil, stirring to dissolve the sugar. Cook the syrup over moderately high heat, brushing down the side of the pan with a damp pastry brush, until it registers 250° on a candy thermometer, about 12 minutes. Immediately pour the hot syrup into the bowl of a stand mixer fitted with the whisk. Scrape in the gelatin mixture and beat at high speed until a smooth white foam forms, about 4 minutes.

3 Spread the marshmallow in the prepared pan and smooth the surface. Press a lightly greased sheet of parchment paper on the surface and let stand overnight, until set.

4 Peel off the parchment. Dust a work surface with cornstarch. Using the foil, lift the marshmallow out of the pan and invert it onto the work surface, then peel off the foil. Dust the top of the marshmallow with cornstarch and, using a lightly greased sharp knife, cut the marshmallow into 1½-inch pieces. Dust the marshmallows with cornstarch.

MAKE AHEAD The cornstarch-dusted marshmallows can be stored in a single layer in an airtight container for up to 2 days.

CINNAMON MARSHMALLOWS

Add ½ tsp. ground Vietnamese cinnamon during the last minute of beating the marshmallow; lightly dust the cut marshmallows with a sifted mixture of ⅔ cup cornstarch, ⅓ cup confectioners' sugar and 1 tsp. cinnamon.

COCONUT-LIME MARSHMALLOWS

Add 1 tsp. pure coconut extract and 2 tsp. finely grated lime zest during the last minute of beating the marshmallow; coat the cut marshmallows with toasted unsweetened shredded coconut.

HAZELNUT MARSHMALLOWS

Add ¼ cup hazelnut praline paste during the last minute of beating the marshmallow; coat the cut marshmallows in coarsely ground roasted hazelnuts

Mousse Cake

The Concord cake at Manhattan's Breads Bakery is a deeply chocolaty, crispy, creamy, chewy meringue-and-mousse confection covered with cocoa meringue sticks. Created by Gaston Lenôtre in 1969 in honor of the Concorde jet (the *e* in the name got lost along the way), it became popular at NYC's now-shuttered Soutine Bakery and has since been revived by Breads owner Gadi Peleg.

Concord Cake

Time	1 hr 30 min active; 2 hr 30 min total plus 6 hr chilling
Makes	one 8-inch cake

CHOCOLATE MOUSSE

- 10 oz. semisweet chocolate (64 percent), finely chopped
- 5 Tbsp. unsalted butter, cut into small pieces
- ½ cup plus 3 Tbsp. granulated sugar
- 2 large egg whites
- ½ vanilla bean, split
- 2 cups heavy cream, chilled

CHOCOLATE MERINGUE

- 2 cups confectioners' sugar, plus more for dusting
- 1 cup unsweetened cocoa powder
- 9 large egg whites
- 1⅓ cups granulated sugar

FOOLPROOF DECORATING

Assembling this rich chocolate dessert (which just happens to be gluten-free) is easy and forgiving: Any imperfections are hidden by the whimsical meringue sticks that cover the cake.

1 Make the mousse In a heatproof medium bowl set over a pot of simmering water, melt the chocolate with the butter, stirring occasionally, until smooth. Remove from the heat and keep warm.

2 In a small saucepan, combine the granulated sugar and ¼ cup water; boil over moderately high heat, without stirring, until the sugar syrup reaches 240° on a candy thermometer, about 7 minutes.

3 Meanwhile, in the bowl of a stand mixer fitted with the whisk, beat the egg whites at medium-high speed until soft peaks form, about 3 minutes.

4 Gradually pour the hot syrup into the egg whites in a steady stream and beat at medium-high speed until the whites are stiff and glossy, about 5 minutes. Using a large rubber spatula, fold in the melted chocolate until no streaks of white remain **(A)**. Scrape the chocolate mixture into a large bowl. Wash and dry the mixing bowl and whisk.

5 In the stand mixer fitted with the whisk, scrape the vanilla bean seeds into the heavy cream. Beat the cream at medium speed until firm. Using a rubber spatula, fold the whipped cream into the chocolate mixture until no streaks remain. Cover the mousse with plastic wrap and refrigerate until firm, at least 2 hours or overnight.

6 Make the chocolate meringue Meanwhile, in a medium bowl, sift the 2 cups of confectioners' sugar with the cocoa powder. Line 4 rimmed baking sheets with parchment paper. Trace an 8-inch circle on 2 of the sheets.

7 In the stand mixer fitted with the whisk, beat the egg whites at low speed until foamy. Increase the speed to medium-high and beat until soft peaks form. Beat in the granulated sugar 3 tablespoons at a time, beating well after each addition. Once all of the sugar has been added, beat the whites until stiff and glossy, about 3 minutes longer. Transfer the meringue to a large bowl and, using a large rubber spatula, gradually fold in the cocoa powder and confectioners' sugar until just a few streaks remain **(B)**.

8 Scrape the meringue into a piping bag fitted with a ½-inch tip. Pipe the meringue into the traced circles in a spiral, beginning at the center; there should be no space between the spirals **(C)**. On the other 2 prepared sheets, pipe the remaining meringue in long sticks, leaving about 1 inch between them **(D)**. Let the meringue rounds and sticks stand at room temperature for 30 minutes.

(continued on next page)

9 Preheat the oven to 350°. Bake the meringue rounds for about 25 minutes, until they are firm and can be lifted off the parchment with an offset spatula. Transfer to racks to cool completely.

10 Bake the meringue sticks for 12 to 14 minutes, until firm enough to be lifted off the parchment. Cut them into 6-inch lengths and transfer to a rack to cool completely. Using a sharp knife, cut the sticks into $1\frac{1}{2}$- to 2-inch lengths **(E)**.

11 Assemble the cake Transfer a meringue round to a cake stand or platter. Spoon half of the chilled chocolate mousse onto the meringue and spread it in an even layer with a large offset spatula **(F)**. Cover with the second meringue round **(G)**. Spread the remaining mousse on top, mounding it slightly in the center. Cover the cake entirely with the meringue sticks. Refrigerate until the mousse is firm, at least 6 hours or overnight. Dust the cake with confectioners' sugar just before serving **(H)**.

MAKE AHEAD The cake can be refrigerated for 1 day.

MERINGUE MAGIC

Two types of meringue work wonders in this amazing cake. The chocolate mousse gets its silky texture from Italian meringue, made by beating hot sugar syrup into whipped egg whites until cool, satiny and stiff. The crunchy-chewy cake layers and sticks are French meringue, made by beating sugar into whipped egg whites until airy and firm.

A

B

C

D

E

F

G

H

A

B

C

D

E

F

G

H

I

Meringues

When you beat egg whites with sugar and bake them, they transform into crisp, chewy meringues. They're delicious on their own, but Oregon pastry chef Daniel Jasso takes these confections to the next level. He layers big chocolate and hazelnut meringue disks and tons of whipped cream to make an epic, towering cake. Keep reading for the recipe, plus Jasso's clever slicing trick.

Hazelnut-and-Chocolate Meringue Cake

Time	35 min active; 4 hr total plus overnight chilling
Makes	8 to 10 servings

1½ cups hazelnuts (7 oz.)

6 large egg whites, at room temperature

Pinch of kosher salt

1½ cups granulated sugar

2 tsp. pure vanilla extract

½ tsp. pure almond extract

1 cup mini chocolate chips (6 oz.)

6 oz. bittersweet chocolate, melted and cooled

3 cups heavy cream

¼ cup confectioners' sugar

Chocolate shavings, for garnish

1 Preheat the oven to 350° and line 2 large baking sheets with parchment paper. Draw two 8-inch rounds on one sheet of the parchment and one 8-inch round on the other **(A)**.

2 Spread the hazelnuts on a third baking sheet and toast for 12 to 14 minutes, until browned. Let cool slightly, then transfer to a towel and rub to remove the skins **(B)**. Chop the nuts **(C)**. Lower the oven temperature to 225°.

3 In the bowl of a stand mixer fitted with the whisk, beat the egg whites with the salt at medium-high speed until soft peaks form **(D)**. Gradually beat in the granulated sugar at high speed until stiff. Beat in the vanilla and almond extracts. Fold in the hazelnuts and chocolate chips **(E)**. Pour the melted chocolate down the side of the bowl and gently fold until the meringue is lightly marbled **(F)**.

4 Spread the meringue in the drawn circles and bake for 2 hours and 30 minutes, until crisp; rotate the pans halfway through baking. Turn off the oven, leave the door ajar and let the meringues cool completely **(G)**.

5 In the bowl of the stand mixer, beat the cream with the confectioners' sugar until firm. Remove the meringues from the parchment paper. Spread the whipped cream on the layers and stack them **(H)**. Refrigerate or freeze the cake overnight. Using a serrated knife, cut into wedges and serve at room temperature. Garnish with chocolate shavings before serving **(I)**.

WINE Nutty, chocolaty Madeira.

MAKE THE CUT

Jasso has nicknamed this cake "the beast," because slicing it can be tricky—the meringue tends to crumble. The solution: Freeze the cake, cut it with a serrated knife and let it return to room temperature before serving.

Peanut Butter Candy

Mirracole Morsels in Kingston, Washington, makes peanut butter candies that are as flaky as the inside of a Butterfinger bar. The secret to the light, layered texture, says owner Nicole Haley, is the aerating power of baking soda. Also essential: using the best, freshest peanuts you can find. Supremely giftable, the candy can be made two weeks ahead of eating.

Miracle Peanut Butter Crunch

Time	20 min plus cooling
Makes	about 3 dozen candies

- 1 cup sugar
- ¾ cup light corn syrup
- 1 Tbsp. unsalted butter
- 1½ cups natural peanut butter
- 1 cup coarsely chopped roasted peanuts
- ¾ tsp. kosher salt
- ¾ tsp. pure vanilla extract
- ½ tsp. baking soda

1 Line a 9-inch square pan with foil. In a medium saucepan, stir the sugar with the corn syrup and 2 tablespoons of water. Add the butter and bring to a boil over high heat, stirring to dissolve the sugar. Attach a candy thermometer to the pan and cook over moderately high heat until the caramel reaches 285°, about 10 minutes.

2 Meanwhile, in a large, heatproof, microwave-safe bowl, combine the peanut butter with the peanuts and salt **(A)**. Heat the mixture in the microwave at high power until melted and hot, about 1½ minutes. Stir well.

3 In a small bowl, whisk the vanilla with the baking soda. As soon as the caramel reaches 285°, carefully stir in the baking soda mixture; the caramel will foam and bubble up **(B)**.

4 Immediately pour the caramel into the melted peanut butter mixture and, using a heatproof spatula, fold together as quickly as possible. You want the mixtures to be combined but not homogenized; the candy will come together very fast.

5 Immediately scrape the hot candy into the prepared pan and press into a flat, even layer **(C)**. Let cool completely. Peel off the foil and cut the candy into squares.

MAKE AHEAD Cut or uncut, the candy can be stored in an airtight container at room temperature for up to 2 weeks.

A

B

C

Nut Milks

Teresa Piro, founder of Can Can Cleanse in San Francisco, creates delicious, additive-free nut milks that customers crave long after their cleanse is over. She sweetens the milks naturally with dates or honey and uses vanilla and salt to bring out the nuts' richness. The two versions here—one made with almonds, another with mixed nuts—are simple to make and as good straight up as in dishes like a silky panna cotta (p. 208).

Almond Milk

Time	20 min active; 1 hr 20 min total plus overnight soaking
Makes	3 cups

1 cup raw almonds
5 cups filtered water, plus more for soaking
4 plump Medjool dates, pitted
¼ tsp. cinnamon
2 pinches of sea salt

1 Soak the almonds In a medium bowl, cover the almonds with filtered water **(A)**. Cover and let stand overnight at room temperature.

2 Make the almond milk Drain and rinse the almonds; transfer to a blender. Add the 5 cups of filtered water, the dates, cinnamon and salt and puree at high speed until very smooth, about 2 minutes. Pour the almond milk through a cheesecloth-lined fine sieve set over a bowl and let drain for 30 minutes **(B)**. Using a spatula, press on the solids to extract any remaining milk **(C)**. Discard the solids. Pour the almond milk into an airtight container and refrigerate until chilled, about 30 minutes. Stir or shake before serving.

MAKE AHEAD The almond milk can be refrigerated for up to 4 days.

(continued on next page)

A   B   C

Mixed-Nut Milk

Time	20 min active; 1 hr 20 min total plus overnight soaking
Makes	4 cups

1   cup raw hazelnuts

½   cup raw almonds

½   cup raw Brazil nuts

1   vanilla bean

5   cups filtered water, plus more for soaking

2   Tbsp. honey

½   tsp. sea salt

1 In a medium bowl, cover the nuts and vanilla bean with filtered water. Cover and let stand overnight at room temperature.

2 Drain and rinse the nuts and vanilla bean; transfer to a blender. Add the 5 cups of filtered water, the honey and the salt and puree at high speed until very smooth, about 2 minutes. Pour the nut milk through a cheesecloth-lined fine sieve set over a bowl and let drain for 30 minutes. Using a spatula, press on the solids to extract any remaining milk; discard the solids. Pour the nut milk into an airtight container and refrigerate until chilled, about 30 minutes. Stir or shake before serving.

MAKE AHEAD The mixed-nut milk can be refrigerated for up to 4 days.

Mixed-Nut-Milk Panna Cotta

Time	30 min active 2 hr 30 min total
Makes	6 servings

2   tsp. unflavored powdered gelatin

3   cups Mixed-Nut Milk

⅓   cup sugar

2   Tbsp. honey

½   vanilla bean, split lengthwise and seeds scraped

Pinch of kosher salt

Vegetable oil, for brushing

Crushed toasted hazelnuts and ¼ cup strawberry jam whisked with 1 Tbsp. water, for serving

📷 opposite page

1 In a small bowl, sprinkle the gelatin over ½ cup of the nut milk and let stand until softened, about 5 minutes. In a medium saucepan, combine the remaining 2½ cups of nut milk with the sugar, honey, vanilla seeds and salt. Bring just to a simmer over moderately high heat. Remove the pan from the heat and whisk in the softened gelatin mixture until dissolved.

2 Lightly brush six ½-cup ramekins with vegetable oil and set them on a baking sheet. Carefully fill the ramekins with the panna cotta mixture and refrigerate until set, at least 2 hours or up to 2 days.

3 Run a knife around each panna cotta and invert onto a plate. Top with crushed hazelnuts and serve with the jam. –*Justin Chapple, F&W Test Kitchen senior editor*

MILK SWAP

You can also make this jiggly panna cotta with 100 percent almond milk for a more delicate and pure almond flavor.

Vermouth

Jackson Cannon of The Hawthorne, Eastern Standard and Island Creek Oyster Bar in Boston makes his own aromatic fortified wine with rosé. It's beautifully balanced, with a freshness no commercial vermouth can match—perfect as an aperitif over ice or stirred into cocktails.

Rosé Vermouth

Time	3 hr plus 2 days infusing
Makes	3 qts

- 1 lb. strawberries, hulled and sliced
- 2¼ cups unaged (clear) brandy, preferably French
- 2¾ cups sugar
- 4 small rosemary leaves
- 7 small sage leaves
- 2 tsp. oregano leaves
- 1 tsp. thyme leaves
- 1 Tbsp. bitter orange peel
- 2 tsp. wormwood root (see below)
- ½ tsp. gentian root (see below)
- ¼ tsp. ground ginger
- One 1½-inch piece of vanilla bean
- Three 750-ml bottles (9½ cups) rosé, preferably Spanish Garnacha
- 1 cup ruby port
- ½ tsp. finely grated orange zest

📷 page 142

1 In a glass jar or pitcher, cover the sliced strawberries with the brandy and let macerate for 2 days at room temperature; the strawberries should be completely submerged **(A)**.

2 Strain the strawberry-infused brandy through a cheesecloth-lined sieve; discard the strawberries.

3 In a large nonreactive saucepan, combine the sugar with ¼ cup of water and cook over moderately low heat, swirling the pan occasionally, until the sugar is dissolved and a medium-amber caramel forms, about 10 minutes. Remove the pan from the heat and carefully add the strawberry-infused brandy **(B)**. The caramel will harden. Cook over low heat, stirring, until the caramel is dissolved. Remove from the heat.

4 In a nonreactive medium saucepan, combine the rosemary, sage, oregano, thyme, bitter orange peel, wormwood, gentian, ginger, vanilla bean and 3 cups of the rosé **(C)**. Bring to a boil, then remove from the heat and let stand for 10 minutes. Stir in the port.

5 Add the infused port and the remaining 6½ cups of rosé to the strawberry-brandy caramel syrup. Stir in the orange zest and refrigerate until cold, about 2 hours.

6 Strain the vermouth through a cheesecloth-lined sieve **(D)**. Pour into bottles and refrigerate. Serve the vermouth as an aperitif or over ice, or use it in a cocktail like the Fifty-Fifty martini **(E)** or Cannon's Frobisher (recipe follows).

STRAIGHT TO THE SOURCE

Vermouth is easier to make than you might think: It doesn't require special equipment or impossible-to-find ingredients (Amazon sells wormwood and gentian).

MAKE-AHEAD TIP

The vermouth can be refrigerated for 4 months.

A

B

Frobisher Cocktail

Time | 15 min
Makes | 1 drink

2 oz. Plymouth gin
¾ oz. Rosé Vermouth (recipe at left)
¼ oz. Luxardo maraschino liqueur
  Ice
1 orange peel
1 maraschino cherry, for garnish

📷 page 142

In a mixing glass, stir the gin with the vermouth and maraschino liqueur. Add ice and stir again until well chilled. Strain into a chilled cocktail glass and twist the orange peel over the drink; discard the peel. Garnish with the cherry.

C

D

E

Level Four

214 Soup Dumplings

218 Tofu

222 Lasagna

226 Raviolo

230 Paella

234 Porchetta

236 Mazemen Ramen

240 Croissants

242 Babka

246 Cinnamon Rolls

248 Ice Cream Cake

252 Cultured Butter

256 Marmalade

260 Bitters

Soup Dumplings

There's something magical about *xiao long bao,* the steamed Shanghainese dumplings filled with hot broth and meat. Dim sum master Joe Ng and restaurateur Ed Schoenfeld, who serve NYC's juiciest version, share the secret to getting the soup inside: Gelatin-rich stock solidifies when chilled, so you can fold the dough around it. Read on to learn their technique.

Pork-and-Crab Soup Dumplings

Time	3 hr active 7 hr 30 min total
Makes	about 4 dozen dumplings

JELLIED STOCK

  One 3-lb. chicken, quartered

1 lb. boneless pork shoulder, sliced 1 inch thick

  Eight ¼-inch slices of fresh ginger

2 scallions, halved

1 large carrot, thinly sliced

2 qts. low-sodium chicken broth

3 envelopes unflavored gelatin

PORK-AND-CRAB FILLING

4 dried shiitake mushrooms

  Boiling water

¾ lb. ground pork shoulder

¼ cup Asian crab paste (optional; see Note)

½ cup finely chopped chives

2 Tbsp. potato starch

2 Tbsp. toasted sesame oil

1½ Tbsp. dark soy sauce

1½ Tbsp. mushroom soy sauce, such as Healthy Boy (see Note)

1 Tbsp. sugar

1 tsp. finely chopped peeled fresh ginger

¾ tsp. kosher salt

½ tsp. white pepper

DOUGH

4½ cups all-purpose flour, plus more for dusting

1½ cups bread flour

  Boiling water

  Large pinch of saffron threads, crumbled

1 Tbsp. fine sea salt

1 Make the jellied stock In a large, deep pot, combine the chicken, pork, ginger, scallions, carrot, broth and 1 quart of water and bring to a boil. Reduce the heat and simmer until the chicken is cooked through, about 30 minutes. Remove the chicken; when cool enough, pull the meat from the bones. Return the bones to the pot and simmer until the broth is very flavorful and reduced to 6 cups, 1½ hours longer; strain and skim the fat from the surface. Reserve the chicken meat and pork for another use.

2 In a small bowl, combine the gelatin with ⅓ cup of cold water and let stand for 5 minutes. Whisk the softened gelatin into 3 cups of the hot stock until melted. (Reserve the remaining stock for another use.) Pour the gelatinized stock into a 2-quart glass or ceramic baking dish and refrigerate until firm, at least 3 hours or overnight **(A)**.

3 Make the pork-and-crab filling In a small bowl, cover the dried mushrooms with boiling water and soak until softened, about 20 minutes. Drain, squeezing out any excess liquid; discard the stems. Finely chop the caps and transfer to the bowl of a stand mixer fitted with the paddle. Add the pork, crab paste, chives, potato starch, sesame oil, dark and mushroom soy sauces, sugar, ginger, salt and white pepper. Beat at medium speed until thoroughly combined, about 5 minutes.

4 In a food processor, pulse the 3 cups of jellied stock until chopped **(B)**. Beat into the pork mixture at medium speed until light and fluffy, 5 minutes.

5 Meanwhile, make the dough In a medium bowl, stir ½ cup of the all-purpose flour, ½ cup of the bread flour and ½ cup of boiling water until combined. Turn the hot-water dough out onto a work surface and knead until fairly smooth, about 5 minutes.

6 In a glass measuring cup, combine 2 cups of room-temperature water with the saffron and let stand for 5 minutes. In the bowl of a stand mixer fitted with the dough hook, blend the remaining 4 cups of all-purpose flour and 1 cup of bread flour with the salt. Add the saffron water and beat at medium speed until a smooth dough forms, about 5 minutes. Add the hot-water dough and beat at medium speed until incorporated, about 5 minutes. Turn the dough out onto a work surface and knead it into a smooth ball. Wrap the dough in plastic and let stand at room temperature for 30 minutes or refrigerate overnight.

(continued on page 217)

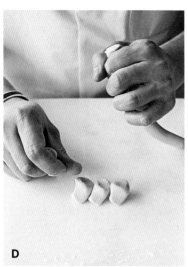

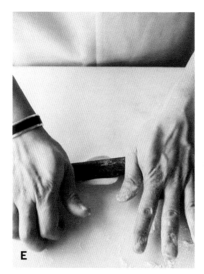

7 Form the dumplings Cut the dough into 4 pieces. Working with 1 piece at a time and keeping the rest covered, roll the piece of dough into a 1-inch-thick rope **(C)**. Pinch or cut the rope into ³/₄-inch pieces and roll them into balls **(D)**. Then, using a small dowel, glass bottle or Chinese-style rolling pin, roll each piece of dough into a thin 3¹/₂-inch round, dusting with flour as necessary **(E)**. Lightly dust the rounds with flour, transfer them to a floured baking sheet and cover with a damp towel to keep them from drying out. Repeat with the remaining dough. You should have about 4 dozen rounds.

8 Line 2 baking sheets with wax paper and dust lightly with flour. Working with 1 dough round at a time and keeping the rest covered, spoon a well-rounded tablespoon of the filling onto the center of the round **(F)**. Using your fingers, pinch and pleat the dough around the filling, leaving a tiny steam vent at the top **(G)**. Transfer to the baking sheet and garnish with a goji berry (optional). Repeat with the remaining dough and filling.

9 Steam the dumplings Fill a pot with 2 inches of water and bring to a boil. Arrange the dumplings in a bamboo steamer basket in batches, leaving at least 1 inch between them **(H)**. Cover and steam over the boiling water until the dough is shiny and the filling is soupy, 5 minutes. Serve with the dipping sauce (see below) while you steam the remaining dumplings.

NOTE Crab paste (a concentrated condiment) and mushroom soy sauce are available at Asian markets and online from amazon.com.

MAKE AHEAD Freeze uncooked dumplings on a baking sheet; seal in a plastic bag and freeze for up to 2 weeks. Steam until cooked, 10 minutes. The jellied stock can be refrigerated in an airtight container for up to 3 days.

DIPPING SAUCE

While Ng's soup dumplings are delicious on their own, they're also good with a very simple sauce of ¹/₄ cup Chinese black vinegar mixed with 1 Tbsp. julienned fresh ginger. Drizzle the sauce on top of each dumpling before eating.

MIX MASTER

Ng runs his jellied stock through a meat grinder to give it the same texture as the pork. A food processor works just as well.

LET OFF STEAM

To avoid burning your mouth on the piping-hot broth, place the dumpling on a spoon and carefully bite a hole at the edge to let steam out.

Tofu

Who says tofu has to be bland? For the creamiest, most indulgent version you've ever tasted, make your own. The key, says Douglas Keane of Two Birds/One Stone in St. Helena, California, is to start with homemade soy milk (most store-bought versions won't work). "It should have a richness to it similar to whole milk. It shouldn't be thin and blue like skim." Follow Keane's steps for crêpe-like "tofu skins," delicate silken tofu and the freshest firm tofu that's anything but boring.

Tofu Skins (Yuba)

Time	1 hr 30 min plus overnight soaking
Makes	about a dozen

1⅓ cups dried soybeans (8 oz.)
6 cups water, preferably filtered

1 Make the soy milk In a large bowl, cover the soybeans with 3 inches of cold water. Cover and let stand overnight at room temperature.

2 Drain the soybeans and transfer them to a blender. Add 3 cups of the filtered water and puree at high speed until as smooth as possible.

3 Line a large sieve with a clean cotton napkin or 3 layers of cheesecloth and set the sieve over a heatproof bowl. In a large pot, bring the remaining 3 cups of filtered water to a boil. Add the soybean puree and bring just to a boil (be careful not to let it boil over). Boil over moderately high heat for exactly 8 minutes, stirring constantly with a heatproof rubber spatula to prevent sticking and scorching.

4 Carefully pour the mixture into the prepared sieve. Let stand until just cool enough to handle, about 20 minutes. Gather the ends of the napkin or cheesecloth and squeeze to extract as much of the soy milk as possible; the remaining solids should be nearly dry. Discard the solids and skim off any foam from the soy milk. You should have about 4 cups of soy milk.

5 Make the tofu skins In a large, clean saucepan, bring the soy milk to just below a simmer. A skin will slowly form on the surface of the soy milk. When the skin is fully formed, use a paring knife to carefully detach it from the side of the saucepan. Carefully slide a chopstick or skewer under the skin and lift it from the milk. Let drain for a few seconds before transferring to a plate. Repeat, stacking the tofu skins, until the soy milk is depleted.

SERVE WITH Dashi, scallions and cilantro.

MAKE AHEAD Stacked tofu skins can be wrapped in plastic and refrigerated overnight.

(continued on page 220)

THIN SKIN

Known as *yuba* in Japan, the layer that forms on the surface of hot fresh soy milk (just as it does on warm cow's milk) has a mild flavor and pleasingly chewy texture. It can be served as is with condiments or fried and stuffed with fillings.

Silken Tofu

Time | 1 hr plus overnight soaking
Makes | about 1 lb

1⅓   cups dried soybeans (8 oz.)
6¼   cups water, preferably filtered
 1   tsp. nigari flakes (see Note)

1 Make the soy milk In a large bowl, cover the soybeans with 3 inches of cold water. Cover and let stand overnight at room temperature.

2 Drain the soybeans and transfer them to a blender. Add 3 cups of the filtered water and puree at high speed until as smooth as possible.

3 Line a large sieve with a clean cotton napkin or 3 layers of cheesecloth and set the sieve over a heatproof bowl. In a large pot, bring 3 cups of the filtered water to a boil. Add the soybean puree and bring just to a boil (be careful not to let it boil over). Boil over moderately high heat for exactly 8 minutes, stirring constantly with a heatproof rubber spatula to prevent sticking and scorching.

4 Carefully pour the mixture into the prepared sieve. Let stand until just cool enough to handle, about 20 minutes. Gather the ends of the napkin or cheesecloth and squeeze to extract as much of the soy milk as possible; the remaining solids should be nearly dry. Discard the solids and skim off any foam from the soy milk. You should have about 4 cups of soy milk.

5 Make the silken tofu In a small measuring cup, dissolve the nigari in the remaining ¼ cup of filtered water. Spoon 2 tablespoons plus 2 teaspoons of the nigari solution into a large heatproof glass bowl. In a clean large saucepan, heat the soy milk to 185°. Gently pour the hot soy milk into the bowl with the nigari solution and quickly stir once or twice just to combine thoroughly; it's easy to scramble the rapidly coagulating tofu. Cover and let stand undisturbed until the silken tofu is fully set, about 5 minutes. Discard the remaining nigari solution.

SERVE WITH Yuzu zest or fresh ginger.

NOTE Nigari (sea salts like magnesium chloride) can be purchased at Japanese markets or online from myworldhut.com.

Firm Tofu

Time	1 hr 15 min plus overnight soaking
Makes	about ½ lb

1⅓ cups dried soybeans (8 oz.)
6¼ cups water, preferably filtered
1 tsp. nigari flakes (see Note)

1 Make the soy milk In a large bowl, cover the soybeans with 3 inches of cold water. Cover and let stand overnight at room temperature.

2 Drain the soybeans and transfer them to a blender. Add 3 cups of the filtered water and puree at high speed until as smooth as possible.

3 Line a large sieve with a clean cotton napkin or 3 layers of cheesecloth and set the sieve over a heatproof bowl. In a large pot, bring 3 cups of the filtered water to a boil. Add the soybean puree and bring just to a boil (be careful not to let it boil over). Boil over moderately high heat for exactly 8 minutes, stirring constantly with a heatproof rubber spatula to prevent sticking and scorching.

4 Carefully pour the mixture into the prepared sieve. Let stand until just cool enough to handle, about 20 minutes. Gather the ends of the napkin or cheesecloth and squeeze to extract as much of the soy milk as possible; the remaining solids should be nearly dry. Discard the solids and skim off any foam from the soy milk. You should have about 4 cups of soy milk.

5 Make the tofu In a small measuring cup, dissolve the nigari in the remaining ¼ cup of filtered water. Spoon 2 tablespoons plus 2 teaspoons of the nigari solution into a large heatproof glass bowl. In a clean large saucepan, heat the soy milk to 185°. Gently pour the hot soy milk into the bowl with the nigari solution and quickly stir once or twice just to combine thoroughly; it's easy to scramble the rapidly coagulating tofu. Cover and let stand undisturbed until the silken tofu is fully set, about 5 minutes. Discard the remaining nigari solution.

6 Set a cheesecloth-lined sieve, colander or other mold with drainage over a bowl and spoon the silken tofu into it. Neatly fold the overhanging cheesecloth over the tofu and top with a small plate or other light weight to gently press out excess water. Let drain for at least 15 minutes or up to 2 hours, depending on the desired firmness. Unwrap and serve.

SERVE WITH Black radish slices and soy sauce, or a miso glaze.

NOTE Nigari can be purchased at Japanese markets or online from myworldhut.com.

MAKE AHEAD Firm tofu can be refrigerated for up to 3 days, covered with water.

SHAPE UP

Firm tofu is silken tofu that's pressed into a block. One great suggestion for an improvised mold: a plastic berry basket lined with cheesecloth.

Lasagna

The ultimate lasagna—say pasta purists—is a creamy tomato-less version. At Pastaria in St. Louis, chef Gerard Craft serves a lush layering of just three elements: delicate egg pasta, béchamel and melted Grana Padano and Fontina cheeses. Instead of baking additional ingredients inside the lasagna, Craft dresses up each slice with seasonal toppings.

Creamy White Lasagna with Toppings

Time	1 hr 30 min active
	3 hr 30 min total
Makes	10 servings

PASTA

3½ cups all-purpose flour, plus more for dusting

1½ tsp. kosher salt

3 large eggs, lightly beaten

BÉCHAMEL

2 sticks unsalted butter

1 medium onion, finely chopped

2 rosemary sprigs

2 thyme sprigs

3 garlic cloves, crushed
  Kosher salt

1 cup all-purpose flour

2 qts. whole milk

(continued on next page)

1 Make the pasta In a food processor, pulse the 3½ cups of flour with the salt. Add the eggs and ½ cup of water and pulse until the dough starts to come together **(A)**. Turn the dough out onto a work surface and knead by hand until smooth and elastic, about 10 minutes **(B)**. If the dough is too sticky to work with, lightly dust it with flour. Wrap the dough in plastic and let rest at room temperature for 1 hour.

2 Meanwhile, make the béchamel In a large saucepan, melt the butter. Add the onion, rosemary, thyme, garlic and a pinch of salt and cook over moderate heat, stirring occasionally, until the onion is softened but not browned, about 8 minutes. Add the flour and cook, stirring constantly, until the roux is light golden, 3 to 5 minutes. Gradually whisk in the milk and bring to a boil, then simmer over moderately low heat, stirring frequently, until no floury taste remains, about 20 minutes. Press the béchamel through a fine sieve into a bowl; discard the solids. Season with salt and let cool.

(continued on next page)

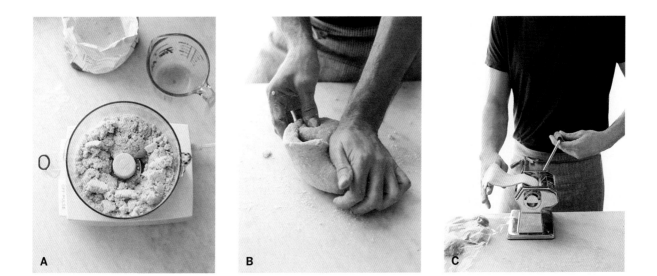

A

B

C

Extra-virgin olive oil

½ lb. imported Fontina cheese, shredded (2½ cups)

5 oz. Grana Padano cheese, freshly grated (1¼ cups)

3 Assemble the lasagna Cut the dough into 8 equal pieces; work with 1 piece at a time, keeping the rest covered with a towel. Flatten the dough slightly. Run it through a pasta machine a total of 6 times: Start at the widest setting, then run through successively narrower settings **(C, D)**. Dust the sheet with flour and lay it on a parchment paper–lined baking sheet. Repeat with the remaining dough, separating the sheets with parchment **(E)**.

4 In a large pot of salted boiling water, cook the pasta sheets until just al dente, 1 to 2 minutes **(F)**. Drain in a colander and cool under running water, then drain again. Return the pasta to the baking sheet and toss with olive oil to prevent the sheets from sticking together.

5 Preheat the oven to 350°. Brush a deep 9-by-13-inch baking dish with oil; spread with ½ cup of the béchamel. Arrange a layer of pasta over the béchamel, trimming to fit. Spread one-fifth of the remaining béchamel over the pasta **(G)**. Sprinkle with ½ cup of the Fontina and ¼ cup of the Grana Padano. Repeat the layering 4 more times, ending with the cheeses **(H)**.

6 Tightly cover the baking dish with foil and bake the lasagna for 45 minutes, until bubbling. Remove from the oven and uncover. Preheat the broiler. Broil the lasagna 6 inches from the heat until lightly browned on top, 2 to 4 minutes. Let rest for 15 minutes, then cut into squares and serve with one of the toppings **(I)**.

MAKE AHEAD The assembled, unbaked lasagna can be refrigerated for 1 day.

WINE Spiced, dark-fruited Chianti Classico.

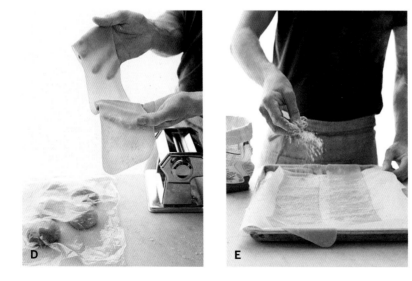

TOPPINGS

ROASTED WILD MUSHROOM Preheat the oven to 450°. In a large bowl, toss 2 lbs. mixed chopped mushrooms (such as maitake, stemmed shiitake, oyster and cremini) with ½ cup extra-virgin olive oil and season with salt. Spread on 2 large rimmed baking sheets and roast for about 30 minutes, stirring once, until golden. Season with fresh lemon juice. The roasted mushrooms can be refrigerated overnight. Reheat gently.

SALSA VERDE In a large bowl, whisk ¾ cup extra-virgin olive oil with 1½ Tbsp. fresh lemon juice, 1 minced garlic clove and 3 Tbsp. each of finely chopped parsley, tarragon, dill, mint and chives. Season with kosher salt. The salsa verde can be refrigerated overnight.

ROASTED CARROT PUREE Preheat the oven to 350°. In a large ovenproof skillet, heat 2 Tbsp. vegetable oil. Add 3 cups chopped carrots (1½ lbs.) and 2 thyme sprigs; cook over moderate heat, stirring, until the carrots are browned, 10 minutes. Transfer to the oven and roast for 10 minutes, until the carrots are tender. Pulse the carrots in a food processor until chopped. With the machine on, drizzle in 1 cup extra-virgin olive oil and ¾ cup water; puree until smooth, about 30 seconds. Season with salt. The carrot puree can be refrigerated overnight. Reheat gently.

LAYER IT ON

At Pastaria, Craft serves lasagna slices with toppings like a tangy salsa verde, carrot puree or his favorite, roasted wild mushrooms. It's like bruschetta that you can customize to your taste.

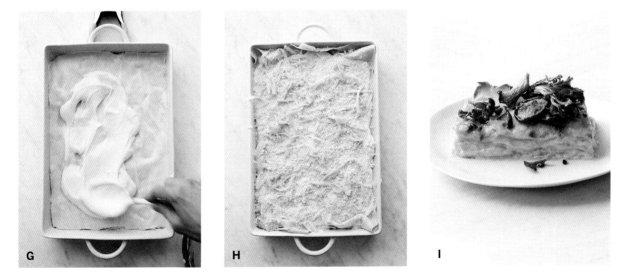

G

H

I

Raviolo

At Chicago's Monteverde, chef Sarah Grueneberg makes an impressive *uovo in raviolo*—a giant pasta round stuffed with fresh ricotta, feta and a runny egg yolk, inspired by one of her favorite Italian dishes, *uova in purgatorio.* She serves the behemoth in a fresh-tasting tomato sauce with basil and a pinch of chile flakes. Here's how to #putanegginit at home.

Uovo in Raviolo with Hand-Grated-Tomato Sauce

Time	1 hr 15 min active
	2 hr total
Makes	8 servings

PASTA DOUGH

- 2 large eggs
- 4 large egg yolks
- 2 cups 00 flour (10 oz.)

FILLING

- 8 oz. soft sheep-milk feta cheese, such as Bulgarian or Spanish
- 8 oz. whole-milk ricotta
- ½ cup (1 oz.) freshly grated Pecorino Romano cheese
- ½ tsp. grated orange zest
- 1 Tbsp. chopped parsley
- 2 tsp. chopped oregano
- Kosher salt

TOMATO SAUCE

- 4 lbs. ripe tomatoes, halved
- 6 Tbsp. extra-virgin olive oil
- 1 garlic clove, minced
- 1 pinch of crushed red pepper
- Kosher salt

RAVIOLI

- Semolina, for dusting
- 8 large egg yolks
- 3 large egg whites, beaten
- 1 cup torn basil leaves, plus small leaves for garnish
- Shaved Pecorino Romano cheese, for garnish

1 Make the pasta dough In a small bowl, whisk the eggs with the egg yolks and ¼ cup of water. Mound the flour on a work surface, make a well in the center and add the eggs. Using a fork, gradually draw in the flour until a dough forms **(A)**. Gather and knead the dough until smooth **(B)**. Form into a ball, cover in plastic wrap and refrigerate for 1 hour.

2 Meanwhile, make the filling In a food processor, pulse the feta until smooth. Scrape into a medium bowl and add the next 5 ingredients. Mix until well blended and season with salt. Refrigerate until ready to use.

3 Make the tomato sauce Grate the tomato halves on the large holes of a box grater set in a bowl until only the skins remain; discard the skins **(C)**. In a large saucepan, heat the olive oil. Add the garlic and cook over moderate heat, stirring, until fragrant, about 2 minutes. Add the grated tomatoes and crushed red pepper and season with salt. Cook over moderate heat, stirring occasionally, until the sauce has thickened and reduced to 3 cups, about 20 minutes.

4 Make the ravioli Divide the pasta dough into 4 pieces. Work with 1 piece at a time, keeping the rest covered. Press the dough to flatten it slightly. Run the dough twice through a pasta machine at the widest setting. Run the dough through 4 successively narrower settings, twice per setting, until the dough is about $\frac{1}{16}$ inch thick **(D)**. Dust a work surface with semolina and lay the pasta sheet on top; dust the pasta generously with semolina and cover with a damp kitchen towel. Repeat with the remaining 3 pieces of pasta dough, keeping the rolled-out sheets covered.

5 Lay 1 of the pasta sheets on a work surface and brush off the semolina. Spoon four ¼-cup mounds of the cheese filling onto the pasta sheet about 4 inches apart **(E)**. Spread the mounds of filling into 3-inch rounds and make a small well in the center of the filling. Slip 1 egg yolk into each well **(F)**. Brush around the filling with the beaten egg whites. Drape another sheet of pasta on top and press around the fillings to push any air pockets out of the ravioli **(G)**. Using a 4-inch fluted cookie cutter, stamp out the ravioli **(H)**. Press the edges to make sure they are sealed. Transfer the ravioli to a semolina-dusted baking sheet. Repeat to form another 4 ravioli; reserve any remaining filling for another use.

(continued on next page)

6 Bring a large pot of water to a boil and season generously with salt. Reheat the tomato sauce in the saucepan. Using a slotted spoon, add 4 of the ravioli to the boiling water and cook until the pasta is al dente, about 3 minutes. Using a slotted spoon, transfer the ravioli to the tomato sauce **(l)**. Add half of the torn basil and cook, stirring gently, until nicely coated, about 1 minute. Transfer the ravioli to plates and spoon some of the sauce on top. Repeat with the remaining 4 ravioli and torn basil. Garnish with Pecorino Romano and basil leaves and serve.

MAKE AHEAD The filling and tomato sauce can be stored separately in the refrigerator for 3 days. The formed ravioli can be covered and refrigerated for 3 hours.

WINE A bright and smoky red from Sicily.

ROUND OFF

If you don't have a cookie cutter, stamp out the ravioli with a 4-inch jar lid or an empty aluminum can.

A

B

C

D

E

F

G

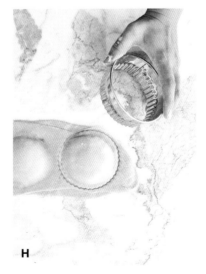

H

I

Paella

Seamus Mullen of New York City's Tertulia has opinions when it comes to Valencia's most famous dish. "True paella," he says, "starts with a thin layer of rice slowly infused with an intense stock. The rice shouldn't be much deeper than the first knuckle on your thumb; that's why you need a proper paella pan that's wide and shallow." For this recipe, Mullen suggests using a 17-inch paella pan set on a grill over a live fire to heat the pan evenly and impart an authentic smoky flavor.

Chicken-and-Seafood Paella with Allioli

Time	2 hr 15 min active
	4 hr 15 min total
Makes	8 servings

LOBSTER-INFUSED CHICKEN STOCK

Two 1¼-lb. lobsters

2 dried ñora chiles (see Note), stemmed and seeded

½ cup boiling water

2 Tbsp. vegetable oil

¼ cup tomato paste

½ cup brandy

2 medium onions, quartered

2 medium carrots, quartered

2 fennel bulbs, quartered and cored

4 garlic cloves, quartered

2 qts. plus 3 cups chicken stock

2 bunches of basil

¼ tsp. loosely packed saffron threads

SOFRITO

1 dried ñora chile, stemmed and seeded

½ cup boiling water

2 Tbsp. extra-virgin olive oil

1 small onion, minced

2 garlic cloves, minced

½ red bell pepper, minced

2 plum tomatoes, grated on a box grater

1 Tbsp. white wine vinegar

Salt and pepper

(continued on next page)

1 Prepare the stock In a large pot, boil the lobsters until just red but still undercooked, 4 minutes; let cool. Remove the meat from the tails, claws and knuckles; discard the intestinal veins and cut the tails into thick slices. Put the meat in a bowl and refrigerate. Chop the bodies and legs.

2 In a heatproof bowl, cover the chiles with the boiling water and let stand for 15 minutes. Meanwhile, in a pot, heat the oil. Add the chopped shells and cook over high heat for 1 minute. Reduce the heat to moderate and cook, stirring, until browned. Stir in the tomato paste and cook for 1 minute. Add the brandy and simmer for 2 minutes, scraping up any browned bits. Add the onions, carrots, fennel and garlic; cook over low heat for 5 minutes.

3 Lift the chiles from the bowl and mince; add with the soaking liquid to the pot. Add the chicken stock and basil; bring to a boil. Cover partially and simmer for 2 hours. Strain the lobster-infused stock. You should have about 10 cups. Add the saffron and let stand for 20 minutes.

4 Meanwhile, make the sofrito In a small heatproof bowl, cover the ñora chile with the boiling water and let stand until softened, about 15 minutes. Lift the pepper from the water and finely chop it. Return the chopped pepper to the soaking liquid.

5 In a medium skillet, heat the olive oil. Add the onion and cook over moderate heat until translucent, about 4 minutes. Add the garlic, bell pepper, grated tomatoes, vinegar and the chopped ñora chile and its soaking liquid. Simmer over low heat, stirring occasionally, until the liquid has evaporated and the vegetables are very soft and browned, about 20 minutes. Season with salt and pepper. You should have about 1 cup.

(continued on next page)

SOFRITO SECRET

The key to sofrito, a mixture of sautéed vegetables that flavors paella? The slower you cook it, the deeper the flavor will be.

2 Tbsp. extra-virgin olive oil

8 chicken drumsticks (about 3 lbs.)

8 chicken thighs (about 3 lbs.)
   Salt and pepper

2¼ cups Bomba or Calasparra rice
   (see Note)

½ lb. romano beans or green beans,
   cut into ½-inch pieces

2 lbs. littleneck clams, scrubbed

1 lb. mussels, scrubbed
   Lemon wedges, for serving

ALLIOLI (GARLIC MAYONNAISE)

3 garlic cloves

1 large egg

2 tsp. white wine vinegar

¼ cup fresh lemon juice
   Pinch of salt

¼ cup canola or grapeseed oil

½ cup extra-virgin olive oil

6 Grill the paella Light a hardwood charcoal or wood fire in a covered grill. When the fire is very hot, set a 17-inch paella pan on the grill. Add the olive oil and heat until shimmering. Season the chicken with salt and pepper and cook until browned, about 4 minutes per side **(A)**. Transfer the chicken to a plate. Add 3 cups of the hot lobster-infused stock to the pan, scraping up the browned bits on the bottom **(B)**. Whisk in the 1 cup of sofrito and bring to a rolling boil **(C)**. Add the rice and romano beans, shaking the pan to distribute them evenly **(D)**. Season with salt and return to a vigorous boil. Cook for 4 minutes, stirring as little as possible; add more lit coals and/or wood to the fire to maintain the temperature **(E)**. Bury the chicken pieces skin side up in the rice and cook until the stock is nearly evaporated, about 6 minutes.

7 Reduce the heat to a simmer; if necessary, use cast-iron trivets to lift the pan higher off the grill to reduce the heat. Add 3 more cups of the lobster-infused stock, 1 cup at a time, shaking the pan from time to time and waiting until the stock is nearly absorbed between additions, 10 minutes **(F)**. The rice should be lightly browned and crisp on the bottom, but not burned. Continue to cook the paella, adding as much of the remaining hot stock as necessary, ½ cup at a time, until the rice is almost tender and still very moist, 5 minutes. Nestle the clams and mussels into the rice, cover the grill and cook until they start to open, 6 minutes **(G, H)**. Arrange the reserved lobster meat all over the paella. Cover and cook until the clams and mussels are wide open and the lobster is heated through, 3 minutes longer **(I)**.

8 Meanwhile, make the allioli In a blender, puree the garlic, egg, vinegar, lemon juice and salt at high speed. With the blender at low speed, add the canola oil in a thin stream and blend until the sauce is creamy, then drizzle in the olive oil until blended.

9 Transfer the paella to the table, cover with a kitchen towel and let stand for 5 minutes. Serve with the allioli and lemon wedges.

NOTE Dried ñora chile peppers and Bomba and Calasparra rice are available at specialty stores or online from tienda.com. If you can't find ñoras, substitute an equal amount of ancho chiles.

WINE Albariño, the crisp Spanish white, has a vibrant minerality that's reminiscent of the sea, making it an easy match for this paella's delicately briny shellfish.

TOP IT OFF

Mullen recommends dolloping the paella with some allioli (garlic mayonnaise). The name comes from the Catalan phrase *all i oli*, which means "garlic and oil."

A

B

C

D

E

F

G

H

I

Porchetta

This Italian showstopper is traditionally a whole pig that's been deboned, stuffed, rolled, tied and roasted. With some smart tweaks, Michael Pirolo of Macchialina in Miami Beach transforms it into a spectacular main course using just the pork belly. The roast fits in a conventional oven yet is big (and impressive) enough to feed a crowd. By omitting the leaner cuts, which are prone to drying out, Pirolo's recipe guarantees amazingly moist meat—all encased in "crack your teeth crispy" skin.

Pork Belly Porchetta

Time	45 min active; 4 hr total plus 2 days brining and seasoning
Makes	10 servings

BRINE

10	rosemary sprigs
10	bay leaves
3	heads of garlic, smashed
⅓	cup juniper berries
3	Tbsp. black peppercorns
2	Tbsp. fennel seeds
1	Tbsp. crushed red pepper
1¼	cups kosher salt
¼	cup sugar
2	Tbsp. honey
	One 9-lb. meaty pork belly with skin (see Note)

RUB

1½	Tbsp. fennel seeds
1	tsp. juniper berries
¾	tsp. black peppercorns
¾	tsp. freshly grated nutmeg
¾	tsp. crushed red pepper
3	Tbsp. very finely chopped rosemary
4	large garlic cloves, minced
	Roasted potatoes, for serving

1 Brine the belly In a large pot, combine the rosemary, bay leaves, garlic, juniper berries, peppercorns, fennel seeds, crushed red pepper and 1 gallon of water. Bring to a simmer over high heat, cover and cook for 10 minutes. Add the salt, sugar and honey and stir until dissolved.

2 Pour the brine into a large roasting pan and let cool completely. Add the pork belly to the brine, skin side up. Cover with plastic wrap and refrigerate overnight.

3 Make the rub In a small skillet, toast the fennel seeds, juniper berries and peppercorns over moderate heat until they are fragrant, about 1 minute. Let cool, then grind to a powder in a spice grinder. Transfer the spice blend to a small bowl and stir in the nutmeg, crushed red pepper, rosemary and garlic.

4 Drain the pork belly and pat dry, then pick off any spices. Turn the belly skin side down and rub the meaty side with the spice blend **(A)**. Transfer the pork belly to the roasting pan, skin side up, and pierce the skin all over with the tip of a knife **(B)**. Refrigerate the pork uncovered overnight.

5 Preheat the oven to 400° and position a rack in the lower third. Set the pork belly skin side down on a work surface. Roll up the belly lengthwise to form a tight cylinder and tie tightly at 2-inch intervals with kitchen twine **(C)**.

A

B

6 Return the pork to the pan and roast for 1 hour. Lower the heat to 300° and roast for 2 hours and 15 minutes longer, until the skin is deep brown and crisp and an instant-read thermometer inserted in the center registers 185°. Transfer the porchetta to a cutting board and let rest for 20 minutes. Remove the twine and slice the porchetta ½ inch thick, using a serrated knife to cut through the skin **(D)**. Serve with roasted potatoes **(E)**.

NOTE Because pork belly can be a very fatty cut, be sure to ask your butcher for one that is very meaty, at least 50 percent lean.

MAKE AHEAD The porchetta can be prepared through Step 5 and refrigerated overnight.

WINE Spicy, dark-fruited Tuscan red.

LOVE YOUR LEFTOVERS

Salumi Serve cold and thinly sliced on a cured-meat board.

Sandwich Layer with melted provolone and sautéed broccoli rabe on toasted ciabatta.

Eggs Fold into an omelet with goat cheese and scallions.

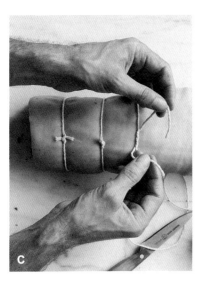

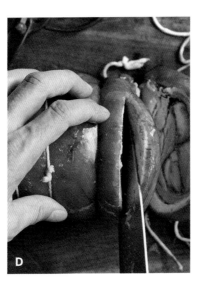

Mazemen Ramen

Ramen obsessive Ivan Orkin takes a labor-intensive approach to the dish; the broth recipe alone fills five pages in his cookbook, *Ivan Ramen.* The most manageable—and still inspiring—recipe for the home cook is the drier-style mazemen. Because the broth is a less critical component, basic chicken stock mixed with instant dashi achieves excellent results. The main project, then, is preparing Orkin's signature toasted rye noodles, luscious pork belly and chile-eggplant sofrito.

Chile-Eggplant Mazemen Ramen with Pork Belly

Time	2 hr 45 min active
	5 hr total
Makes	8 servings

PORK BELLY

One 2-lb. piece of skinless meaty pork belly

1 Tbsp. canola oil

Kosher salt and black pepper

3 cups chicken stock or low-sodium broth

CHILE-EGGPLANT SOFRITO

1 cup canola oil

1 large onion, minced (2 cups)

½ small eggplant, minced (1½ cups)

2 medium tomatoes, minced (1¼ cups)

2½ tsp. chipotle chile powder

Kosher salt

SHOYU TARE

⅓ cup canola oil

1 large onion, minced

3 Tbsp. minced peeled fresh ginger

2 tsp. minced garlic

⅔ cup reduced-sodium soy sauce

½ cup dry sake

½ cup mirin

2 cups chicken stock or low-sodium broth

1 Tbsp. instant dashi, such as Ajinomoto Hon Dashi

(continued on page 239)

1 Prepare the pork belly Preheat the oven to 425°. Rub the pork belly on both sides with the oil, season with salt and pepper and set it on a rack in a medium roasting pan. Add the stock to the pan, cover and roast the pork for about 2½ hours, until very tender. Let the pork rest for 30 minutes. Strain the rendered fat through a cheesecloth-lined sieve into a bowl; the stock will have evaporated. Cut the pork into ½-inch-thick slices and keep warm **(A)**.

2 Meanwhile, make the sofrito In a large saucepan, heat the oil. Add the onion and eggplant and cook over low heat, stirring occasionally, until the vegetables are very soft, about 1 hour. Add the tomatoes and cook, stirring occasionally, until the tomatoes have almost melted, about 1 hour. Stir in the chipotle powder and cook for 15 minutes longer; season with salt. Transfer the sofrito to a bowl and let cool to room temperature. Drain the sofrito in a sieve; discard the oil or reserve it for another use.

3 Make the shoyu tare In a medium saucepan, heat the oil. Add the onion and cook, stirring occasionally, until softened, about 5 minutes. Add the ginger and garlic and cook, stirring occasionally, until lightly caramelized, about 10 minutes. Add the soy sauce, sake and mirin and bring to a boil; simmer for 2 minutes. Add the stock and dashi powder and simmer for 3 minutes. Keep warm.

(continued on page 239)

A

B

C

D

E

F

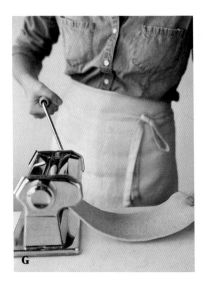

G

H

I

TOASTED RYE NOODLES

- 20 g. (1 Tbsp. plus ¾ tsp.) baking soda
- 70 g. (¼ cup plus 2½ Tbsp.) rye flour
- 620 g. (4 cups) bread flour
- 300 g. (2 cups) cake flour
- 13 g. (1½ Tbsp.) kosher salt
- 430 ml (2 cups plus 2 Tbsp.) cool water

  Cornstarch, for dusting

  Thinly sliced scallions and chipotle chile powder, for garnish

---

RAMEN 101

Noodles In Japan, cooks use *kansui* (an alkaline solution) to give ramen noodles their springy texture; here, Orkin substitutes baking soda that's been baked to increase its potency. This dough may seem too dry at first, but adding extra water will result in noodles that are too soft.

Shoyu tare *Tare*—a mixture of ingredients like shoyu (soy sauce), sake and mirin—is the main seasoning in ramen.

Sofrito Borrowing from Latin American, Italian and Spanish cooking, Orkin tops his ramen with sofrito: vegetables sautéed in oil until almost melting.

4 Make the toasted rye noodles Preheat the oven to 275°. In a small ovenproof skillet lined with aluminum foil, spread the baking soda in an even layer and bake for 1 hour **(B)**. Let cool.

5 Meanwhile, in a small nonstick skillet, toast the rye flour over moderately low heat, stirring, until fragrant, about 4 minutes **(C)**. Using a rubber spatula, scrape the toasted rye flour into the bowl of a stand mixer fitted with the dough hook. Add the bread flour and cake flour. In a medium bowl, stir the baked baking soda and salt with the cool water until dissolved **(D)**. With the mixer at low speed, slowly blend the baking soda solution into the flour in 3 additions. Mix, scraping down the bowl frequently, until the dough starts to come together. At medium speed, knead the dough until it forms a shaggy ball, about 10 minutes. Cover the bowl with plastic wrap and let stand at room temperature for 30 minutes.

6 Pat the dough into a disk and cut into 8 equal pieces **(E, F)**. Work with 1 piece at a time and keep the rest of the dough covered with a damp kitchen towel: Flatten the dough about ¼ inch thick. Roll the dough through a pasta machine at the widest setting. Fold the dough in thirds, like a letter, and roll it again at the widest setting. Repeat this folding and rolling until the dough feels smooth and elastic, about 3 more times. Roll the dough through successively narrower settings, two times per setting without folding, until the sheet of dough is ¹⁄₁₆ inch thick **(G)**. Cut the sheet of dough into roughly 12-inch lengths and transfer them to a baking sheet or work surface lightly dusted with cornstarch. Lightly dust the pasta sheets with cornstarch and cover with a dry kitchen towel. Repeat with the remaining dough, slightly overlapping the pasta sheets on the baking sheet.

7 Run each sheet of pasta through the spaghetti cutter **(H)**. Gently toss the noodles with cornstarch and spread them on a baking sheet or work surface in a single layer in 8 even portions (roughly 5 ounces each) **(I)**.

8 Assemble the ramen Pour ⅓ cup of the warm shoyu tare and 1 teaspoon of the reserved rendered pork fat into a bowl. Boil 1 portion of noodles in unsalted water just until al dente, about 1 minute. (If you are assembling multiple bowls of ramen, you can cook up to 4 portions of noodles together at the same time.) Drain the noodles well and add to the bowl. Top with ¼ cup of the sofrito and a slice of pork belly. Garnish with scallions and chipotle powder and serve.

MAKE AHEAD The pork belly and its rendered fat, the chile-eggplant sofrito and the shoyu tare can be refrigerated separately for up to 3 days. The 5-ounce portions of noodles can be refrigerated overnight in individual resealable plastic bags or frozen for up to 2 weeks. Cook the noodles from frozen.

Croissants

In Washington, DC, the best power breakfasts involve crackly croissants from Frenchie's bakery. Here, owner Erica Skolnik simplifies the notoriously fussy shaping process by "turning" (rolling out and folding) her butter and dough just two times, not the traditional four.

Frenchie's Croissants

Time	1 hr 15 min active; 10 hr total plus 2 overnight restings
Makes	18 croissants

SPONGE

1¼ cups all-purpose flour

⅔ cup water, at room temperature

One ¼-oz. package active dry yeast

DOUGH

Extra-virgin olive oil, for greasing

1¾ cups plus 1 Tbsp. whole milk

3 cups all-purpose flour

3 cups bread flour

⅓ cup plus 1 Tbsp. sugar

1½ Tbsp. kosher salt

Two ¼-oz. packages active dry yeast

5 sticks (1¼ lbs.) cold unsalted European-style butter (82 percent butterfat), such as Plugrá

2 large eggs

1 Make the sponge In a medium bowl, combine the flour, water and yeast and mix well with a wooden spoon. Cover with plastic wrap and refrigerate overnight.

2 Make the dough Let the sponge stand at room temperature for 30 minutes. Lightly grease a large bowl with olive oil.

3 In a small saucepan, heat the milk until lukewarm. In the bowl of a stand mixer fitted with the dough hook, combine both flours with the sugar, salt and yeast. Scrape in the sponge. At low speed, drizzle in the lukewarm milk and mix just until the dough comes together. Let stand for 10 minutes.

4 Knead the dough at low speed until it forms a ball, about 3 minutes. Transfer to the prepared bowl, cover with plastic wrap and let stand at room temperature for 30 minutes. Punch down and refrigerate for 3 hours.

5 Meanwhile, on a sheet of parchment paper, arrange the sticks of butter side by side so they touch. Cover with another sheet of parchment. Using a rolling pin, pound the butter flat and roll out to a 10-by-12-inch rectangle **(A)**. Refrigerate until ready to use.

6 Remove the butter from the refrigerator and let stand at room temperature for about 10 minutes, until soft and pliable–the butter should yield gently when you press it with your finger and hold the indent, like a ripe avocado. On a lightly floured surface, using a lightly floured rolling pin, roll out the dough to a 12-by-28-inch rectangle. If the dough springs back, cover it with a kitchen towel and let rest for 5 minutes before rolling. Arrange the butter

A

B

C

in the center of the dough so the short sides are parallel. Fold over the 2 short sides of the dough so they meet in the center; pinch together to seal **(B)**. Pinch the long sides of the dough together to completely seal in the butter. Turn the dough so that a long side is facing you and roll out to a 12-by-28-inch rectangle. Starting from the bottom, fold the dough into thirds like a letter **(C)**. Brush off any excess flour and wrap the dough in plastic. Chill until firm but pliable, about 1 hour.

7 Arrange the dough on a lightly floured surface with a short side facing you. Using a lightly floured rolling pin, roll out the dough to a 12-by-28-inch rectangle. Fold into thirds like a letter, wrap in plastic and freeze overnight. Before baking, let thaw in the refrigerator until semi-firm and pliable, about 3 hours.

8 Shape the croissants Line 3 baking sheets with parchment paper. On a lightly floured surface, using a lightly floured rolling pin, roll out the layered dough to a 13-by-36-inch rectangle. Using a pizza cutter or sharp knife, cut the dough crosswise to form nine 13-by-4-inch strips. Halve each strip lengthwise on the diagonal to make 18 long triangles. Starting at the shortest side, roll each triangle into a crescent shape **(D)**. Arrange the croissants on the prepared sheets, tip side down and spaced 3 inches apart. Cover loosely with plastic wrap and let rise at room temperature until doubled in size, 1 to 2 hours.

9 Preheat the oven to 400°. In a small bowl, beat the eggs with 1 tablespoon of water. Brush the croissants with the egg wash **(E)**. Bake until deep golden brown and crisp, 20 to 23 minutes. Transfer the croissants to a rack to cool, then enjoy with butter and jam **(F)**.

MAKE AHEAD The baked croissants can be frozen for 1 month. Reheat in a 350° oven until warm and crisp.

BIGGER IS BETTER

Skolnik makes her croissants larger than the classic kind. "There are more layers to unravel," she says. "People feel like they're getting something special."

D

E

F

Babka

Melissa Weller, master baker of Sadelle's in New York City, is obsessed with breakfast pastries—both eating and making them. Her thickly glazed babkas are next-level delicious, with whorls of chocolate and chocolate-cookie crumbs or raisin-walnut filling inside tender, buttery dough. Learn how she makes these two varieties of the classic and her genius twisting technique.

Raisin-Walnut Babka

Time	1 hr 30 min active; 6 hr total plus overnight resting
Makes	two 9-inch babkas

DOUGH

- 4 cups all-purpose flour, preferably King Arthur
- ⅓ cup plus 2 Tbsp. granulated sugar
- 2 tsp. fine sea salt
- 1 cup whole milk, warmed
- 1 package active dry yeast
- 1 large egg plus 1 large egg yolk
- 1 stick plus 2 Tbsp. unsalted butter, cut into tablespoons, at room temperature
- Baking spray

FILLING

- 3 cups golden raisins, soaked in warm water for 10 minutes and drained
- ¾ cup granulated sugar
- 6 Tbsp. unsalted butter, softened
- 1 Tbsp. ground cinnamon
- 1½ tsp. fine sea salt
- ½ cup dark raisins, soaked in warm water for 10 minutes and drained
- ¾ cup walnuts, toasted and coarsely chopped

GLAZE

- 1 stick unsalted butter
- 6 Tbsp. whole milk
- 1½ cups confectioners' sugar
- 2 Tbsp. ground cinnamon
- ¼ tsp. fine sea salt

1 Make the dough In a medium bowl, whisk the flour with the granulated sugar and salt. In a stand mixer fitted with the dough hook, combine the milk with the yeast and let stand until foamy, about 5 minutes. Add the egg and egg yolk and sprinkle the dry ingredients on top. Mix at low speed for 2 minutes. Scrape down the side of the bowl and mix at medium speed until all of the dry ingredients are incorporated and the dough is smooth, 5 minutes. Add all of the butter at once and mix at low speed until it is fully incorporated and a tacky dough forms, 3 minutes; scrape down the side of the bowl as needed during mixing. Cover the bowl with plastic wrap and let the dough stand at room temperature for 1 hour.

2 Line a large baking sheet with parchment paper and coat the paper generously with nonstick baking spray. Scrape the dough out onto the parchment paper and cut the dough in half. Pat each piece into a neat square. Cover with plastic wrap and refrigerate overnight.

3 Make the filling Combine all of the ingredients except the dark raisins and walnuts in a food processor and puree until smooth.

4 Roll the dough Coat two 9-by-4-inch loaf pans with nonstick baking spray and line with parchment paper, allowing 2 inches of overhang on each of the long sides. Roll out each square of dough to a 16-inch square. Using an offset spatula, spread all but ½ cup of the raisin puree in an even layer over the dough squares to within ½ inch of the edges. Sprinkle the dough evenly with the dark raisins and toasted walnuts. Starting at the edge nearest you, tightly roll up each dough square jelly roll–style into a tight log.

5 Twist the dough Using a sharp knife, cut the logs in half crosswise. Using an offset spatula, spread ¼ cup of the reserved filling on the top and sides of 2 of the halves. Set the other halves on top in the opposite direction to form a cross. Twist the coated and uncoated logs together to form spirals and transfer to the prepared pans. Cover the loaves with a towel and let stand in a warm place until doubled in bulk, about 2 hours.

6 Bake Preheat the oven to 375°. Bake the loaves in the center of the oven for about 45 minutes, until puffed and well browned. Let cool slightly, then use the parchment paper to lift the babkas out of the pans and onto a rack set over a large rimmed baking sheet. Discard the paper.

7 Make the glaze In a small saucepan, melt the butter in the milk. Whisk in the remaining ingredients. Spread the glaze on the warm babkas and let stand until set, about 30 minutes.

(continued on next page)

Chocolate Babka

Time	1 hr 15 min active; 6 hr total plus overnight resting
Makes	two 9-inch babkas

DOUGH

- 4 cups all-purpose flour, preferably King Arthur
- ⅓ cup plus 2 Tbsp. sugar
- 2 tsp. fine sea salt
- 1 cup whole milk, warmed
- 1 package active dry yeast
- 1 large egg plus 1 large egg yolk
- 1 stick plus 2 Tbsp. unsalted butter, cut into tablespoons, at room temperature
-   Baking spray

FILLING

- 9 oz. milk chocolate, finely chopped
- 3 oz. bittersweet chocolate, finely chopped
- 1½ sticks unsalted butter, cubed
- 1½ cups finely ground chocolate wafer cookies
- 3 Tbsp. honey

GLAZE

- 12 oz. bittersweet chocolate, finely chopped
- 4 oz. milk chocolate, finely chopped
- 1½ sticks unsalted butter, cubed
- 2 Tbsp. light corn syrup

1 Make the dough In a medium bowl, whisk the flour with the sugar and salt. In a stand mixer fitted with the dough hook, combine the milk with the yeast and let stand until foamy, about 5 minutes. Add the egg and egg yolk and sprinkle the dry ingredients on top. Mix at low speed for 2 minutes. Scrape down the side of the bowl and mix at medium speed until all of the dry ingredients are incorporated and the dough is smooth, about 5 minutes. Add all of the butter at once and mix at low speed until it is fully incorporated and a tacky dough forms, about 3 minutes; scrape down the side of the bowl as needed during mixing **(A)**. Cover the bowl with plastic wrap and let the dough stand at room temperature for 1 hour.

2 Line a large baking sheet with parchment paper and coat the paper generously with nonstick baking spray. Scrape the dough out onto the parchment paper and cut the dough in half. Pat each piece into a neat square. Cover with plastic wrap and refrigerate overnight.

3 Make the filling In a large heatproof bowl set over a saucepan of simmering water, melt both chocolates with the butter, stirring occasionally, until smooth. Let cool to room temperature, then stir in the cookie crumbs and honey.

4 Roll the dough Coat two 9-by-4-inch loaf pans with nonstick baking spray and line with parchment paper, allowing 2 inches of overhang on each of the long sides. Roll out each square of dough to a 16-inch square **(B)**. Using an offset spatula, spread all but ½ cup of the filling in an even layer over the dough squares to within ½ inch of the edges **(C)**. Starting at the edge nearest you, tightly roll up each dough square jelly roll–style into a tight log **(D)**.

5 Twist the dough Using a sharp knife, cut the logs in half crosswise. Using an offset spatula, spread ¼ cup of the reserved filling on the top and sides of 2 of the halves. Set the other halves on top in the opposite direction to form a cross **(E)**. Twist the coated and uncoated logs together to form spirals **(F)**. Transfer the loaves to the prepared pans, cover them with a towel and let stand in a warm place until doubled in bulk, about 2 hours **(G)**.

6 Bake Preheat the oven to 375°. Bake the loaves in the center of the oven for about 45 minutes, until puffed and well browned. Let cool slightly, then use the parchment paper to lift the babkas out of the pans and onto a rack set over a baking sheet. Discard the paper.

7 Make the glaze In a heatproof bowl set over a saucepan of simmering water, melt both chocolates with the butter; stir until smooth. Stir in the corn syrup. Spread the glaze on top of the warm babkas and let stand until set, about 30 minutes **(H)**.

RAISING THE BABKA BAR

Weller spreads the filling on the inside and outside of the dough before twisting, which guarantees an ample swirl. Then, instead of the usual crumb topping, she opts for a thick glaze—chocolate, as in the recipe here, or cinnamon, for the raisin-walnut version.

A

B

C

D

E

F

G

H

A

B

C

D

E

F

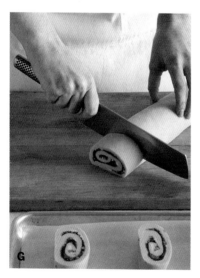

G

H

I

Cinnamon Rolls

Pastry chef Megan Garrelts has a cult following for her all-American sweets. At Bluestem in Kansas City, Missouri, her cinnamon rolls require at least two days to make, and they're served one at a time in individual mini skillets. In this streamlined method, the rolls are swirled with pecans, sugar, cinnamon and sour cream, then baked in big batches.

Glazed Cinnamon Rolls with Pecan Swirls

Time	1 hour active
	10 hr 30 min total
Makes	2 dozen rolls

DOUGH

- 2¼ tsp. instant dry yeast
- 2 Tbsp. warm water
- ¼ cup plus 1 tsp. granulated sugar
- 6 large eggs
- 4½ cups sifted all-purpose flour (1¼ lbs.), plus more for rolling
- 1½ tsp. salt
- 3 sticks unsalted butter, cut into ½-inch cubes and chilled

FILLING

- 4 oz. pecans (1 cup)
- 1½ cups packed light brown sugar
- 1 Tbsp. cinnamon
- 1 cup sour cream
- 2 large eggs beaten with ¼ cup of water

SUGAR GLAZE

- 1½ cups confectioners' sugar
- 4 Tbsp. unsalted butter, softened
- ¼ cup heavy cream
- 1 tsp. pure vanilla extract

MAKE-AHEAD TIP

The unbaked cinnamon rolls and sugar glaze can be frozen separately for up to 1 month.

1 Make the dough In a medium bowl, combine the yeast with the warm water and 1 teaspoon of the granulated sugar and let stand until foamy, about 5 minutes. Whisk in the 6 eggs **(A)**. In a stand mixer fitted with the dough hook, mix the 4½ cups of sifted flour with the salt and the remaining ¼ cup of granulated sugar. Add the egg mixture and beat at medium speed until the dough is just moistened and very stiff. Add the butter a few cubes at a time, waiting until it is partially kneaded into the dough before adding more **(B)**. Continue kneading until the butter is fully incorporated and the dough is silky, 8 to 10 minutes. Transfer the dough to an oiled bowl, cover with plastic wrap and refrigerate until chilled and slightly risen, at least 2 hours or overnight **(C)**.

2 Make the filling Preheat the oven to 350°. Spread the pecans in a pie plate and toast for about 8 minutes, until fragrant and browned. Let cool, then finely chop the pecans. Transfer to a medium bowl and stir in the brown sugar and cinnamon **(D)**.

3 Line 2 baking sheets with parchment paper. On a floured surface, cut the dough into 2 pieces. Working with 1 piece at a time (while keeping the other refrigerated), roll the dough out to a 12-by-16-inch rectangle. Transfer the dough to a baking sheet and refrigerate until chilled. Repeat with the remaining dough.

4 Spread half of the sour cream over 1 sheet of dough, leaving a ½-inch border all around. Sprinkle with half of the pecan filling **(E)**. Brush the long sides with some of the egg wash. Roll up the dough from a long side into a tight cylinder and pinch the ends to seal **(F)**. Freeze the dough log until it is chilled, about 2 hours. Repeat with the remaining dough, sour cream and filling. Cover and refrigerate the remaining egg wash.

5 Transfer the logs to a work surface and cut each one into 12 even slices. Set the slices on the baking sheet, cut side up **(G)**. Cover with plastic wrap and freeze until firm, at least 3 hours and preferably overnight.

6 Unwrap the rolls and let stand at room temperature for 1 hour.

7 Preheat the oven to 350°. Brush the tops and sides of the rolls with the egg wash **(H)**. Bake in the center of the oven for 35 to 40 minutes, until golden and risen.

8 Meanwhile, make the sugar glaze In a medium bowl, using a hand mixer, beat the confectioners' sugar with the butter, cream and vanilla until thick and smooth. Spread the glaze on the hot cinnamon rolls and let cool for 20 minutes before serving **(I)**.

Ice Cream Cake

Laura Sawicki loves celebrating birthdays. At Launderette in Austin, she makes an epic layered ice cream birthday cake that's a nostalgic nod to the Carvel and Baskin-Robbins creations she adored as a kid. The recipe she shares here—with a devil's food base, cold hot fudge, chocolate crunchies and a seriously thick chocolate ganache glaze—will make chocoholics swoon.

Ice Cream Birthday Cake

| Time | 1 hr 30 min active; 5 hr total plus overnight freezing |
| Makes | 16 servings |

DEVIL'S FOOD CAKE

- 1 cup all-purpose flour
- ½ tsp. baking powder
- ½ tsp. baking soda
- ½ tsp. kosher salt
- ½ cup plus 1 Tbsp. unsweetened cocoa powder
- ½ cup hot water
- 4 Tbsp. unsalted butter, at room temperature
- 1¾ cups dark brown sugar
- 1 large egg plus 1 large egg yolk
- ½ cup buttermilk
- ½ tsp. pure vanilla extract

HOT FUDGE

- 1 cup heavy cream
- 6 Tbsp. dark brown sugar
- 4½ Tbsp. unsweetened cocoa powder
- ¼ cup plus 2 Tbsp. light corn syrup
- 9 oz. bittersweet chocolate, coarsely chopped
- 1½ Tbsp. unsalted butter
- ½ tsp. kosher salt

CAKE ASSEMBLY

- 2 pints chocolate chip ice cream, softened slightly
- 2 pints strawberry ice cream, softened slightly
- 2½ cups heavy cream, chilled
- 3 Tbsp. granulated sugar
- 8 oz. bittersweet chocolate, coarsely chopped
- Maraschino cherries and rainbow sprinkles, for decorating (optional)

1 Make the devil's food cake Preheat the oven to 350°. Spray an 8-inch springform pan with nonstick cooking spray. In a medium bowl, whisk the flour with the baking powder, baking soda and salt. In a small bowl, whisk the cocoa powder with the hot water until a smooth paste forms. In the bowl of a stand mixer fitted with the paddle, beat the butter with the brown sugar at moderate speed for 3 minutes. Beat in the egg, egg yolk, buttermilk and vanilla. At low speed, beat in the dry ingredients and cocoa paste in 2 alternating batches.

2 Scrape the batter into the prepared pan **(A)**. Bake for 30 to 35 minutes, until a toothpick inserted in the center comes out with a few moist crumbs attached. Let the cake cool for 15 minutes, then remove the ring and let the cake cool completely on a rack. Leave the oven on.

3 Using a serrated knife, cut a ¼-inch-thick layer off the top of the cake **(B)**. In a food processor, pulse the cake top until fine crumbs form. Spread the crumbs on a small rimmed baking sheet and bake for 10 to 12 minutes, turning the pan halfway through, until the crumbs are crisp **(C)**. Let the crunchies cool completely.

4 Make the hot fudge In a small saucepan, combine the cream with the brown sugar, cocoa powder and corn syrup and bring to a boil over moderate heat, whisking constantly. Reduce the heat to low and simmer for 1 minute. Remove from the heat and add the chocolate, butter and salt; whisk until smooth. Scrape the hot fudge into a bowl and let cool to room temperature.

5 Assemble the cake Using scissors, trim a sheet of clear acetate to 6-by-24 inches. Wrap the acetate around the cake and secure it with tape. Secure the springform pan ring around the acetate-wrapped cake **(D)**.

6 Using an offset spatula, spread half of the hot fudge evenly over the cake **(E)**. Top with half of the cake crunchies Freeze until the fudge is firm, about 20 minutes.

7 Using the spatula, spread the chocolate chip ice cream over the fudge layer **(F)**. Top with the remaining cake crunchies and press down to help them adhere. Freeze the cake for 20 minutes, until firm.

(continued on page 251)

A

B

C

D

E

F

G

H

I

8 Remove the cake from the freezer and spread the remaining fudge over the crunchies. Freeze for 20 minutes. Spread the strawberry ice cream over the fudge and freeze for another 20 minutes.

9 In the bowl of a stand mixer fitted with the whisk, beat 1½ cups of the heavy cream with the granulated sugar until it holds soft peaks. Spread 2 cups of the whipped cream over the strawberry ice cream layer; refrigerate the rest of the whipped cream for decorating. Freeze the cake overnight.

10 Place the chocolate in a heatproof medium bowl. In a small saucepan, bring the remaining 1 cup of heavy cream to a boil. Pour the hot cream over the chocolate and let stand until melted, about 5 minutes **(G)**. Stir until smooth, then tap the bowl on the counter to pop any air bubbles. Let the ganache cool down to 80°, about 30 minutes.

11 Carefully remove the springform ring and peel the acetate off the cake **(H)**. Transfer the cake to a rack set over a rimmed baking sheet. Working quickly, pour the ganache onto the center of the cake in one fluid motion, allowing the excess to drip over the side. Freeze the cake until the ganache is firm, about 30 minutes.

12 Meanwhile, whisk the reserved whipped cream until stiff peaks form. Transfer to a pastry bag fitted with a star tip. Pipe whipped cream around the edge of the cake and garnish with maraschino cherries and rainbow sprinkles, if desired. Freeze the cake for 30 minutes before serving **(I)**.

MAKE AHEAD The cake can be assembled through Step 11; once the ganache is firm, wrap the cake in plastic and freeze for up to 1 week. Decorate the cake the day you plan to serve it. For neat slices, use a sharp knife warmed in hot water and wipe it off between cuts.

SMOOTH FINISH

You'll need an acetate collar to make this tall cake. You can buy them presized or cut one yourself with scissors. They're readily available at baking supply stores and from amazon.com.

Cultured Butter

It doesn't take much more than a brief lapse in attention to make butter, as anyone who's mistakenly whipped heavy cream for too long well knows. The European-style cultured variety, however, doesn't happen by accident. Adeline Druart of the excellent Vermont Creamery shows how to make the pleasingly tangy and nutty butter at home using a stand mixer as a churner.

European-Style Cultured Butter

Time	1 hr plus 1 to 2 days culturing
Makes	¾ lb

1 qt. good-quality heavy cream (at least 40 percent butterfat)

⅓ cup buttermilk or crème fraîche

Ice water

1 In a large bowl, whisk the heavy cream with the buttermilk or crème fraîche. Cover with plastic wrap and let stand at room temperature until thickened, at least 12 hours and up to 48 hours.

2 Scrape the cultured cream into the bowl of a stand mixer, cover with plastic wrap and refrigerate until well chilled, about 45 minutes.

3 Cover the rim of the bowl well with plastic to catch any splatter; alternatively, use the pouring-shield attachment. Beat the cultured cream with the whisk at high speed until the butter solids start to form a ball, about 4 minutes **(A)**. Drain the butter solids in a fine sieve set over a bowl and reserve the buttermilk for another use **(B)**.

4 Transfer the butter to a large bowl and, using gloved hands or a large fork, knead to expel any excess buttermilk. Pour ¼ cup of ice water over the butter, knead and drain **(C)**. Repeat, adding ice water, kneading and draining 3 more times. Continue kneading until the butter no longer expels any water.

5 Form the butter into a cylinder or block, wrap it in cheesecloth and gently squeeze to remove any remaining moisture. Discard the cheesecloth and wrap the butter tightly in plastic, followed by parchment paper, and refrigerate for up to 1 week.

WASTE NOT, WANT NOT

The leftover cultured buttermilk in Step 3 can be refrigerated for up to 6 days and used for making biscuits and pastries, or for culturing heavy cream for another batch of butter.

A

B

C

Cultured Butter
page 252

Marmalade
page 257

Marmalade

In its complex balance of bitter and sweet, marmalade is the thinking man's answer to jelly and jam. Rachel Saunders of California's Blue Chair Fruit Company shows how to make three of her artisanal preserves using the same lemon jelly base. The recipes take three days to make, but the active time is minimal—just two hours. Follow our instructions for an easy-to-follow play-by-play.

Valencia Orange Marmalade

Time	2 hr active
	3 days total
Makes	ten ½-pt jars

LEMON JELLY BASE

2 lbs. lemons, cut into 8 wedges each

MARMALADE

2 lbs. Valencia oranges—cut lengthwise into 8 wedges each, seeded and very thinly sliced crosswise

8 cups sugar (3½ lbs.)

¼ cup fresh lemon juice

1 On Day 1, start the lemon jelly base In a large nonreactive saucepan, cover the lemon wedges with 2 inches of water (about 8 cups) and let stand at room temperature overnight.

2 Meanwhile, start the marmalade In another large nonreactive saucepan, cover the oranges with 2 inches of water (about 8 cups). Let stand overnight.

3 On Day 2, finish the lemon jelly base Bring the lemons to a boil. Simmer over moderate heat, stirring occasionally, until the lemons are very tender and the liquid is reduced by half, about 2 hours and 15 minutes. Pour the lemons into a fine sieve set over a large heatproof bowl; let cool completely. Cover the sieve and bowl with plastic wrap and let drain overnight at room temperature; discard the lemon wedges.

4 Meanwhile, continue making the marmalade Bring the oranges to a boil and simmer over moderate heat, stirring occasionally, until the oranges are very tender, about 40 minutes. Let stand covered at room temperature overnight.

5 On Day 3, finish the marmalade Add the lemon jelly base to the oranges in the saucepan. Stir in the sugar and lemon juice and bring to a boil. Simmer over moderate heat, without stirring, until the marmalade darkens slightly, about 30 minutes; skim off any foam as necessary.

6 Test for doneness Spoon 1 tablespoon of the marmalade onto a chilled plate and refrigerate until it is room temperature, about 3 minutes; the marmalade is ready when it thickens like jelly and a spoon leaves a trail when dragged through it. If it's not ready yet, continue simmering and testing every 10 minutes until it passes the test, up to 1½ hours.

7 Jar the marmalade Spoon the marmalade into ten ½-pint canning jars, leaving ¼ inch of space at the top. Screw on the lids. Using canning tongs, lower the jars into a large pot of boiling water; boil for 15 minutes. Remove the jars with the tongs; let stand until the lids seal. Store the marmalade in a cool, dark place for up to 6 months.

(continued on next page)

Lemon Marmalade

Time | 2 hr active
     | 3 days total
Makes | ten ½-pt jars

LEMON JELLY BASE

2 lbs. lemons, cut into 8 wedges each

MARMALADE

2 lbs. lemons—cut lengthwise into 8 wedges each, seeded and very thinly sliced crosswise

8½ cups sugar (3¾ lbs.)

¼ cup fresh lemon juice

1 On Day 1, start the lemon jelly base In a large nonreactive saucepan, cover the lemon wedges with 2 inches of water (about 8 cups) and let stand at room temperature overnight **(A)**.

2 On Day 2, finish the lemon jelly base Bring the lemon wedges to a boil. Simmer over moderate heat, stirring occasionally, until the lemons are very tender and the liquid is reduced by half, about 2 hours and 15 minutes **(B)**. Pour the lemon wedges into a fine sieve set over a large heatproof bowl; let cool completely **(C)**. Cover the sieve and bowl with plastic wrap and let drain overnight at room temperature; discard the lemon wedges.

3 Meanwhile, start the marmalade In a large nonreactive saucepan, cover the lemon slices with 2 inches of water (about 8 cups) **(D)**. Bring to a boil, then simmer over moderately high heat for 5 minutes, stirring occasionally **(E)**. Drain the lemon slices in a fine strainer; discard the cooking liquid **(F)**. Return the lemon slices to the saucepan and cover with 1 inch of water (about 4 cups). Bring to a boil and simmer over moderate heat, stirring occasionally, until the lemons are very tender, about 40 minutes; let stand covered at room temperature overnight.

4 On Day 3, finish the marmalade Add the lemon jelly base to the lemon slices in the saucepan. Stir in the sugar and lemon juice and bring to a boil. Simmer over moderate heat, without stirring, until the marmalade darkens slightly, about 30 minutes; skim off any foam as necessary **(G)**.

5 Test for doneness Spoon 1 tablespoon of the marmalade onto a chilled plate and refrigerate until it is room temperature, about 3 minutes **(H)**. The marmalade is ready when it thickens like jelly and a spoon leaves a trail when dragged through it **(I)**. If it's not ready yet, continue simmering and testing every 10 minutes until it passes the test, up to 1½ hours.

6 Jar the marmalade Spoon the marmalade into ten ½-pint canning jars, leaving ¼ inch of space at the top. Screw on the lids. Using canning tongs, lower the jars into a large pot of boiling water; boil for 15 minutes. Remove the jars with the tongs; let stand until the lids seal. Store the marmalade in a cool, dark place for up to 6 months.

MEYER LEMON VARIATION Prepare the lemon jelly base as described in Steps 1 and 2 above. On Day 2, cut 2 lbs. Meyer lemons lengthwise into 8 wedges each, then seed them and very thinly slice them crosswise. Add the lemon slices to a large nonreactive saucepan, cover with 1 inch of water (about 4 cups) and let stand covered at room temperature overnight.

On Day 3, bring the Meyer lemons to a boil. Simmer over moderate heat, stirring occasionally, until the lemons are very tender, about 40 minutes. Add the lemon jelly base to the saucepan. Stir in 7½ cups sugar and ¼ cup fresh lemon juice and bring to a boil. Simmer over moderate heat, without stirring, until the marmalade darkens slightly, about 30 minutes; skim off any foam as necessary. Proceed with Steps 5 and 6 above.

SWEET TALK

"People are shocked by how much sugar goes into marmalade," says Saunders. "But the sugar acts as a thickener." If you skimp, the preserves may not set.

Bitters

"People say bitters are the salt and pepper of the bar, but really, they're like the spice rack," says Brad Thomas Parsons, the mixologist author of *Bitters*. Infused with herbs and roots, these intensely flavored concoctions add depth and balance to mixed drinks. Here, Parsons shares three recipes inspired by what he calls "the holy trinity"—Angostura (woodsy and spiced), Peychaud's (anise-scented) and orange—along with the best cocktail recipes to show them off.

Cranberry-Anise Bitters

Time	20 min plus about 3 weeks steeping
Makes	14 oz

- 2 cups high-proof vodka (such as Stolichnaya Blue 100 Proof)
- 1½ cups fresh or thawed frozen cranberries, each one pierced with a toothpick
- 1 cup dried cranberries
- 2 Tbsp. chopped candied ginger
- 2 star anise pods
- One 3-inch cinnamon stick
- One 1-inch piece of fresh ginger, peeled and sliced ¼ inch thick
- 1 tsp. gentian root (see below)
- ½ tsp. white peppercorns
- 2 Tbsp. simple syrup (see Note)

1 In a 1-quart glass jar, combine all of the ingredients except the syrup. Cover and shake well. Let stand in a cool, dark place for 2 weeks, shaking the jar daily.

2 Strain the infused alcohol into a clean 1-quart glass jar through a cheesecloth-lined funnel. Squeeze any infused alcohol from the cheesecloth into the jar; reserve the solids. Strain the infused alcohol again through new cheesecloth into another clean jar to remove any remaining sediment. Cover the jar and set aside for 1 week.

3 Meanwhile, transfer the solids to a small saucepan. Add 1 cup of water and bring to a boil. Cover and simmer over low heat for 10 minutes; let cool completely. Pour the liquid and solids into a clean 1-quart glass jar. Cover and let stand at room temperature for 1 week, shaking the jar once daily.

4 Strain the water mixture through a cheesecloth-lined funnel set over a clean 1-quart glass jar; discard the solids. If necessary, strain again to remove any remaining sediment. Add the infused alcohol and the syrup. Cover and let stand at room temperature for 3 days. Pour the bitters through a cheesecloth-lined funnel or strainer and transfer to glass dasher bottles. Cover and keep in a cool, dark place.

NOTE To make simple syrup, in a small saucepan, dissolve 1 cup of granulated sugar in 1 cup of water over moderate heat. Let cool before using, and reserve the rest for another use.

MAKE AHEAD The bitters can be stored at room temperature indefinitely. For best flavor, use within 1 year.

BITTERS GLOSSARY

Sarsaparilla A vine with the flavor of root beer.

Cassia chips Cinnamon-flavored bark from Asia.

Devil's club root Has a deeply woodsy scent.

Black walnut leaf A tannic, mildly bitter ingredient.

Gentian root From a mountain plant; very bitter.

Wild cherry bark Has a slight cherry-fruit aroma.

Cinchona bark The natural source of anti-malarial quinine.

All of these ingredients are sold at dandelionbotanical.com.

CRANBERRY-SPICE COCKTAIL

Mince two 1-inch pieces of candied ginger, transfer to a cocktail shaker and muddle with 1 orange wedge and 10 cranberries. Add 2 oz. Aperol, 1 oz. Lillet blanc, 4 dashes of Cranberry-Anise or Peychaud's bitters and ice. Shake well. Double-strain the drink into an ice-filled Collins glass and top with 4 oz. hard cider. Garnish with 3 cranberries skewered on a pick with a slice of candied ginger. Makes 1 drink.

Woodland Bitters

Time	20 min plus about 3 weeks steeping
Makes	14 oz

2 cups overproof bourbon (such as Wild Turkey 101)

1 cup pecans, toasted

1 cup walnuts, toasted

4 cloves

Two 3-inch cinnamon sticks

1 whole nutmeg, cracked

1 vanilla bean, split

2 Tbsp. devil's club root

1 Tbsp. cinchona bark

1 Tbsp. chopped black walnut leaf

1 Tbsp. wild cherry bark

½ tsp. cassia chips

½ tsp. gentian root

½ tsp. sarsaparilla root

3 Tbsp. pure maple syrup

1 In a 1-quart glass jar, combine all of the ingredients except the syrup. Cover and shake well. Let stand in a cool, dark place for 2 weeks, shaking the jar daily.

2 Strain the infused alcohol into a clean 1-quart glass jar through a cheesecloth-lined funnel. Squeeze any infused alcohol from the cheesecloth into the jar; reserve the solids. Strain the infused alcohol again through new cheesecloth into another clean jar to remove any remaining sediment. Cover the jar and set aside for 1 week.

3 Meanwhile, transfer the solids to a small saucepan. Add 1 cup of water and bring to a boil. Cover and simmer over low heat for 10 minutes; let cool completely. Pour the liquid and solids into a clean 1-quart glass jar. Cover and let stand at room temperature for 1 week, shaking the jar once daily.

4 Strain the water mixture through a cheesecloth-lined funnel set over a clean 1-quart glass jar; discard the solids. If necessary, strain again to remove any remaining sediment. Add the infused alcohol and the syrup. Cover and let stand at room temperature for 3 days. Pour the bitters through a cheesecloth-lined funnel or strainer and transfer to glass dasher bottles. Cover and keep in a cool, dark place.

MAKE AHEAD The bitters can be stored at room temperature indefinitely. For best flavor, use within 1 year.

HARVEST COCKTAIL

In a medium saucepan, combine ½ cup water, ½ cup sugar and 2 cinnamon sticks. Boil over moderately high heat, stirring occasionally, until the sugar is dissolved, about 5 minutes. Let the syrup cool. Discard the cinnamon sticks. In an ice-filled cocktail shaker, combine ½ tablespoon of the cinnamon syrup with 2 oz. apple brandy, ½ oz. Snap liqueur and 4 dashes of Woodland or Angostura bitters. Shake well. Strain the drink into an ice-filled rocks glass and garnish with an apple slice. Makes 1 drink.

TASTE TEST

To understand how bitters can enhance a drink, Parsons suggests mixing a Manhattan with and without them: "One will be beautifully complex, and the other will be overly sweet and cloying."

Figgy-Orange Bitters

Time	20 min plus about 3 weeks steeping
Makes	14 oz

- 2 cups overproof bourbon (such as Wild Turkey 101)
- 1 cup dried figs (about 6 oz.), halved
- 8 green cardamom pods, crushed
- 4 cloves
- 2 fresh figs, halved
- Strips of zest from 3 oranges
- 1 Tbsp. cinchona bark
- ½ tsp. gentian root
- ¼ cup dried orange peel
- One 3-inch cinnamon stick
- 1 vanilla bean, split
- 2 Tbsp. rich syrup (see Note)

1 In a 1-quart glass jar, combine all of the ingredients except the syrup. Cover and shake well. Let stand in a cool, dark place for 2 weeks, shaking the jar daily.

2 Strain the infused alcohol into a clean 1-quart glass jar through a cheesecloth-lined funnel. Squeeze any infused alcohol from the cheesecloth into the jar; reserve the solids. Strain the infused alcohol again through new cheesecloth into another clean jar to remove any remaining sediment. Cover the jar and set aside for 1 week.

3 Meanwhile, transfer the solids to a small saucepan. Add 1 cup of water and bring to a boil. Cover and simmer over low heat for 10 minutes; let cool completely. Pour the liquid and solids into a clean 1-quart glass jar. Cover and let stand at room temperature for 1 week, shaking the jar once daily.

4 Strain the water mixture through a cheesecloth-lined funnel set over a clean 1-quart glass jar; discard the solids. If necessary, strain again to remove any remaining sediment. Add the infused alcohol and the syrup. Cover and let stand at room temperature for 3 days. Pour the bitters through a cheesecloth-lined funnel or strainer and transfer to glass dasher bottles. Cover and keep in a cool, dark place.

NOTE To make rich syrup, in a small saucepan, dissolve 2 cups of demerara or turbinado sugar in 1 cup of water over moderate heat. Let cool before using, and reserve the rest for another use.

MAKE AHEAD The bitters can be stored at room temperature indefinitely. For best flavor, use within 1 year.

FIGGY-ORANGE COCKTAIL

In an ice-filled cocktail shaker, combine 2 oz. bourbon, ½ oz. Punt e Mes, 1 Tbsp. fresh orange juice, ½ Tbsp. simple syrup (see Note on p. 261) and 4 dashes of Figgy-Orange or Regan's Orange Bitters No. 6. Shake well. Strain the drink into a chilled coupe and garnish with freshly grated nutmeg. Makes 1 drink.

BITTERS BACKSTORY

Sometimes still marketed as digestive aids, bitters were once sold as medicine; they later became a key ingredient in classic drinks like the Manhattan. Today's craft-cocktail enthusiasts are resurrecting 100-year-old "lost" bitters recipes and creating out-there new flavors like Jamaican jerk and Mexican mole.

Spicy Mapo Tofu Dumplings
Page 148

INDEX

A

ALMONDS
Almond Milk, **206,** 207
Catalan Fish Stew, 73
Chicken Tikka Masala, 84, **85**
Mixed-Nut Milk, **206,** 208
Mixed-Nut-Milk Panna
  Cotta, 208, **209**
APPLES
Apple-Brined Turkey, 16, **17**
Double-Crust Apple-Apricot
  Pie, 120, **122**
Four-Herb Turkey with Crispy Skin, 19
Homemade Sauerkraut with Caraway
  and Apples, 100, **101**
ARUGULA
Soft-Shell Crab Sandwiches with
  Pancetta and Remoulade, **78,** 79
Squash and Arugula Pizza, **66,** 67

B

BACON
Beef Medallions with Bacon
  and Carrots, 29
Beef Medallions with Bacon
  and Morels, **28,** 29
French (Canadian) Onion
  Soup, 144, **145**
Soft-Shell Crab Sandwiches with
  Pancetta and Remoulade, **78,** 79
BASIL
Chicken-and-Seafood Paella
  with Allioli, **230,** 231
Chicken Pho, **86,** 87
Green Curry Chicken, **90,** 91
Margherita Pizza, **63,** 67
Provençal-Style Chicken
  Sausage, 169

PAGE NUMBERS
IN **BOLD** INDICATE
PHOTOGRAPHS.

Uovo in Raviolo with Hand-Grated-
  Tomato Sauce, **226,** 227
BEEF. See also VEAL
Barbacoa Beef Tacos with
  Two Sauces, 170, **171**
Beef Chuck Eye Roast with Paprika-
  Herb Rub, 26, **27**
Beef Medallions with Bacon and
  Carrots, 29
Beef Medallions with Bacon and
  Morels, **28,** 29
Black Pepper Jerky, 52
Cheddar-and-Onion Smashed
  Burgers, 22, **23**
Lemon-and-Garlic-Marinated
  Flat Iron Steak, 29
Red Wine Vinegar–Marinated
  Flat Iron Steak, 29
Sweet and Spicy Jerky, 52, **53**
Umami Burgers with Port and
  Stilton, **24,** 25
BEETS
Seakraut, **101,** 103
BERRIES
Blueberry-Nectarine
  Pandowdy, 36, **37**
Cranberry-Anise Bitters, **260,** 261
Cranberry-Spice Cocktail, **260,** 261
Doughnuts with Tart Cranberry
  Glaze, **190,** 191
Mixed-Berry Conserve, 114, **115**
Mixed-Fruit Cornmeal Cobbler, **38,** 39
Rosé Vermouth, **142,** 210
Strawberry Sauce, 40, **41**
**BREADS. See also PIZZA;
SANDWICHES**
Chocolate Babka, **242,** 244
Croissants, **1,** 240
Crusty White Bread, 182, **183**
German-Style Pretzels, 186, **187**
Glazed Cinnamon Rolls with Pecan
  Swirls, **246,** 247
Jessamyn's Sephardic
  Challah, **184,** 185
Orange Popovers, 106, **107**
Oversize Breakfast Biscuits, 30, **31**
Parker House Rolls, **180,** 181
Raisin-Walnut Babka, **242,** 243
Scandinavian Rye Bread, **104,** 105

BREAKFAST & BRUNCH
Almond Milk, **206,** 207
Chocolate Babka, **242,** 244
Croissants, **1,** 240
Glazed Cinnamon Rolls with Pecan
  Swirls, **246,** 247
Greek-Style Yogurt, **112,** 113
Gruyère Cheese Soufflé, **108,** 109
Mixed-Nut Milk, **206,** 208
Orange Popovers, 106, **107**
Oversize Breakfast Biscuits, 30, **31**
Pastrami Breakfast Biscuit, 30
Raisin-Walnut Babka, **242,** 243
Rothschild Soufflé, 110, **111**
Sausage-Cheddar Breakfast
  Biscuit, 30
Strawberry Jam Breakfast Biscuit, 30
Vanilla Raised Doughnuts, 188, **189**
BURGERS
Cheddar-and-Onion Smashed
  Burgers, 22, **23**
Umami Burgers with Port and
  Stilton, **24,** 25
BUTTERMILK
Creole-Spiced Fried Chicken, **82,** 83
Double-Chocolate Layer
  Cake, **116,** 118
European-Style Cultured
  Butter, 252, **254**
Ice Cream Birthday Cake, 248, **249**
Mixed-Fruit Cornmeal Cobbler, **38,** 39
Oversize Breakfast Biscuits, 30, **31**

C

CABBAGE
Homemade Sauerkraut with
  Caraway and Apples, 100, **101**
Indian-Spiced Sauerkraut, **101,** 102
Seakraut, **101,** 103
CAKES
Brown-Butter Layer Cake, **116,** 117
Concord Cake, **198,** 199
Double-Chocolate Layer
  Cake, **116,** 118
Hazelnut-and-Chocolate Meringue
  Cake, **202,** 203

Ice Cream Birthday Cake, 248, **249**

CANDY & CONFECTIONS
Chai Caramels with Salted
 Pepitas, **136,** 137
Cinnamon Marshmallows, **195,** 197
Citrus Lollipops, 134, **135**
Coconut-Lime
 Marshmallows, **195,** 197
Hazelnut Marshmallows, **195,** 197
Light and Fluffy
 Marshmallows, **195,** 196
Miracle Peanut Butter
 Crunch, 204, **205**
Soft and Chewy
 Marshmallows, **195,** 197
Vanilla-Mint Marshmallows, **132,** 133

CARROTS
Barbacoa Beef Tacos with
 Two Sauces, 170, **171**
Beef Medallions with Bacon
 and Carrots, 29
Braised Lamb Neck with
 Turnip, **98,** 99
Carrot and Ricotta Ravioli, **154,** 155
Classic Chicken Stock, **54,** 55
Four-Herb Turkey with Crispy Skin, 19
Osso Buco with Citrus
 Gremolata, **94,** 95
Roasted Carrot Puree Lasagna
 Topping, 225

CELERY
Barbacoa Beef Tacos with
 Two Sauces, 170, **171**
Bouillabaisse à l'Américaine, **160,** 161
Braised Lamb Neck with
 Turnip, **98,** 99
Four-Herb Turkey with Crispy Skin, 19
Master Fish Stock, 70
Osso Buco with Citrus
 Gremolata, **94,** 95
Seafood Gumbo, **74,** 75
Slow-Cooked Duck with Green Olives
 and Herbes de Provence, **164,** 165

CHEESE. See also PARMESAN; RICOTTA
Cheddar-and-Onion Smashed
 Burgers, 22, **23**
Creamy White Lasagna with
 Toppings, 223, **225**
French (Canadian) Onion
 Soup, 144, **145**
Fresh Mozzarella, 48, **49**
Gougères, 126
Gruyère Cheese Soufflé, **108,** 109
Macaroni and Cheese with Buttery
 Crumbs, **14,** 15
Margherita Pizza, **63,** 67
Sausage and Olive Pizza, **66,** 67
Sausage-Cheddar Breakfast
 Biscuit, 30

Squash and Arugula Pizza, **66,** 67
Umami Burgers with Port and
 Stilton, **24,** 25
Uovo in Raviolo with Hand-Grated-
 Tomato Sauce, **226,** 227

CHICKEN
Chicken-and-Seafood Paella
 with Allioli, **230,** 231
Chicken Pho, **86,** 87
Chicken Tikka Masala, 84, **85**
Classic Chicken Stock, **54,** 55
Creole-Spiced Fried Chicken, **82,** 83
David Chang's Freeze-Dried
 Chicken Stock, 55
Green Curry Chicken, **90,** 91
Provençal-Style Chicken
 Sausage, 169
Silky Hot and Sour Soup, 56, **57**

CHILES
Barbacoa Beef Tacos with
 Two Sauces, 170, **171**
Chicken Tikka Masala, 84, **85**
Chile-Eggplant Mazemen Ramen
 with Pork Belly, 236, **237**
Fiery Moroccan Lamb
 Merguez, 166, **167**
Green Curry Chicken, **90,** 91
Happy Pancakes, **58,** 59
Hmong Spicy Pork Sausage, 169
Hyderabadi Lamb Biryani, **176,** 177
Salsa Verde Cruda, 170
Spicy Mapo Tofu Dumplings, 148, **149**
Tamales with Red-Chile-Braised
 Pork, **172,** 173

CHIVES
Spicy Mapo Tofu Dumplings, 148, **149**

CHOCOLATE
Chocolate Babka, **242,** 244
Chocolate Corn-Flake
 Clusters, 44, **45**
Chocolate-Hazelnut
 Baklava, **124,** 125
Concord Cake, **198,** 199
Cream Puffs with Chocolate Pastry
 Cream, 126, **127**
Dark Chocolate Mousse
 Filling, **116,** 119
Double-Chocolate Layer
 Cake, **116,** 118
Hazelnut-and-Chocolate Meringue
 Cake, **202,** 203
Hot Fudge Sauce, 40, **41**
Ice Cream Birthday Cake, 248, **249**
Rich Chocolate Buttercream, **116,** 119

CILANTRO
Barbacoa Beef Tacos with
 Two Sauces, 170, **171**
Chicken Pho, **86,** 87
Green Curry Chicken, **90,** 91
Hyderabadi Lamb Biryani, **176,** 177
Salsa Verde Cruda, 170

CINNAMON
Cinnamon Marshmallows, **195,** 197
Glazed Cinnamon Rolls with Pecan
 Swirls, **246,** 247
Harvest Cocktail, 262

COCONUT
Coconut–Lime
 Marshmallows, **195,** 196
Doughnuts with Kaffir Lime–Coconut
 Glaze, **191,** 192
Green Chicken Curry, **90,** 91

COFFEE
Sweet and Spicy Jerky, 52, **53**

**CONDIMENTS, PRESERVES & SPREADS.
See also PICKLES**
European-Style Cultured
 Butter, 252, **254**
Ginger-Peach Conserve, 114, **115**
Lemon Marmalade, **256,** 258
Meyer Lemon Marmalade, **255,** 258
Mixed-Berry Conserve, 114, **115**
Sunchoke Pickle Relish, 33, **33**
Valencia Orange
 Marmalade, **255,** 257

CORNMEAL
Creole-Spiced Fried Chicken, **82,** 83
Crispy Fried Tamales, 174
Mixed-Fruit Cornmeal Cobbler, **38,** 39
Tamales with Red-Chile-Braised
 Pork, **172,** 173
Tamal Pie, 174

CRAB
Pork-and-Crab Soup
 Dumplings, 214, **215**
Seafood Gumbo, **74,** 75
Soft-Shell Crab Sandwiches with
 Pancetta and Remoulade, **78,** 79

CUCUMBERS
Bread-and-Butter Pickles, 32, **32**
Cucumber-Dill Yogurt
 (Tzatziki), 114, **115**
Salmon with Cucumbers, 80

CURRY
Green Curry Chicken, **90,** 91

D

**DESSERTS. See also CAKES;
CANDY & CONFECTIONS; PIES**
American-Style Ice Cream, 130, **131**
Blueberry-Nectarine
 Pandowdy, 36, **37**
Butterscotch Sauce, 40, **41**
Chocolate Corn-Flake
 Clusters, 44, **45**
Chocolate-Hazelnut
 Baklava, **124,** 125
Chouquettes, 126

Cream Puffs with Chocolate Pastry
   Cream, 126, **127**
French-Style Ice Cream, 130, **131**
Fresh Pineapple Sauce, **41,** 43
Hot Fudge Sauce, 40, **41**
Lemon-Ricotta Pudding, **34,** 35
Mixed-Fruit Cornmeal Cobbler, **38,** 39
Mixed-Nut-Milk Panna
   Cotta, 208, **209**
Rothschild Soufflé, 110, **111**
Strawberry Sauce, 40, **41**
Vanilla Raised Doughnuts, 188, **189**
Wet Mixed Nuts, **41,** 43
DOUGH
Pâte à Choux, 126
Perfectly Flaky Yogurt-Butter Pie
   Dough, 120, **121**
Slow-Rising Pizza Dough, 64, **65**
Vanilla Raised Doughnuts, 188, **189**
DRINKS
Aged Bamboo, 141
Aged Chrysanthemum, 140
Aged El Presidente, 141
Aged Martini, 138, **139**
Aged Negroni, **139,** 140
Aged White Manhattan, 138, **139**
Almond Milk, **206,** 207
Cranberry-Anise Bitters, **260,** 261
Cranberry-Spice Cocktail, **260,** 261
Figgy-Orange Bitters, 263
Figgy-Orange Cocktail, 263
Frobisher, **142,** 211
Harvest Cocktail, 262
Mixed-Nut Milk, **206,** 208
Rosé Vermouth, **142,** 210
Woodland Bitters, 262
DUCK
Slow-Cooked Duck with Green Olives
   and Herbes de Provence, **164,** 165
Spiced Duck à l'Orange, 92, **93**
DUMPLINGS
Pork-and-Crab Soup
   Dumplings, 214, **215**
Pork and Shrimp Dumplings, **146,** 147
Spicy Mapo Tofu Dumplings, 148, **149**

E

EGGPLANT
Chile-Eggplant Mazemen Ramen
   with Pork Belly, 236, **237**
Vegetable Tempura with Ginger-
   Ponzu Dipping Sauce, **50,** 51
EGGS
Concord Cake, **198,** 199
French-Style Ice Cream, 130, **131**
Gruyère Cheese Soufflé, **108,** 109
Hazelnut-and-Chocolate Meringue
   Cake, **202,** 203
Lemon Meringue Pie, 192, **194**

Pâte à Choux, 126
Rothschild Soufflé, 110, **111**
Silky Hot and Sour Soup, 56, **57**
Uovo in Raviolo with Hand-Grated-
   Tomato Sauce, **226,** 227

F

FENNEL
Bouillabaisse à l'Américaine, **160,** 161
Chicken-and-Seafood Paella with
   Allioli, **230,** 231
Master Fish Stock, 70
FIGS
Figgy-Orange Bitters, 263
Figgy-Orange Cocktail, 263
FISH. See also SALMON
Bouillabaisse à l'Américaine, **160,** 161
Maki Rolls, 76, **77**
Master Fish Stock, 70
Provençal Fish Stew, **71,** 73
Sicilian Fish Stew, 72
FRUIT. See also specific fruits
Blueberry-Nectarine
   Pandowdy, 36, **37**
Double-Crust Apple-Apricot
   Pie, 120, **122**
Fresh Pineapple Sauce, **41,** 43
Ginger-Peach Conserve, 114, **115**
Mixed-Fruit Cornmeal Cobbler, **38,** 39
Rothschild Soufflé, 110, **111**

G

GARLIC
Barbacoa Beef Tacos with
   Two Sauces, 170, **171**
Bouillabaisse à l'Américaine, **160,** 161
Chicken-and-Seafood Paella with
   Allioli, **230,** 231
Deep-Fried Turkey with Berbere
   Spices, 19
Fiery Moroccan Lamb
   Merguez, 166, **167**
French (Canadian) Onion
   Soup, 144, **145**
Garlicky Rouille, 162, **163**
Happy Pancakes, **58,** 59
Hmong Spicy Pork Sausage, 169
Lemon-and-Garlic-Marinated
   Flat Iron Steak, 29
Osso Buco with Citrus
   Gremolata, **94,** 95
Pork Belly Porchetta, 234, **235**
Provençal-Style Chicken
   Sausage, 169
Seafood Gumbo, **74,** 75

Slow-Cooked Duck with Green Olives
   and Herbes de Provence, **164,** 165
Tamales with Red-Chile-Braised
   Pork, **172,** 173
GINGER
Chile-Eggplant Mazemen Ramen
   with Pork Belly, 236, **237**
Cranberry-Spice Cocktail, **260,** 262
Green Curry Chicken, **90,** 91
Hmong Spicy Pork Sausage, 169
Pecan Pie with Candied Ginger and
   Rum, 122, **123**
Pork and Shrimp Dumplings, **146,** 147
Spicy Mapo Tofu Dumplings, 148, **149**
Vegetable Tempura with Ginger-
   Ponzu Dipping Sauce, **50,** 51
GRAINS. See also RICE
Scandinavian Rye Bread, **104,** 105
GRAPEFRUIT
Citrus Lollipops, 134, **135**
GREEN BEANS
Chicken-and-Seafood Paella with
   Allioli, **230,** 231
GREENS. See also specific greens
Spiced Duck à l'Orange, 92, **93**
Vegetable Tempura with Ginger-
   Ponzu Dipping Sauce, **50,** 51

H

HAM
Meat Ravioli, 152, **153**
HAZELNUTS
Chocolate-Hazelnut
   Baklava, **124,** 125
Hazelnut-and-Chocolate Meringue
   Cake, **202,** 203
Hazelnut Marshmallows, **195,** 197
Mixed-Nut Milk, **206,** 208
Mixed-Nut-Milk Panna
   Cotta, 208, **209**
HERBS. See also specific herbs
Apple-Brined Turkey, 16, **17**
Beef Chuck Eye Roast with Paprika-
   Herb Rub, 26, **27**
Bouillabaisse à l'Américaine, **160,** 161
Classic Chicken Stock, **54,** 55
Cranberry-Anise Bitters, **260,** 261
Cranberry-Spice Cocktail, **260,** 262
Cucumber-Dill Yogurt
   (Tzatziki), 114, **115**
Figgy-Orange Bitters, 263
Figgy-Orange Cocktail, 263
Four-Herb Turkey with Crispy Skin, 19
Harvest Cocktail, 262
Master Fish Stock, 70
Pork Belly Porchetta, 234, **235**
Provençal-Style Chicken
   Sausage, 169
Rosé Vermouth, **142,** 210

Salsa Verde Lasagna Topping, 225
Seafood Gumbo, **74,** 75
Slow-Cooked Duck with Green Olives
  and Herbes de Provence, **164,** 165
Slow-Roasted Turkey with Herb
  Salt, 18, **18**
Woodland Bitters, 262

I

ICE CREAM
American-Style Ice Cream, 130, **131**
French-Style Ice Cream, 130, **131**
Ice Cream Birthday Cake, 248, **249**

J

JAMS. See CONDIMENTS, PRESERVES
& SPREADS

K

KALE
Vegetable Tempura with Ginger-
  Ponzu Dipping Sauce, **50,** 51

L

LAMB
Braised Lamb Neck with
  Turnip, **98,** 99
Fiery Moroccan Lamb
  Merguez, 166, **167**
Hyderabadi Lamb Biryani, **176,** 177
Lamb Steak Frites, 99
Slow-Roasted Leg of Lamb, 96
Vadouvan-Spiced Lamb Ribs, 96, **97**
LEEKS
Bouillabaisse à l'Américaine, **160,** 161
Chicken Pho, **86,** 87
Classic Chicken Stock, **54,** 55
LEMONS
Citrus Lollipops, 134, **135**
Lemon-and-Garlic-Marinated
  Flat Iron Steak, 29
Lemon Marmalade, **256,** 258
Lemon Meringue Pie, 192, **194**
Lemon-Ricotta Pudding, **34,** 35
Meyer Lemon Marmalade, **255,** 258
Osso Buco with Citrus
  Gremolata, **94,** 95
Valencia Orange
  Marmalade, **255,** 257
Vegetable Tempura with Ginger-
  Ponzu Dipping Sauce, **50,** 51

LIMES
Citrus Lollipops, 134, **135**
Doughnuts with Kaffir Lime–Coconut
  Glaze, **190,** 191
Green Curry Chicken, **90,** 91
Hmong Spicy Pork Sausage, 169
Sweet and Spicy Jerky, 52, **53**

M

MAYONNAISE
Chicken-and-Seafood Paella with
  Allioli, **230,** 231
Garlicky Rouille, 162, **163**
MEAT. See BEEF; LAMB; PORK
MINT
Hyderabadi Lamb Biryani, **176,** 177
MUSHROOMS
Beef Medallions with Bacon and
  Morels, **28,** 29
David Chang's Freeze-Dried Chicken
  Stock, 55
Green Curry Chicken, **90,** 91
Happy Pancakes, **58,** 59
Pork-and-Crab Soup
  Dumplings, 214, **215**
Pork and Shrimp Dumplings, **146,** 147
Roasted Wild Mushroom Lasagna
  Topping, 225, **225**
Shiitake and Swiss Chard Soup with
  Hand-Cut Noodles, 60, **62**
Silky Hot and Sour Soup, 56, **57**
MUSTARD
Carolina Pulled Pork with Eastern
  Carolina Sauce, 20, **21**
Soft-Shell Crab Sandwiches with
  Pancetta and Remoulade, **78,** 79

N

NOODLES
Chicken Pho, **86,** 87
Chile-Eggplant Mazemen Ramen
  with Pork Belly, 236, **237**
Shiitake and Swiss Chard Soup with
  Hand-Cut Noodles, 60, **62**
Shrimp Pad Thai, 157, **159**
NUTS. See also ALMONDS;
PEANUTS & PEANUT BUTTER; PECANS;
WALNUTS
Mixed-Nut Milk, **206,** 208
Mixed-Nut-Milk Panna
  Cotta, 208, **209**
Wet Mixed Nuts, **41,** 43
Woodland Bitters, 262

O

OATS
Scandinavian Rye Bread, **104,** 105
OLIVES
Sausage and Olive Pizza, **66,** 67
Sicilian Fish Stew, 72
Slow-Cooked Duck with Green Olives
  and Herbes de Provence, **164,** 165
ONIONS
Bouillabaisse à l'Américaine, **160,** 161
Bread-and-Butter Pickles, 32, **32**
Cheddar-and-Onion Smashed
  Burgers, 22, **23**
Chicken-and-Seafood Paella
  with Allioli, **230,** 231
Chile-Eggplant Mazemen Ramen
  with Pork Belly, 236, **237**
French (Canadian) Onion
  Soup, 144, **145**
Happy Pancakes, **58,** 59
Hyderabadi Lamb Biryani, **176,** 177
Osso Buco with Citrus
  Gremolata, **94,** 95
Slow-Cooked Duck with Green Olives
  and Herbes de Provence, **164,** 165
Sunchoke Pickle Relish, 33, **33**
ORANGES
Figgy-Orange Bitters, 263
Figgy-Orange Cocktail, 263
Orange Popovers, 106, **107**
Osso Buco with Citrus
  Gremolata, **94,** 95
Rosé Vermouth, **142,** 210
Spiced Duck à l'Orange, 92, **93**
Valencia Orange
  Marmalade, **255,** 257

P

PAPRIKA
Beef Chuck Eye Roast with Paprika-
  Herb Rub, 26, **27**
PARMESAN
Carrot and Ricotta Ravioli, **154,** 155
Meat Ravioli, 152, **153**
Milanese Risotto, 68, **69**
Potato Gnocchi with Butter and
  Cheese, **150,** 151
PARSLEY
Apple-Brined Turkey, 16, **17**
Milanese Risotto, 68, **69**
Osso Buco with Citrus
  Gremolata, **94,** 95
Red Wine Vinegar–Marinated
  Flat Iron Steak, 29
Salsa Verde Lasagna Topping, 225
Slow-Cooked Duck with Green Olives
  and Herbes de Provence, **164,** 165

Short ribs for Barbacoa
Beef Tacos with Two Sauces
Page 170

Slow-Roasted Leg of Lamb, 96
PASTA. See also NOODLES
Carrot and Ricotta Ravioli, **154,** 155
Creamy White Lasagna with
  Toppings, 223, **225**
Macaroni and Cheese with Buttery
  Crumbs, **14,** 15
Meat Ravioli, 152, **153**
Potato Gnocchi with Butter and
  Cheese, **150,** 151
Uovo in Raviolo with Hand-Grated-
  Tomato Sauce, **226,** 227
PEANUTS & PEANUT BUTTER
Miracle Peanut Butter
  Crunch, 204, **205**
Shrimp Pad Thai, 157, **159**
PECANS
Glazed Cinnamon Rolls with
  Pecan Swirls, **246,** 247
Pecan Pie with Candied Ginger
  and Rum, **122,** 123
Wet Mixed Nuts, **41,** 43
Woodland Bitters, 262
PEPPERS. See also CHILES
Chicken-and-Seafood Paella with
  Allioli, **230,** 231
Seafood Gumbo, **74,** 75
PICKLES
Bread-and-Butter Pickles, 32, **32**
Sunchoke Pickle Relish, 33, **33**
PIES
Double-Crust Apple-Apricot
  Pie, 120, **122**
Lemon Meringue Pie, 192, **194**
Pecan Pie with Candied Ginger
  and Rum, **122,** 123
PINEAPPLE
Fresh Pineapple Sauce, **41,** 43
PIZZA
Margherita Pizza, **63,** 67
Sausage and Olive Pizza, **66,** 67
Squash and Arugula Pizza, **66,** 67
PORK. See also BACON; HAM; SAUSAGES
Carolina Pulled Pork with Eastern
  Carolina Sauce, 20, **21**
Chile-Eggplant Mazemen Ramen
  with Pork Belly, 236, **237**
Crispy Fried Tamales, 174
French (Canadian) Onion
  Soup, 144, **145**
Happy Pancakes, **58,** 59
Hmong Spicy Pork Sausage, 169
Meat Ravioli, 152, **153**
Pork-and-Crab Soup
  Dumplings, 214, **215**
Pork and Shrimp Dumplings, **146,** 147
Pork Belly Porchetta, 234, **235**
Silky Hot and Sour Soup, 56, **57**
Spicy Mapo Tofu Dumplings, 148, **149**

Tamales with Red-Chile-Braised
  Pork, **172,** 173
Tamal Pie, 174
POTATOES. See also SWEET POTATOES
Bouillabaisse à l'Américaine, **160,** 161
Garlicky Rouille, 162, **163**
Potato Gnocchi with Butter
  and Cheese, **150,** 151
Thrice-Cooked Fries, 12, **13**
POULTRY. See CHICKEN; DUCK; TURKEY

R

RADISHES
Radishes Three Ways, 80, **81**
RAISINS
Raisin-Walnut Babka, **242,** 243
RICE
Chicken-and-Seafood Paella
  with Allioli, **230,** 231
Hyderabadi Lamb Biryani, **176,** 177
Maki Rolls, 76, **77**
Milanese Risotto, 68, **69**
RICOTTA
Carrot and Ricotta Ravioli, **154,** 155
Lemon-Ricotta Pudding, **34,** 35
Uovo in Raviolo with Hand-Grated-
  Tomato Sauce, **226,** 227
ROSEMARY
Pork Belly Porchetta, 234, **235**
Slow-Roasted Leg of Lamb, 96

S

SALMON
Maki Rolls, 76, **77**
Salmon with Cucumbers, 80
SALSA
Salsa Verde Cruda, 170, **171**
Salsa Verde Lasagna Topping, 225
SANDWICHES. See also BURGERS
Carolina Pulled Pork with Eastern
  Carolina Sauce, 20, **21**
Pastrami Breakfast Biscuit, 30
Sausage-Cheddar Breakfast
  Biscuit, 30
Soft-Shell Crab Sandwiches with
  Pancetta and Remoulade, **78,** 79
Strawberry Jam Breakfast Biscuit, 30
SAUCES. See also SALSA
Butterscotch Sauce, 40, **41**
Eastern Carolina Sauce, 20
Fresh Pineapple Sauce, **41,** 43
Garlicky Rouille, 162, **163**
Hot Fudge Sauce, 40, **41**
Perfect Pizza Sauce, 67
South Carolina Sauce, 20
Strawberry Sauce, 40, **41**

Vanilla Bean and Fleur de Sel Caramel
  Sauce, **128,** 129
Western Carolina Sauce, 20
SAUERKRAUT
Homemade Sauerkraut with Caraway
  and Apples, 100, **101**
Indian-Spiced Sauerkraut, **101,** 102
Seakraut, **101,** 103
SAUSAGES
Fiery Moroccan Lamb
  Merguez, 166, **167**
Hmong Spicy Pork Sausage, 169
Provençal-Style Chicken
  Sausage, 169
Sausage and Olive Pizza, **66,** 67
Sausage-Cheddar Breakfast
  Biscuit, 30
Seafood Gumbo, **74,** 75
SCALLIONS
Beef Medallions with Bacon and
  Morels, **28,** 29
Chicken Pho, **86,** 87
Happy Pancakes, **58,** 59
Lemon-and-Garlic-Marinated
  Flat Iron Steak, 29
Pork and Shrimp Dumplings, **146,** 147
**SEAFOOD. See CRAB; FISH; SHELLFISH;
SHRIMP**
SEAWEED
Maki Rolls, 76, **77**
Seakraut, **101,** 103
Shiitake and Swiss Chard Soup with
  Hand-Cut Noodles, 60, **62**
SHELLFISH. See also CRAB; SHRIMP
Bouillabaisse à l'Américaine, **160,** 161
Catalan Fish Stew, 73
Chicken-and-Seafood Paella with
  Allioli, **230,** 231
Master Fish Stock, 70
Provençal Fish Stew, **71,** 73
Seafood Gumbo, **74,** 75
Sicilian Fish Stew, 72
SHRIMP
Bouillabaisse à l'Américaine, **160,** 161
Catalan Fish Stew, 73
Happy Pancakes, **58,** 59
Pork and Shrimp Dumplings, **146,** 147
Provençal Fish Stew, **71,** 73
Seafood Gumbo, **74,** 75
Shrimp Pad Thai, 157, **159**
Sicilian Fish Stew, 72
SNACKS
Black Pepper Jerky, 52
Bread-and-Butter Pickles, 32, **32**
Chocolate Corn-Flake
  Clusters, 44, **45**
German-Style Pretzels, 186, **187**
Sweet and Spicy Jerky, 52, **53**

SOUFFLÉS
Gruyère Cheese Soufflé, **108,** 109
Rothschild Soufflé, 110, **111**
SOUPS & STOCKS. See also STEWS
Bouillabaisse à l'Américaine, **160,** 161
Chicken Pho, **86,** 87
Classic Chicken Stock, **54,** 55
David Chang's Freeze-Dried
  Chicken Stock, 55
French (Canadian) Onion
  Soup, 144, **145**
Master Fish Stock, 70
Shiitake and Swiss Chard Soup with
  Hand-Cut Noodles, 60, **62**
Silky Hot and Sour Soup, 56, **57**
SOYBEANS
Firm Tofu, 221
Silken Tofu, 220
Tofu skins, 218
SPINACH
Spiced Duck à l'Orange, 92, **93**
SQUASH
Squash and Arugula Pizza, **66,** 67
Vegetable Tempura with Ginger-
  Ponzu Dipping Sauce, **50,** 51
STARTERS
Fresh Mozzarella, 48, **49**
Gougères, 126
Pork-and-Crab Soup
  Dumplings, 214, **215**
Pork and Shrimp Dumplings, **146,** 147
Spicy Mapo Tofu Dumplings, 148, **149**
Vegetable Tempura with Ginger-
  Ponzu Dipping Sauce, **50,** 51
STEWS
Catalan Fish Stew, 73
Provençal Fish Stew, **71,** 73
Seafood Gumbo, **74,** 75
Sicilian Fish Stew, 72
SWEET POTATOES
Vegetable Tempura with Ginger-
  Ponzu Dipping Sauce, **50,** 51
SWISS CHARD
Shiitake and Swiss Chard Soup with
  Hand-Cut Noodles, 60, **62**

T

TACOS
Barbacoa Beef Tacos with
  Two Sauces, 170, **171**
TAMALES
Crispy Fried Tamales, 174
Tamales with Red-Chile-Braised
  Pork, **172,** 173
Tamal Pie, 174
TOFU
Firm Tofu, 221
Shrimp Pad Thai, 157, **159**
Silken Tofu, 220

Silky Hot and Sour Soup, 56, **57**
Spicy Mapo Tofu Dumplings, 148, **149**
Tofu Skins, 218
TOMATOES
Bouillabaisse à l'Américaine, **160,** 161
Chicken Tikka Masala, 84, **85**
Chile-Eggplant Mazemen Ramen with
  Pork Belly, 236, **237**
Hyderabadi Lamb Biryani, **176,** 177
Osso Buco with Citrus
  Gremolata, **94,** 95
Perfect Pizza Sauce, 67
Seafood Gumbo, **74,** 75
Uovo in Raviolo with Hand-Grated-
  Tomato Sauce, **226,** 227
TURKEY
Apple-Brined Turkey, 16, **17**
Deep-Fried Turkey with Berbere
  Spices, 19
Four-Herb Turkey with Crispy Skin, 19
Slow-Roasted Turkey with Herb
  Salt, 18, **18**

V

VEAL
Osso Buco with Citrus
  Gremolata, **94,** 95
VEGETABLES. See also specific vegetables
Braised Lamb Neck with
  Turnip, **98,** 99
Seafood Gumbo, **74,** 75
Seakraut, **101,** 103
Sunchoke Pickle Relish, 33, **33**
Vegetable Tempura with Ginger-
  Ponzu Dipping Sauce, **50,** 51

W

WALNUTS
Raisin-Walnut Babka, **242,** 243
Wet Mixed Nuts, **41,** 43

Y

YOGURT
Chicken Tikka Masala, 84, **85**
Cucumber-Dill Yogurt
  (Tzatziki), 114, **115**
Greek-Style Yogurt, **112,** 113
Hyderabadi Lamb Biryani, **176,** 177
Perfectly Flaky Yogurt-Butter Pie
  Dough, 120, **121**
Salmon with Cucumbers, 80

Photo Contributors

ANTONIS ACHILLEOS 81, 153, 154,
186–187, 219

LUCAS ALLEN 139

MATTHEW ARMENDARIZ 10, 12, 13, 15, 21,
31, 32, 33, 34, 35, 45, 50, 53, 57, 58, 59,
61, 68, 69, 78, 79, 85, 90, 94, 107, 124,
128, 145 (A–G), 150, 164, 168, 184, 202,
246, back cover (center right)

CHRIS CHEN 71, 72

CHRIS COURT 234–235

TARA FISHER 1, 4 (top), 41, 42, 46, 49,
82, 93, 104, 105, 204, 205, 206, 207,
209, 212, 240–241, back cover (top left,
bottom center)

CHRISTINA HOLMES 6, 17, 18, 108, 109,
111, 180, 181, 195, 196, 226, 229, 255,
256, 259, back cover (bottom left,
bottom right)

RAYMOND HOM 172, 175

JOHN KERNICK 4 (bottom), 5 (bottom),
8, 27, 28, 37, 38, 54, 63, 65, 66, 77, 97,
98, 112, 115, 121, 122, 123, 131, 146, 149,
215, 216, 230, 233, 237, 238, 252, 253,
254, 264, 272

DAVID MALOSH 2, 9, 89, 132, 134, 135,
136, 137, 142, 160, 163, 167, 176, 179,
183, 189, 190, 191, 193, 194, 198, 201,
210–211, 249, 250, back cover
(top center)

KATE MATHIS 145 (H)

WILLIAM MEPPEM 14

JOHNNY MILLER 127

MARCUS NILSSON 22, 23, 24

PERNILLE PEDERSEN 116

CON POULOS cover, 5 (top), 62, 74, 86,
156, 157, 158, 159, 171, 222, 223, 224–
225, 242, 245, 269, back cover (top
right, center left)

DAVID PRINCE 101

JONNY VALIANT 260

More books from
FOOD&WINE

Annual Cookbook
More than 615 recipes from the world's best cooks, including star chefs like Thomas Keller, Marcus Samuelsson, Michael Symon and Alex Guarnaschelli.

Staff Favorites
From the thousands of recipes published by FOOD & WINE over the last 30+ years, the editors have selected this collection of more than 150 of our all-time favorites.

Mad Genius Tips
Did you know that you can poach a dozen eggs in a muffin tin? Or grate ginger with a fork? Or ripen bananas in the oven? Discover clever shortcuts and unexpected uses for everyday tools in a book that's as helpful as it is entertaining. Justin Chapple, the star of FOOD & WINE's Mad Genius Tips video series, shares more than 90 hacks for 100+ easy, fun and delicious recipes.

TO ORDER, CALL 800-284-4145 OR VISIT **FOODANDWINE.COM/BOOKS**